3
L

US &
★ THEM

Also by James M. Perry

**The New Politics: The Expanding Technology
of Political Manipulation**

US ★ & THEM

How the Press Covered the 1972 Election

by James M. Perry

 Clarkson N. Potter, Inc./Publisher NEW YORK

DISTRIBUTED BY CROWN PUBLISHERS, INC.

Contents

Foreword

This book grows out of my reporting for the *National Observer*. That relationship is now more than a decade old, and it has been a happy one.

My editors have been indulgent and I would mention three of them by name: John F. Bridge, who handles my copy and who doesn't often agree with what I have to say (but who is always generous); my old editor-in-chief, William E. Giles; and my new editor-in-chief, Henry Gemmill.

I would add too the name of Vermont Royster of the *Wall Street Journal*. Not so long ago, he pulled me out of an editor's chair and got me back on the street, where I belong.

This is a book about my peers—the national political writers. They are good men and most of them are (and have been) lively company. Some of them may be offended by what I have to say in this book; most of them will believe, I hope, that my intentions were honorable.

I am especially indebted to my wife, Peggy, who maintained my files, an essential task that made this book possible. My daughters,

Kathie and Greta, were bemused and permitted their father to pursue his folly without frequent interruption.

I would add finally (I've always wanted to say this) that I typed my own manuscript.

JAMES M. PERRY

Washington, D.C.
March 1973.

US—1 ★

1

Who We Are

The Middle Political Journalist is a 45-year-old white male reared in the suburbs of Peoria, Ill., whose wife is a member of the PTA.

To know that the Middle Political Journalist went to a public high school and to his state university, that he is not very liberal and not very conservative, that he is not an intellectual but surely not an ignoramus, that he is overworked and probably underpaid, that he drinks too much and exercises too little, that he cheers for the Redskins and rents a vacation cottage at Ocean City, Md.—to know all of this is the beginning of contemporary wisdom about the nabobs Spiro Agnew has nattered against.

We are, in fact, *you*—middle-class, middle-income, and middle-age Americans.

We are only special because we live in or near Washington, D.C. (near, mostly; we are suburbanites), and because we are the people who, year in and year out, bring you the news about the men (and an occasional woman) who run, or want to run, this country.

3

Because our job is so special, we are some of the most remarkably ordinary people in the world.

This book is about *us,* the political reporters, including me, and *them,* the people who wanted to be President in 1972.

Riding in crowded buses and cluttered airplanes, working 18 hours a day, writing stories on portable typewriters balanced on our knees, tossing our copy on the run to Western Union messengers, shabby, tired, frequently disoriented about both time and place, poorly fed and rarely rested, cranky, crotchety, hungover, we try to make sense of the most complicated political system in the world.

That we often fail is no surprise; that we sometimes succeed is a miracle.

We are filters. It is through our smudgy, hand-held prisms that the voters meet the candidates and grow to love them or hate them, trust them or distrust them. We are the voters' eyes and ears, and we are more than that, for, sometimes, we perform a larger and, some would say, a more controversial function. We write the rules and we call the game.

In the beginning there are only a handful of us. We are the reporters based almost exclusively in Washington who write about politics all the time, year in and year out. Other reporters cover the White House or the Pentagon or Congress; we cover candidates and would-be candidates, for every office from big-city mayor to President of the United States. We are writers; we work in print. The point is important, perhaps surprising. This, McLuhan tells us, is an electronic age, but we are old-fashioned, linear reporters with pencils in our pockets. Every four years, we meet in New Hampshire when the White Mountains are still red and gold. We are the first to arrive and what we say, think, and write sets the tone and the theme for everything that follows. Walter Cronkite plays by our rules and Roger Mudd accepts our wisdom.

As the nation awakens slowly, even grumpily, to the realization that another campaign year has begun, those of us who were there at the beginning start to fade away, like the cicada. Once, when hardly anyone was looking, we had the field to ourselves. But, when the game really begins and the spectators are in the stands, a swarm of other reporters, columnists, and commentators arrives. For some of them, covering political campaigns is quadrennial; for others, this is the first campaign they have ever seen. The full-timers are bumped and jarred, sometimes by new people from their own offices. Finally, that mighty army that is network TV marches in, trailing a ganglion of wires that leads to regiments of technicians who are connected to truckloads of equipment. With rare exceptions, we resent their noisy, garish, and bewildering intrusion. Except for an occasional guerrilla attack—kicking a plug from a socket, stumbling into a light stand—there is nothing we can do about it. Like them or not, they will be with us, night and day, for the rest of the campaign.

In the beginning of the 1972 campaign, there were David Broder and R. W. "Johnny" Apple, Jr. Broder is the national political writer for the *Washington Post;* Apple is his counterpart at *The New York Times.* All of us would agree that these are two of us. Broder and Apple are the nation's two most visible full-time political writers because they are employed by the two publications that everyone seriously involved in the American political system reads, regularly, even religiously. Broder and Apple wear the robes of very high office; they *are* the *Washington Post* and *The New York Times.*

Just as important, more than two hundred papers subscribe to the news service supplied by the *Post* and the *Los Angeles Times,* and more than 1300 papers subscribe to *The New York Times*'s news service. Their influence may originate in the East, but it spreads through those services to every corner of the nation.

The rest of the list is short, for there are not many publications that assign reporters to national politics *full time.** Standing just behind Broder and Apple are Jules Witcover, who covered the recent campaign for the *Los Angeles Times* (but left, in frustration, after it was over, to join the *Washington Post*), and Jack W. Germond, Washington bureau chief for the Gannett newspapers. Both operated under something of a handicap, because most of us and most people working in the campaign did not read what they wrote. Witcover compensates by writing valuable books. Germond's influence is stretched by the sheer force of his personality. People listen to him.

---

* Almost every paper assigns a reporter to cover *local* politics, and some of these reporters take on larger roles in national elections. The best of the local reporters are highly regarded by the national press; their brains are picked constantly.

Walter Mears writes about politics for the Associated Press (AP), the largest newsgathering organization in the world. He is good, and he is blindingly fast. What he writes comes chattering into our offices on a ticker. Steve Gerstel is Mears's counterpart at United Press International (UPI), which is Avis to AP's Hertz. That is his handicap.

Other regulars include Paul Hope of the *Washington Evening Star* (now the *Star-News*), our second hometown paper, Ted Knap of the Scripps-Howard papers, Martin Nolan of the *Boston Globe,* Saul Kohler of the Newhouse papers, Loye W. Miller, Jr., of the Knight papers, Arlen J. Large of the *Wall Street Journal,* Thomas W. Ottenad of the *St. Louis Post-Dispatch,* Jim Squires of the *Chicago Tribune,* Godfrey Sperling, Jr., of the *Christian Science Monitor,* and my own highly skilled friend and colleague at the *National Observer,* James R. Dickenson. He writes it straight, most of the time. I write a column.

There are others who should be included, even if they are not full-timers and even if they are not strictly reporters. Columnists Evans (Rowland) and Novak (Robert), the odd couple of American journalism, specialize in national politics. They strike real fear in the hearts of candidates and campaign managers. Columnist Bruce Biossat specializes in politics too, and his encyclopedic knowledge of delegate counts, primary laws, and so much of the mechanics of politics that confuses most of us is universally respected.

It is curious that only two newsmagazine reporters, John Lindsay and Dick Stout of *Newsweek,* are widely known among political reporters. Even so, we don't ever know exactly what it is they tell their editors. Stories in *Time* and *Newsweek* are anonymous; they are distilled in a way that tends to reduce almost everything they print to conventional wisdom we've already heard, mixed, always, with the kind of minutiae that seems to be essential to the newsmagazine concept.

The television networks had only one correspondent who watched politics on a fairly regular basis—the veteran William Lawrence of ABC, who died covering the New Hampshire primary. No other TV reporter or commentator is widely respected for his (or her) political expertise. One who did show great promise, CBS's Michele Clark, was killed weeks after the election in an airplane crash.

There are political writers based in New York some of us read—Richard Reeves, for example, of *New York* and *Harper's* magazines, and Jack Newfield of the *Village Voice.* I admire both of them. Then there was Hunter S. Thompson, who transmogrified from Aspen, Colorado, to cover politics in 1972 for the *Rolling Stone.* Thompson's coverage was mind-blowing. I liked it.

But now we are getting pretty far afield. If we include Reeves, Newfield, and Thompson, we'd have to include Tom Wicker, William F. Buckley, Jr., the Alsop brothers, Kevin Phillips, James Reston, Tom Braden, Alan S. Otten, William S. White, Joseph Kraft, Marianne Means, Mary McGrory, Harriet van Horne, and many more. They cover politics irregularly.

And then there are the White House reporters, world-weary veterans of Presidential trips to Kuala Lumpur and Paris and Moscow and Peking. They give us daily reports on what the President is doing and saying, even on those rare occasions when they know. They live, we think, in a journalistic cocoon, emerging every four years to see the rest of the country in company with a campaigning President. In 1972, they had a special problem—the President wouldn't come out of his warm, safe cocoon.

I'm sure the list is incomplete but, essentially, these are the people who write about politics on a more or less full-time basis. They are the inner circle.

On or about January 1 of any recent Presidential year, the outer circle begins to form. These are the new people, and there are, quite literally, hundreds of them. The major newspapers assign reporters to all of the candidates they deem, in their own ultimate wisdom, to be important. The networks assign reporters, cameramen, and technicians to the same people.

In 1972, as in earlier years, some of the new people became vitally important. Consider, for example, James M. Naughton of *The New York Times:* he covered Edmund Muskie and then George McGovern. It was from outer-circle Naughton, not inner-circle Johnny Apple, that we learned about these two Democrats in *The New York Times.* Apple's role, so crucial in the preprimary phase, diminished as the campaign began; Naughton's role expanded. So, too, at the *Washington Post,* where Broder, the national political correspondent, virtually disappeared in the campaign's final stages He and a colleague,

Haynes Johnson, examined, in one series after another, what the voters were thinking. *Post* reporters like Lou Cannon and William Greider took over the coverage of the candidates.

Any good reporter lives on ego. Praise is what he seeks because, God knows, he isn't going to get much else. A reporter covering national politics for a newspaper earns between $15,000 and $30,000 a year; a handful earn more. Famous columnists can earn $100,000 a year. TV correspondents start at $35,000 and the anchor men make $200,000 and more.

It is possible that a brilliant reporter can make $18,000 a year and never be read by anyone outside his own hometown. He loses on both counts. He won't make much more until he expands his reputation, but he can't do that because no one outside his hometown knows how good he really is. It is the ultimate frustration.

It is probably true that the bigger the paper, the better the staff. But I suspect that some smaller papers disprove the rule. The *Baltimore Sun,* for example, the world's best unread newspaper, may have covered the campaign as well as *The New York Times* or the *Washington Post.* Maybe better. But their best people, reporters such as Adam Clymer and Bruce Winters, got little credit for it.

What the *Baltimore Sun,* the *Kansas City Star,* the *Philadelphia Bulletin,* and dozens of other newspapers did in the 1972 campaign is outside the scope of this book. I didn't read them. Richard Nixon didn't read them, or McGovern or Muskie or Lindsay or any other candidate, except on those occasions when their campaigns rolled into Baltimore or Kansas City or Philadelphia. They and their people may be superb, but the sad fact is that—on a national scale—they are not, except in special circumstances, significant.

This book is about what I read, and what I made of it. Not because my reading habits are exceptional, but because they are typical.* The reporters covering the campaign and the candidates and the politicians involved in the campaign were all reading pretty much the same material. And so were the faceless editors in New York and Washington who decided what the voters should know in their publications and on their networks.

---

* I know they are because I surveyed 55 political writers, 44 of whom were kind enough to fill out a long questionnaire. Our reading habits are strikingly similar.

I read, regularly, *The New York Times,* the *Washington Post,* the *Wall Street Journal,* the *National Observer,* the *Rolling Stone, Village Voice, Time, Life, Newsweek, New York, Harper's,* the *New Republic,* and *Congressional Quarterly;* I read, irregularly, the *Washington Evening Star,* the *Baltimore Sun,* the *Los Angeles Times,* the *New York Daily News,* the *Manchester* (N.H.) *Union Leader,* the *Milwaukee Journal,* the *Miami Herald, U.S. News & World Report, Atlantic, Esquire,* the *National Review,* the *Boston Globe, Human Events, Monday,* the *Ripon Forum,* the *New Democrat,* the *Christian Science Monitor, Playboy,* the *National Journal,* the *Progressive, Public Opinion Quarterly,* and the *Public Interest.*

I watched, when I could, NBC, CBS, and ABC, along with N-PACT, which produced a political series on PBS, the "educational" network.

I also read, and was influenced by, of all things, books. The importance of books in shaping the opinions of political reporters probably is vastly underrated. Garry Wills's and Jules Witcover's books about Nixon, and the collection of John Osborne's *New Republic* columns about Nixon were influential. So were biographies about Muskie (by Theo Lippman and Donald C. Hansen), McGovern (by Robert Sam Anson), and Agnew (again by Witcover). *The Real Majority,* by Richard Scammon and Ben J. Wattenberg, and *The Emerging Republican Majority,* by Kevin Phillips, told one side of the argument, *The Greening of America,* by Charles Reich, told another. *The Ticket Splitters,* by Lance Tarrance and Walter DeVries, made us think about what we had read in Joe McGinniss's *The Selling of the President 1968.*

There were others, but I suppose the one book that has influenced this generation of political reporters most is Theodore H. White's series, *The Making of the President,* starting in 1960, repeated in 1964 and 1968, and scheduled again in 1972, 1976, 1980, and 1984.

The influence of White, I think, has been bad, and that will be a theme of this book. White showed us that a great many fascinating things occur behind the scenes in every campaign. He showed, by his exceptional writing skill, that the story of a campaign can be told in vivid, chronological detail. He made us think that we were missing most of it. And so, I would argue, consciously or unconsciously, we began to imitate his technique and even, sometimes, his style. We have become nit-pickers, peeking into dusty corners, looking for the squabbles, celebrating the trivia, and leaping to those sweeping, cosmic, melodramatic conclusions and generalities that mark the Teddy White view of American politics.

One point is worth noting: White tells us what it all meant after the election is over. Often, I think, he tells us what it meant badly. It is a different matter to try to do the same sort of thing *during* a campaign.

We cannot do it, most of the time.* We can't run down all the details. The situation is too chaotic; events are moving much too rapidly. Even if we tried, our sources might not level with us. The truth, during a campaign, can hurt. White talks to people ex post facto, when the tempo is slower and when truth is possible. But even White is an instant historian, with all the drawbacks that implies.

If we play White's game, we risk a certain dereliction of what I think is our duty. We fail to keep the voters informed about who the candidates really are and what they are trying to do and to say. Often, it seems, that is what interests us least; it is what should motivate us most.

Thanks to White, our coverage is sometimes out of focus. We are too interested in the kinds of details he treasures. We are too interested in "images." Last but not least, we are far too interested in trying to find out who's going to win. White has us there; he *knows.* Our who's-ahead mentality is reckless; more than anything else, in 1972, it helped to damage our credibility and confound our readers, because, quite simply, there was no way we could have been right. We are bound to be wrong, some of the time. In 1972, we were wrong most of the time. We were prepared, before the first primary, to award the nomination to Muskie. We read Dr. Gallup's famous poll and wrote off poor George McGovern. We never imagined Wallace would run in primaries in the North, and we couldn't know he would be shot. We waited, breathlessly, for Lindsay to make up his mind; he, we said, would put an end to this McGovern nonsense. Meanwhile,

---

* I will use the pronoun in the collective sense, but a caveat: I do not suggest by it collective guilt. In almost every instance, one of "us" wrote something else, which I may or may not have read. What I mean to suggest, in these situations, is that there was a consensus among the people I'm talking about.

we destroyed Lindsay by nit-picking about his manipulation of the media. We said Jackson was an anachronism, when we said anything about him at all. We thought Humphrey was old and foolish, and we were embarrassed for him. He almost won.

We couldn't decide whether we were entering the Age of Aquarius or the First American Reich.

When we couldn't go anywhere with Nixon, we went with Agnew. That seemed to solve the problem.

Then, at least in our editorials, we said McGovern had to dump Eagleton. He did and his campaign fell apart.

We said Vietnam wasn't an issue because Kissinger was taking care of it. "Peace was at hand." A month after the election, the bombs were falling again.

No group of reporters in the history of journalism has guessed so wrong so often. And it was silly; we shouldn't even have been in the predicting business. Maybe, if we have any sense, we won't be again.

If our performance (and mine, in taking note of it) gives some satisfaction to Spiro Agnew, well, so be it. Some of the things he has said about us are valid; other things are worth thinking about. And much of what he has said is nonsense.

He began his attack on the press—his chief target has been television—on November 13, 1969, in Des Moines, when he complained about a "gaggle of commentators" who, days earlier, had subjected the President's speech on Vietnam to "instant analysis and querulous criticism."

Agnew said the President has "a right to communicate directly with the people who elected him . . . without having [his] words and thoughts characterized through the prejudices of hostile critics before they can be digested."

A small group of men—no more, Agnew thought, than a dozen —"can elevate men from local obscurity to public prominence within a week. They [the dirty dozen] can reward some politicians with national exposure and ignore others."

These men and their producers "live and work in the geographical and intellectual confines of Washington, D.C., or New York City —the latter of which James Reston terms the 'most unrepresentative community in the entire United States.' "

The news 40,000,000 Americans receive each night is determined by a handful of men "responsible only to their corporate employers and filtered through a handful of commentators who admit to their own set of biases."

Members of this little group "talk constantly to one another, thereby providing artificial reinforcement to their shared viewpoints."

Agnew's criticism is, of course, self-serving. He was sent on the attack by the White House because the President didn't like what this "gaggle of commentators" was saying about him and his policies. Agnew welcomed the assignment.

And we can, I think, dismiss Agnew's contention that he was "not asking for government censorship or any other kind of censorship." Of course he was; at the end of his Des Moines speech, he challenged his listeners to write to the networks and local stations to let them know that "they want their news straight and objective."

When complaints such as this are made to local TV stations, the Federal Communications Commission can draw its own conclusions when the time comes for license renewal. The point to remember is that broadcasting is licensed and monitored by the federal government, and the Vice-president of the United States was doing the talking.

If Nixon and Agnew had federal intervention in mind, that was sinister, and that's what most media leaders worried about. Agnew, by implication, was making some threats that were not entirely veiled.

Agnew, at the very least, was asking the networks and the local stations to impose voluntary censorship. He wanted less opinion from them, more facts. He wanted them to hire new people, who might be more representative of American opinion, which is to say, more sympathetic to Nixon and the Republican Party.

Reaction to what Agnew said concentrated on the implied threats to freedom of the press. That reaction was understandable and proper. Events in 1972 have underlined this concern. A correspondent for my own newspaper, Peter Bridge, was jailed in New Jersey for refusing to tell a grand jury information he had been given in confidence. More recently, John Lawrence, the Washington bureau chief of the *Los Angeles Times,* was jailed for refusing to turn over tapes of conversations between two of his reporters and a figure in the Watergate investigation. The press is caught in a serious constitutional squeeze, and Agnew's performance may in some ways have precipitated it.

Much of that, however, is beyond the scope of this book. Separate Agnew from these other considerations and the question becomes: Is his criticism valid?

In part, yes. He uses the same word I have already used—filter—to describe the process by which we communicate information about him, and the rest of them, to the voters. We can, and do, "elevate men from local obscurity to public prominence." We can, and do, "reward some politicians with national exposure and ignore others." And obviously we do "live and work in the intellectual confines of Washington, D.C., or New York City." And many of us do "talk constantly to one another."

Where I think Agnew and most conservatives err is in believing that this small, willful band of men tilts the news to the left. The record of 1972 that we will explore fails to bear out any such contention. Rather, the record shows that the press, most of the time, is devoid of ideology. It is not interested in ideology. It will not explore questions of ideology.

There is probably one serious exception—the war in Vietnam. Hundreds of reporters have been to Vietnam, and most of them have come home appalled at what they have observed. Reporters, columnists, and commentators generally believed that the war should be stopped. Those who disagreed—most famously, Joe Alsop—stick out like chimneys among the rubble.

I am not convinced the press's antiwar attitude is an indication of bias to the left, or any other direction. It is simply a journalistic observation: the war has been bad for the United States, not to mention Southeast Asia. With some reporters, it was a moral question; with others, a practical one. Either way, the press wanted it ended. It is a bias, I suppose, and I share it. There are times, I think—once in every century, perhaps—when the cause of objectivity asks too much.

Most of the time, reporters are not deeply committed, or even seriously interested, in issues. Which is not to say that reporters in both print and on television don't take strong points of view. They do, all the time, far too much of the time. But not on issues, not on ideology. They are more interested in such questions as a candidate's style (or, more frequently, his lack of it), his professionalism, his ability as a performer, the quality of his staff, the reaction by the crowd to his speeches, and, finally and most importantly, his chances for success.

If, in fact, as Agnew says, our bias is to the left, we should have celebrated George McGovern, the Aquarius, Consciousness III candidate. Instead, in 1971 when he was trying so hard to catch our attention, we ignored him.

Even though he was the leading antiwar candidate, sharing our bias, we wrote him off—because he lacked style, because important people in the party (who did not always share his and our antiwar views) did not take him seriously, and because he was low in Dr. Gallup's poll, and that meant to us he was a loser. When McGovern showed he could win, we about-faced. He was, we said, a professional. He had the best organization, and maybe style wasn't so important after all.

I suppose the press admired John Kennedy more than any other modern American politician. He had style and he was a professional. It is easy to forget, though, that the press was beginning to express reservations even about Kennedy, just before he was killed. By then, it seemed to many of us, he was losing legislative battles we thought he could have won.

Nixon, obviously, is disliked by most reporters. He lacks style and he took four years to get us out of Vietnam. But he does get some grudging respect because he works hard and he is a professional.

Nixon is seen as devious, introverted, inconsistent, opportunistic, humorless, and sanctimonious. He would surely be more popular if he were straightforward, extroverted, consistent, philosophical, humorous, and unpretentious.

Why, we seem to ask, can't he be more like *us?*

And that may get us closer to the problem posed by the fact that the news is written and produced in Washington and New York. Perhaps Easterners prefer a distinctive life-style and a special kind of personality.

Perhaps because we live in the East (though most of us grew up elsewhere), because we are middle class and middle income, because almost all of us are college graduates, we do seek qualities in politicians that are not quite so important elsewhere. Perhaps.

In any event, there's not much that can be done about it, short of moving the capital to Des Moines and transferring the networks, the newsmagazines, and the book publishers from New York to Peoria.

Whatever our deficiencies, at least not very many of us are "effete," fewer still are "snobs," and only Walter Cronkite and Joe Alsop are "nabobs." As I began to say, we are pretty ordinary middle-class Americans trying to do a difficult job.

Let us now see how difficult that job, covering *them,* can sometimes be.

part two

★
THEM

2

Nixon

THE WHITE HOUSE

TRIP OF THE PRESIDENT TO
NEW YORK CITY AND CHICAGO
NOVEMBER 9-10   1971

2:30 P.M.	Baggage call, Room 87, EOB.
3:45 P.M.	Press buses depart Southwest Gate en route Andrews Air Force Base.
4:00 P.M.	Press checks in at Andrews Air Force Base.
4:30 P.M.	Press plane departs Andrews Air Force Base en route LaGuardia Airport, New York City.
	Flying time: 1 hr.
	No time change

It was Tuesday, Nov. 9, 1971, and that's when the Republican Presidential campaign of 1972 began for me, and perhaps for Richard Milhous Nixon too. That day set the tone for all the 363 days that were to follow.

Because on November 9, 1971, the 52 members of the press who traveled with the man many of us call The Trick never saw him.

So this is how it was that day for me and for whatever other reporters were trying to make some sense of Richard Nixon and the kind of campaign he was about to begin. I wrote a diary.

3:45 P.M. Board chartered bus at the southwest gate of the White House for the ride to Andrews Air Force Base, where we will board a chartered TWA jet. The jet will take us to New York, where we will hear the President address a Republican fund-raising dinner. These two dinners are among 20 being held all over the country to raise $5,000,000 for the Republicans. They will all be connected by closed-circuit television. I know this is so because the AP and *The New York Times* already have told me it is so, and I have their clippings stashed in my briefcase.

4:10 P.M. Arrive Andrews in suburban Maryland, board TWA jet. I can see, 100 yards away, *Air Force One,* recently renamed *Spirit of '76.* I can say that for sure; I've accompanied that beautiful blue-and-white 707 to such places as Kuala Lumpur and Cam Ranh Bay. Seven of *us* will fly in it with *them*—the members of the "pool": AP, UPI, NBC, *Time, Chicago Tribune,* AP Photos, and UPI Photos. On our plane (it really is ours, we'll pay for chartering it), stewardesses pass down the aisle, taking orders for drinks. One of them is a smashing redhead in hot pants.

(A few of the faces on the press plane are familiar. Hearst's Harry Kelly, for example, who will be a good companion in the weeks to come, and "the real" John Lindsay of *Newsweek* magazine, who insists he's the most anonymous political reporter in America. Maybe he is all of that, but most of us who think we're not so anonymous listen to him. Other faces are unfamiliar. I'm not a White House reporter; I'm a political reporter. They have their own club; we have ours. We don't think much of them; they don't think much of us. We're pretty good; they're pretty bad. So I don't say hello to the *Washington Post*'s Carroll Kilpatrick and he doesn't say hello to me. I would have said hello to *The New York Times*'s Robert B. Semple, Jr., because he's an old friend; we worked together in our early Washington days. But he's not on this trip; filling in for him is a *Times* man

I've never seen before, James Naughton. As I mentioned earlier, he will become a key man in this campaign, perhaps the most important of all of us, because he will cover, first, Edmund Muskie, and, finally, George McGovern, for *The New York Times.*

4:30 P.M. "Wheels up," in the dreadful vernacular of the White House press corps. Stewardesses now serve us appetizers—barbecued spareribs and what seems to be a very small shish kebab.

5:30 P.M. "Wheels down" at LaGuardia, say good-bye to red-headed stewardess, board press bus for trip downtown to the garish Americana Hotel. Lots of traffic and jokes about the corruption of the police who are trying to help us. My schedule shows that the President, at about this very moment, is departing the south lawn of the White House by helicopter, en route to Andrews and the *Spirit of '76.*

6:15 P.M. Arrive Americana Hotel, herded to Press Room, Royal Blue A, mezzanine level. Diligent investigation reveals that the ball-room, where the speechmakin', in Lyndon's word, will take place, is just across the hall. The ballroom is filled with prosperous Republicans in gowns and dinner jackets. But guards at the door won't let me in. One of the guards stops Nelson Rockefeller, who is wearing a dinner jacket but who seems to have forgotten his ticket. I tell the guard that Rockefeller is, well, Rockefeller. He scowls, but his wife, Happy, smiles nicely. The guard relents and the Rockefellers are allowed inside. I return to the press room, where TV consoles have been installed so we can watch what's happening 100 yards away. This, after all, is the age of television, and this program is being carried to Republicans in 20 cities by TNT Productions.

7:05 P.M. The press room doors are closed by Secret Service agents; the President is about to arrive. I decide to go to the men's room, which is guarded by five policemen. They inspect the credentials hanging on a chain around my neck and allow me to go inside. There, a Secret Service agent is looking for bombs in the toilet bowls. I return to the press room and settle down in front of one of the TV sets, checking, first, to see that my little tape recorder (we all use tape recorders these days, perhaps because we have forgotten how to take notes) is working. It is.

7:10 P.M. Bob Hope comes swimming into focus, in living color. He begins his routine. John Lindsay, he says, smirking, would have been here, but he's attending his *bar mitzvah.* Governor Rockefeller, Hope says, was so surprised by Lindsay's defection to the Democrats that he dropped his glass of champagne. The $500-a-plate Republicans, from Robert H. Abplanalp to Mr. and Mrs. Howard R. Young, respond with polite laughter. Hope fades away and now I see Sen. Robert Dole of Kansas, chairman of the Republican National Committee. The President, he says, is going to give America a "generation of peace." GOP, he says—get it?—generation of peace. "That," says a reporter watching the TV set next to me, "has got to be the most tasteless acronym of the year."

Now I see Nelson Rockefeller who, once upon a time, didn't think much more of Richard Nixon than he now thinks of John Lindsay. "In times of crisis," Rockefeller says, reading painfully from a prepared text, "a leader emerges" and America is again fortunate to have a great leader in a time of great crisis. He is talking about Richard Nixon. Vision. Boldness. Imagination. Realism. My God, I think to myself, does this man feel no shame? And so, Rockefeller concludes, I give you the President of the United States and the *next* President of the United States!

7:28 P.M. And here he is! Here's The Trick; I can see him on the screen and some of the applause from across the hall comes filtering into the press room. It gives us all a sense of participation. We start taking notes and fumbling with our Sonys. Sssh, the President is talking.

"This is a great event," he says. "What you have done is to have made this event, these dinners across the nation, the biggest events of their kind in a nonelection year in America's history in either party." Great, but not all that great. A great with an asterisk.

But it's not an occasion for partisanship, he says. (Why not?) It's time to talk about the nation's agenda for the future. (It is?) Such a great event deserves a great cause (It does?)—and we have that cause (We do?). Peace is in sight now, while, three years ago, we were at war. And now it's time to build a full generation of peace "and beyond that."

"This, in truth," the President says, ever so solemnly, "is a great goal."

He is going to Moscow and Peking, he says, because negotiation offers us a chance for peace. And that's what we owe to the future. He is doing his part.

Oh, he says, it's so easy for members of Congress to vote against maintaining our military strength and to vote against mutual assistance for "countries abroad." He was once in the House and he remembers just how easy it was. But this is not the time to take the easy way; that just means the world will become more unstable. So, he says, we must face up to the challenges of peace.

And then there are the problems at home. He says we need to get the economy moving to compete with Western Europe and Japan, and the cities and the states are in big trouble, and he has programs—revolutionary programs—to solve those problems. But Congress won't act.

He's reaching his peroration now. Great civilizations have fallen because their leaders lost their will and their drive. We must not let that happen to us. Let us have the courage to meet the challenge by not turning away from greatness.

7:47 P.M. He's finished and we run for the press buses, which take us to the Wall Street helipad. We board Marine helicopters and noisily whirl off to the airport, where the redheaded stewardess welcomes us home.

9:45 P.M. (Chicago time). Arrive O'Hare, take helicopters to Meigs Field, in downtown Chicago. Take bus to Conrad Hilton Hotel, where I stayed during the 1968 convention. Can't smell stink bombs anymore. We enter the hotel through the basement and are herded into another press room. This one has a bar and, one senses, it has been open for some time.

10:05 P.M. Look for the ballroom, but can't find it. Someone says it's upstairs (seeing we're in the basement, that sounds reasonable) but guards are stationed at the escalators, and we can't get by. Settle down, once again, in front of a TV console.

10:10 P.M. Gov. Ronald Reagan is talking, apparently from a dinner somewhere in California. He is quoting Pope Pius XII. Now Art Linkletter is talking, from someplace else. He is putting the blast on Ramsey Clark, the "chief dove in the war on crime." Now Attorney General John Mitchell, presumably the chief hawk in that war, is talking. Linkletter, I surmise, must have been introducing him.

10:13 P.M. Now Linkletter and Bob Hope are *both* talking. Where's Hope? I ask somebody, *anybody,* in mounting desperation. In Chicago, I'm told. So where's Linkletter? In Los Angeles. Split-screen technique. Hope, I'm told, has been spirited from New York to Chicago to warm up a second audience. John Wayne is in Cleveland. Jackie Gleason is in Miami. Julie Eisenhower is back in Washington, where we could have watched this whole damn thing. Pat Buttram is in San Francisco.

10:17 P.M. Hope introduces Spiro Agnew. The golf swing that's launched a thousand ambulances, Hope says. Agnew has a better line. Hope, he says, is getting ready to take his troupe overseas—to entertain Henry Kissinger. Then Agnew gets serious, rains praise on Nixon. Camera cuts to Nixon. He is humble.

10:19 P.M. Two complete television crews—two cameramen, two sound men, two lighting men—come rocking past me. They stagger up to my TV set, dragging wires behind them, and begin taking pictures of the television pictures on my television screen. And nobody seems to think it's curious, even though I keep pointing at what's happening. I sense that people think *I'm* crazy. But I can't grapple with it. TV taking pictures of TV pictures? Why, it's downright bizarre. And where will it lead us? I'm not prepared to deal with that.

10:21 P.M. A drunk in a dirty blue shirt, baggy pants, and muddy boots walks up to me. "What the hell's going on here?" he asks. I have no reply nearly adequate to the occasion. Hope is still talking. Vice-presidents, he's saying, are supposed to buy a knife and a piece of wood and whittle for four years. But before they could get the knife away from Agnew he'd cut up three television networks and two newspapers.

10:54 P.M. Finally, Nixon. But here in the press room in Chicago, hardly anyone seems to be listening or watching. The bar is still open. My friend the drunk has engaged someone else in conversation about school busing. Nixon gives pretty much the same speech he gave in New York, but he adds one provocative new line: "You are leaders. You would not be able to afford this dinner unless you were leaders."

11:15 P.M. (Chicago time); 12:15 P.M. (our time). The President finishes. We run for our buses and head for the Drake Hotel. The press room is the Georgian room (15 long-distance telephones and 3 Telex machines). The President, according to the schedule, is spending the night at the Continental Plaza Hotel.

8:15 A.M. Wednesday. Baggage call for the press, in the hotel lobby. Buses leave for the airport at 8:45.

9:15 A.M. We arrive at the airport and board our TWA jet. The redheaded stewardess, offering me a Bloody Mary, asks politely how the President is doing.

9:16 A.M. I reply, "How the hell would I know?" The stewardess takes her tray elsewhere.

10:10 A.M. "Wheels up" for Washington.

3

Muskie

Comedian Jack E. Leonard once sized up Senator Edmund S. Muskie of Maine and asked him, "Why don't ya split a rail or somethin'?"

That was long, long ago when we called him the front-runner, before we began calling him Bullwinkle. That was when we presumed he would be the Democratic candidate for President and when some of us, including the *Washington Post*'s David Broder, perhaps the most celebrated of all of us, thought he would be the next President.

Well, Muskie was no Lincoln—but, then, who is?—and we never gave him much of a chance. Muskie was destroyed *in* the press, if not *by* the press. What happened to him and to us is one of the shabbiest stories of the 1972 campaign. We will begin that story, to be continued later, here.

We and almost every other reasonably alert American first took serious note of Ed Muskie on September 25, 1968. We met him, through the evening TV news, in Washington, Pennsylvania, where he was campaigning as Hubert Humphrey's running mate. But, once again, he couldn't give his speech because of the hecklers.

"Stop the war! Stop the war!" they shouted.

Muskie had a proposal. "I will suggest something right now to you young gentlemen," he said. "You pick one of your number to come up here right now, and I'll give him ten minutes of uninterrupted attention." Then, he said, they'd have to give him their uninterrupted attention.

The students' choice was Rick Brody, 21, a senior at nearby Washington and Jefferson College. According to Theo Lippman, Jr., of the *Baltimore Sun,* and Donald C. Hansen, of the Guy Gannett newspaper chain, authors of *Muskie,* Brody was "almost straight out of central casting." His hair was long and his jeans were dirty.

"Thank you," Brody began. "This is a chance we usually don't get, and I think it's fine. You guys [referring to older people in the audience jeering him] say we are dirty and unwashed. We are the true Americans. . . . The reason I am out here in the streets is because no one listened to us at Chicago when Senator McCarthy showed through the primaries that seventy percent of the American Democratic Party was dissatisfied with President Lyndon Baines Johnson's stand on Vietnam and domestic issues. . . ." Brody's speech was downhill after that; he talked about "an anti-election," in which he seemed to be saying people shouldn't vote for either party. He implied that the system had failed.

Muskie took it from there. What Brody had said led naturally into a favorite theme of Muskie's, one we heard over and over again in 1972. Muskie started talking quietly about his father, Stephen Marciszewski, born in 1882 in Poland, a poor boy, uneducated, apprenticed at the age of 12 to a tailor. He left Poland when he was 17, ostensibly to avoid conscription in the Russian czar's army. He went to England, worked there for three years, and then came to America in 1903.

His father, Muskie said, "tore himself out of his homelife, tore himself away from a family he would never see again, to go to a foreign land with only five years' formal education, with a newly learned trade as a tailor, to take up life and to find opportunity for himself and for children who were yet unborn. And the year before he died his son became the first Polish-American ever elected governor of an American state.

"Now that may not justify the American system to you, but it sure did to him."

The crowd applauded; even the students cheered.

What the crowd in Washington, Pennsylvania, felt isn't important. That's a point some reporters have yet to learn. It doesn't matter what a few hundred people listening to the candidate in person think. What really matters is how it looks on the evening news.

And Muskie's performance looked just beautiful. It appeared on all three network news shows, the kind of hat trick every campaigner aims for. Far and away, it was the best coverage Muskie received in the campaign.

In early September, Louis Harris reported that 33 percent of his national sample preferred Muskie for Vice-president; 30 percent preferred Agnew. By October 21, it was 41 percent for Muskie, 24 percent for Agnew.

Muskie was a kind of instant hero. The American voters had been introduced to him, in their living rooms, and they were favorably impressed.

But what was it that impressed them? Muskie's quickness, I suppose. He reacted, it seemed, instantaneously, and turned what appeared to be a disaster into a triumph. Yet, we know now, Muskie had been thinking about just such a stratagem for weeks; in fact, he'd suggested to the beleaguered Humphrey that he try it. Humphrey refused.

And Muskie's coolness. But that too grew out of the fact that this was a situation he'd been planning for and thinking about. So what I'm suggesting is that Muskie first appeared on the national stage in a role that was staged; a role, more importantly, that was not truly representative of his own character.

For Muskie is not quick and, God knows, he is not cool. He is a very special breed—a plodder with a roaring temper. It takes him weeks, sometimes years, to make up his mind about things like equal rights and the war in Vietnam, and then it takes mere seconds to unleash lightning and thunder on those who wonder why it took him so long.

". . . when Muskie is frustrated and bored," Richard Stewart, then of the *Boston Globe,* wrote in June of 1970, "his irritability threshold is down around his ankles. The public appearance of calm and control belies the monumental temper he can display in private." Stewart knew Muskie as well as any correspondent in Washington, and he would soon become his press secretary.

Humphrey lost, narrowly, to Richard Nixon, and some people said that if the Democratic ticket had been reversed it would have won. Muskie began thinking quietly about 1972. He traveled around the country and he made a trip to Russia, Europe, and the Middle East. Almost everywhere he went, though, he kept hearing about Senator Edward M. Kennedy. Muskie was on the verge of saying the hell with it when, on July 18, Kennedy and Mary Jo Kopechne plunged off the Dike Bridge into Poucha Pond. Miss Kopechne died and so—most of us said—did Kennedy's chances for the Presidency.

It was on November 2, 1970, the nation met Ed Muskie again. He had been chosen as the Democrats' spokesman to answer charges made by the Republicans in what was surely the most poisonous off-year election in recent history. Muskie spoke from somebody's kitchen in Cape Elizabeth, Maine.

The half-hour program was produced by Robert Squier, Muskie's newly hired media advisor. Most of the speech was written by Richard Goodwin, who is very good at writing speeches.

". . . there are those who seek to turn our common distress to partisan advantage—not by offering better solutions—but with empty threat, and malicious slander," Muskie said, somberly. "They imply that Democratic candidates for high office in Texas and California, in Illinois and Tennessee, in Utah and Maryland, and among my neighbors from Vermont and Connecticut—men who have courageously pursued their convictions, in the service of the republic in war and in peace—that these men actually favor violence, and champion the wrongdoer.

"That is a lie.

"And the American people know it is a lie."

What made Muskie's performance all the more memorable was its contrast to President Nixon's half-hour program that appeared just in front of it. Somebody—nobody has ever taken the blame— decided to air a tape of a Nixon speech delivered in Phoenix a few days earlier. It was an outrageous speech about law and order and crime, implying the Democrats were somehow responsible for it. It was, in John Mitchell's memorable words, Nixon running for sheriff. To make it worse, the tape was of poor quality and what Nixon said came across garbled and full of static.

Muskie, commentators said, looked like the President; Nixon looked like the desperate opponent.

I don't suppose either speech, or the speeches taken together, changed very many votes. But this can be said: Republicans, the next day, did not fare well at the polls.

Late November, 1970. It's a good time to pause. Because, then, everything seemed so obvious. Nixon vs. Muskie. That's how I figured it; that's how almost everyone else figured it. Most of us thought it would be a good match-up. Nixon, we told each other, was seen as tricky, not quite trustworthy. He didn't have very many principles, and all the principles we thought he had he threw away. We were to see him go to Peking and China. We were to watch as he became a Keynesian. We were to see him impose wage and price controls.

Against all that, the man of candor and honesty, the rugged man from rugged, poor little Maine: Ed Muskie. Lincolnesque.

I was especially impressed by Muskie's performance on the tube. That, I thought, was what would take him to the nomination and maybe even to the Presidency. I blame Bob Squier, who knows more about television than I. He said Muskie was good and that the rest were bad. He told me that if you close your eyes when you watch George McGovern, you'll think you're hearing Liberace.

The work that went into every Muskie appearance on TV was impressive. In May, he showed up on NBC's "Dinah's Place," where he mesmerized a lobster named Fred for the edification of some 4,000,000 housewives. Muskie grasped the lobster firmly and began to stroke his back. The lobster somersaulted rapturously, landed on his head, and froze.

"Oh," said Dinah Shore, "isn't that sweet?"

Squier and his wife, Jane, had been preparing Muskie for that show for two weeks. The Squiers even suggested that Miss Shore conclude the show by singing "Jet Plane," you know, the one that begins, "All my bags are packed, I'm ready to go. . . ."

The Squiers supplied still photographs of Ed and Jane Muskie's trip to Russia, Europe, and the Middle East. The last photo showed Muskie with his arm around Jane, asleep on a bench at the London airport, fogged in by the weather, waiting to come home. It was a touching finale.

"I couldn't put a price on that show," Squier told me. "You just couldn't get a situation or an audience like that for any amount of cash."

He was right; you couldn't. But it was still the familiar image— decent, steady, just-folks Ed Muskie, as quick to mesmerize a lobster as to mesmerize a crowd of angry kids.

And then the nit-picking began. Muskie's staff, it was said, was second-rate. And Muskie's dull; where's the star quality? He's indecisive, we were told. A joke made the rounds. "If Ed Muskie had been Paul Revere, he would have ridden out of Boston shouting, 'The British have been here, the British have been here—and I deplore it.' "

By April of 1971, the attacks were getting pretty serious. James Reston of *The New York Times* reported on the twenty-eighth that the other Democratic candidates "are sniping at the senator from Maine," privately. "Muskie, they complain, is poorly organized, indecisive, inexperienced on urban questions and foreign policy, an Adlai Stevenson without Stevenson's eloquence, experience, or big-state political base."

Evans (Rowland, the thin, aristocratic member of the team) and Novak (the round, rumpled, bourgeois one) detected Muskie moving dangerously to the left. On April 19, they said: "The fact that Muskie endorsed Saturday's antiwar demonstration here without considering its domination by Trotskyist Communists typifies the cloak of respectability inadvertently provided for the far left by liberals."

Evans and Novak sustained this sort of prose for months. They became the self-appointed, self-anointed conscience of the center of the Democratic Party, whatever that was in 1972. They preached the gospel of Richard M. Scammon and Ben J. Wattenberg again and again—and again.*

Not many voters, I suspect, paid much attention to Evans and

---

* Scammon and Wattenberg wrote another book we all read, *The Real Majority: An Extraordinary Examination of the American Electorate.* To win, the authors said, you've got to find the center and stick to it. They didn't say how you find it, stick to it, and go about winning the Democratic nomination.

Novak or me or anyone else. According to a famous study of voting behavior by Berelson, Lazarsfeld, and McPhee, Americans aren't very interested in politics, know next to nothing about the issues, rarely display any political principles, and throw away all logic when they enter the voting booth. They simply confirmed what H. L. Mencken was trying to tell us all those years.

In September of 1971, something did happen, I think, that caught an inattentive nation's attention.

BLACK VP
DISCOUNTED
BY MUSKIE

. . . the headline in the *Washington Post* (buried inside the paper) said. It was an Associated Press story and it began this way:

"Los ANGELES, Sept. 8 (AP)—Sen. Edmund S. Muskie (D-Maine) said today that there are blacks who are eminently qualified to be Vice-president but that he doesn't believe 'at this point in history' he could be elected president with a Negro running mate."

Muskie had set out September 5 on a four-month, 32-state tour to "galvanize what we sense is widespread support into hard support," his campaign manager, Berl Bernhard, had said. And this, on the third day of that tour, was the big headline he got.

How it all happened is one of the most fascinating stories of the campaign, and one of the most important, I suspect, because this is where the seeds of doubt were sown. This is where we first saw an Ed Muskie who didn't quite fit the perceptions we had formed of him in our living rooms.

The story begins with Richard Bergholz, a political reporter for the *Los Angeles Times*. Bergholz is a traditionalist, in harmony with his paper's traditionalist concept of how political news should be reported, and he was worried. Muskie, he discovered, had a lamentable habit of wandering around California without a reporter following him. So Bergholz suggested to Dick Stewart, Muskie's press secretary, there ought to be a "pool" arrangement of some kind.* Bergholz

---

* Stewart is one of the truly free spirits in American journalism. He had been one of *us,* and when he defected to *them* we figured Muskie couldn't be all bad. On September 7, the day before the blooper, Stewart opened a press conference in

meant that at least one reporter should be assigned to Muskie at all times and that he would share his findings with all the other reporters.

Stewart agreed and a pool arrangement took effect on Tuesday, September 7. Not so surprisingly, Bergholz was assigned as the pool reporter. And that was why Bergholz was the only reporter traveling with Muskie when he left San Francisco the morning of September 7 in Frank Sinatra's private jet. The rest of the press followed behind in a creaky old DC-6.

The Sinatra jet was late arriving in Los Angeles, which meant that things became a little hectic right at the outset. Bergholz tagged along with Muskie to the Century Plaza Hotel, where the senator met with a group of prospective contributors to his financially distressed campaign.

Then off they went to dedicate the Martin Luther King, Jr., Hospital, where the rest of the press, freshly arrived in the DC-6, joined up.

When the dedication was over, Bergholz climbed in the telephone car in the tiny motorcade. He presumed he was still the pool man and, anyway, he had some calls to make. His schedule—and the schedule for all the other reporters—indicated that everyone was going to the Century Plaza Hotel for rest and relaxation.

But, to Bergholz's considerable surprise, the little motorcade headed towards Watts, the black section of Los Angeles ravaged by riot in 1965, and pulled up in front of Ralph's Supermarket. The press bus was nowhere to be seen. Bergholz went along with Muskie's aides and found himself in a room above the supermarket normally used by the employees for their coffee breaks.

Bergholz looked around the room and saw many blacks he recognized immediately—Tom Bradley, for example, the black city councilman who almost defeated Sam Yorty for mayor in 1969, Roosevelt Grier, the retired football player and one-time aide to

San Francisco this way: "Gentlemen, my name is Dick Stewart. I'm the senator's press secretary. I mention that for anybody who needs an extra name for his expense account." Stewart is prone to do his impression of Clyde McCoy's "Sugar Blues" on almost any occasion and he will tell his joke about the gorilla and the two Englishmen without provocation or invitation. Stewart is now the *Boston Globe*'s national editor.

Robert Kennedy, and Chester Washington, editor of a black newspaper. Next to Washington was a young woman, notebook in hand, pencil at the ready. Missing, of course, were Press Secretary Stewart and the rest of the traveling press. They were relaxing at the hotel, just as the schedule said they should be.

Muskie walked into the little room above Ralph's Supermarket, took off his jacket, and began an informal give-and-take session with the assembled blacks—30 or 35 of them. Bergholz began taking notes and so did that young woman seated next to Editor Washington. One of Muskie's aides sidled up to Bergholz, and whispered to him that the session was off the record. Bergholz stopped taking notes. But he noticed, later, that no one had told the young woman to stop taking notes. She was writing, copiously.

At one point in the discussion, Muskie was asked if he would consider a black running mate, should he win the nomination, and he gave the reply that was to become famous.

No, he said in essence (there is no transcript of what he said), "it is my judgment that such a ticket is not electable now." He went on to say that he regretted this was so—it shouldn't be, he said—but a ticket with a black man on it would be defeated and that would be a setback to the efforts of those who are committed to equality for blacks.

No one pressed him on what he had said; there was no criticism. The discussion turned to other matters.

When he got back to the Century Plaza, Bergholz gave a "pool report" to the other reporters. He said a meeting had been held with black leaders in Watts and that Muskie's remarks were off the record.

But Bergholz was still worried about Editor Washington and that young woman taking all those notes. He told Press Secretary Stewart that he had no complaint about the session being off the record but that he did worry about being scooped by the black newspaper. He neglected to tell Stewart what Muskie had said in Watts.

Dutifully, Stewart checked with Editor Washington and was assured by him that no story would run in his newspaper. He was there as a black leader, not as a newspaperman, he said. But what about the young woman? Extensive investigation finally determined that she was an employe of the supermarket chain, on assignment to write a story for the chain's house organ. The Muskie people contacted officials of the supermarket and won *their* assurance that the house organ wouldn't run anything embarrassing.

That should have put an end to it—but, of course, it didn't. Bergholz, in giving his pool report, mentioned the names of several of the blacks (Tom Bradley among them) who had attended the session. On the basis of that information, one enterprising reporter, Bill Stall of the Associated Press, took it upon himself to ask Bradley if Muskie had said anything interesting.

Bradley was glad to oblige. Nobody had told him the session was off the record. Quite the contrary; he had seen Dick Bergholz at the meeting, and so he presumed it was *on* the record. So Stall filed a story, and all hell broke loose.

That evening, Muskie appeared at a fund-raiser at the Beverly Hills Hotel, pursued by a press corps that was in full, deep-throated cry. Tom Bradley, in the words of a Muskie aide, was "humbly apologetic" for breaking the story.

Back at the Century Plaza, Muskie's aides, according to some observers, were in a state bordering on panic. Some of them, it was said, believed the nomination, the election—everything—was lost. It was even suggested that Tom Bradley hold a midnight press conference to clear things up. Some of the reporters demurred; it was hardly that urgent, they felt.

So the press conferences were delayed until the following day, when the "pool man" was James Naughton of *The New York Times.* In his pool report (this was one of the first of the many Jim Naughton would write, and they were all models of their kind) he said:

"Back at the Century Plaza, Muskie told your pooler that he believed the political implications of this issue would not be harmful to him. 'I expect now every candidate will have to face this question,' he said with a smile. 'There are only three answers: yes, no, or maybe. I chose what I thought was the honest answer.' "*

And so there it was, hanging like a fat curve ball. Muskie doesn't

---

* Naughton handles details nicely. In this pool report, he was impressed by the appearance of a mistress of ceremonies who interviewed Muskie that day on KABC-TV: "The hostess, Stephanie Edwards, was wearing a marvelous knit purple pair of hot pants and matching halter under a knit long gown in purple, red, and beige stripes." Dick Stout of *Newsweek* (whose editors, just like *Time*'s, relish these pettifogging details) said later, in jest, that Naughton could have a job with *Newsweek* simply on the basis of the way he described menus in his pool reports.

think the nation is ready to vote for a black man for Vice-president and what do all you other politicians think about that, eh?

Not much, as it turned out. The reaction was as predictable as it was outrageous.

George McGovern's comment was typical. "I am not going to rule anybody off the ticket on the basis of race or sex," he said (only on the basis of previous mental-health history, as it turned out). Birch Bayh, Hubert Humphrey, Henry Jackson, and every .200 hitter in politics said just about the same thing.

I suppose Mayor Sam Yorty sank the lowest. The man who defeated Tom Bradley in what most observers think was a pure racist campaign said this: "I'm not going to be the man to tell a Negro boy he can never become Vice-president."

And let us not forget the President of the United States. He intoned: "I believe it is, frankly, a libel on the American people to suggest that they are too prejudiced to vote for an individual of a certain religion, race, or national heritage."

The year's most scurrilous publication—and that's the word, scurrilous, meaning the language of low indecency or abuse—was *Monday,* the publication of the Republican National Committee edited by John Lofton, who received early training from a man we will meet later, William Loeb of the *Manchester* (N.H.) *Union Leader.*

Lofton rarely missed an opportunity for low buffoonery. His riposte to the Muskie blooper was a fictional wire-service story:

"WASHINGTON (AP)—President Abraham Muskie said today that he doesn't believe 'at this point in history' he could be re-elected President if he were to issue the Emancipation Proclamation, even though there are many blacks who are eminently qualified to be free."

In a practical sense, Muskie's judgment that a white-and-black ticket almost surely would lose is probably correct. And Yorty and Nixon and all the others surely agreed with that verdict privately (which, of course, is why their sanctimonious reactions are so deplorable). In April 1969, in fact, the Gallup poll reported that 67 percent of its national sample would vote for a Negro, if he were properly qualified to be President. But 23 percent said they would not vote for a qualified Negro and 10 percent said they weren't sure.

But that's not the kind of poll we were interested in. We were interested in the who's-ahead polls. Because if the American people are interested in anything about politics, it's about who's going to win, "on all fours," with our interest "in the World Series, the Kentucky Derby, and the annual Rose Bowl football game," according to Stuart Chase.

That being all too true, the little band of believers—the reporters and the politicians and the activists really interested in politics—read George Gallup's figures as if they were chiseled in stone. At this early stage of the game, they were, in fact, scribbled in sand.

The trouble is that most people—stubborn bastards—continue to believe that a poll taken in November of 1971 tells us something about what's going to happen in November of 1972. It doesn't, of course; it simply suggests to us what would happen if the election were held at the precise moment the poll was taken. But that's spurious; in November of 1971, a full year before the election, nobody gave a damn.

But it was all we had, and we marveled at the precision of the little figures. Watch this procession: On August 1, Gallup reported that Muskie and Kennedy were tied (among Democratic voters). On September 19, Kennedy was ahead. On November 14, Muskie took an 11-point lead over Kennedy. But, at that same time, Louis Harris, in *his* poll, showed Kennedy leading Muskie by 7 points. Then, on December 6, Kennedy came storming back with a 5-point lead over Muskie.

In retrospect, it's easy to see how absurd, how meaningless all of this really was. These who's-ahead polls at this stage of a campaign (a noncampaign, really, if the interest of the voters is taken into consideration) should be abolished.

But, alas, we listened and so did the professionals who should have known better. We decided, in concert, that Muskie's nomination was inevitable, even if he was appeasing the Trotskyists, even if he did store his red wine in the refrigerator (as one magazine told us).

We forgot what a little headline in the Sunday *New York Times* told us. "Muskie's Waterloo?" it asked. The story that went with it talked about Muskie's indiscretion and it remarked that nameless people were calling it his "Waterloo." That really wasn't it; if anything, it was Muskie's "Trafalgar." The ultimate defeat was to come later, in the cold drizzle of New Hampshire.

For now, Muskie remained the front-runner and nobody thought much about poor old George McGovern, aground on rock bottom at 6 percent in Mr. Gallup's poll.

4

McGovern

My friend Bruce Biossat, columnist for Newspaper Enterprise Association and a lovable, crotchety den father to the national political press, refused to go campaigning with Senator George S. McGovern of South Dakota.

"I don't waste my time with six percenters," he said.

I agreed with him. I can't think of anybody who didn't agree. George McGovern, we told each other, was a decent sort of fellow, but . . .

That attitude left McGovern staffers babbling in frustration and rage. For them, it was a classical dilemma: you won't write about us because we're only at 6 percent in the polls but we can't climb in the polls unless you tell the voters who we are.

"To hell with you," Gary Hart, the McGovern organizer, told me once. "If we have to, we'll go to Miami Beach still at 6 percent in the polls—and we'll win the nomination."

Obviously, we underestimated the man we called, patronizingly, McGoo.

—We underestimated the organization Hart was so carefully building.

—We underestimated the importance of the party reforms that McGovern had shaped.

I am still puzzled by my own reluctance to make much of McGovern's striking advantage in organizational skills. Surely what he was doing was nothing new. Kennedy, in the primaries of 1960, did much the same thing. Larry O'Brien's little manual became something of a minor classic. "Volunteers," he said, "are essential to the success of any political campaign."

Volunteers were essential to John Kennedy's success. "The organizational secret of Kennedy politics was so simple that it was often overlooked: it was a politics of personal involvement, on a massive scale," David Broder wrote in his book, *The Party's Over.*

In 1968, I wrote a book, *The New Politics: The Expanding Technology of Political Manipulation.* In it, I suggested that candidates could now go directly to the voters, bypassing the party's organizational structure, with new techniques, including paid TV and radio commercials, computerized direct mail, highly sophisticated demographics, and much, much more. It was almost an antiparty phenomenon I was examining, and it was working because political organizations no longer were effective in the face of it.

Broder argues that the two-party system is breaking down, and he deplores it (and recommends ways of doing something about it). I was demonstrating that candidates using these new techniques were moving into the vacuum created by the breakdown of the party system.

There is a point I may not have considered seriously enough: a candidate can create his own political organization, complete with precinct, ward, county, district, and state chairmen, run by loyal, enthusiastic volunteers, aimed at bypassing the regulars and carrying the message to all the voters. In West Virginia, for example, John Kennedy did almost just that. What he did was exclusionary only in the sense that most political leaders in the state refused to participate.

That was not Kennedy's way. He wanted everyone to join, and the doors were always open.

I suppose you could say Gene McCarthy, in 1968, and George McGovern, in 1972, wanted everyone to join too, and that their doors were always open.

Yet, John Kennedy was not a one-issue candidate; he was not really an ideologue at all. He was one candidate, out of many, trying to win the Presidential nomination and what he was saying was not that much different from what everyone else was saying. If you *like* me, Kennedy implied, work for me. If you *agree* with me, McCarthy and McGovern implied, you may work for me.

If you agree with me that the war in Vietnam must end, now: that was the test, for both McCarthy and McGovern. In 1968, the press was slow to realize that the issue was so powerful; in early 1972, we were reluctant to admit that it remained powerful.

Maybe, in fact, it had faded; perhaps McGovern's 6 percent in the polls represented the hard core of Americans who felt deeply and emotionally about what was happening in Vietnam.

But from that 6 percent came the people who gave the thrust to McGovern and for party reform. From that 6 percent came the only people who really cared enough to work hard within a party system that was undergoing sweeping change. And their candidate was George McGovern and remained George McGovern, despite prose-lytizing by Harold Hughes of Iowa, Fred Harris of Oklahoma, Birch Bayh of Indiana, Gene McCarthy himself, and, at last, Mayor John Lindsay of New York, the one we took most seriously.

That was what George McGovern began with and it was enough —barely enough—to carry him all the way to Miami Beach and the nomination for President of the United States.

I saw what was happening in New Hampshire, where it all be-gan for George McGovern, but I didn't quite believe it. And I suppose I was influenced by the fact that my colleagues saw what was hap-pening and they didn't quite believe it either.

It was something of a lark, my first trip to New Hampshire with George McGovern in early May 1971. We traveled around the state in a station wagon—McGovern, his aide Gordon Weil, Tom Ottenad of the *St. Louis Post-Dispatch,* and me. "So here we were," I wrote, "the all-time champion early-bird caravan, seeking out friendly faces on the streets of Berlin, a backyard garden in Keene, a Fellowship in Israel dinner in Nashua."

But, I said, McGovern needs all the time he can get in New Hampshire. I was pessimistic because I'd been reading polls again. A few days earlier, the *Boston Globe* published a professional survey taken by Becker Research Corporation and based on interviews with 1,021 New Hampshire Democrats. In an eight-way race the results were: Muskie, 45 percent; Kennedy, 20; Humphrey, 14; McGovern, 6; Lindsay, 3; Bayh, 2; Jackson, 2; Hughes, 1; and undecided, 7.

Narrowing it down to three candidates, the results were: Muskie, 58 percent; Kennedy, 26; McGovern, 9; and undecided, 7.

Reacting to this, I parroted the conventional wisdom: "Given his choice, McGovern would rather avoid New Hampshire. It is a conservative state and McGovern is the most liberal candidate around. Further, Muskie lives right next door in Maine, and Muskie, like so many of New Hampshire's Democrats, is a Roman Catholic. McGovern is the son of a Plains state Methodist preacher, and he looks and sounds like it."

This, for the record, is the first statement of the propinquity factor: that candidates who come from next door do better than candidates who live across town. But, as McLuhan says, we live in a global village. The propinquity factor doesn't mean a thing anymore.

I plunged on.

"McGovern's style (if not his content)," I wrote, "is nicely tailored to New Hampshire. He is pleasant, candid, hardworking, intelligent, sincere, trustworthy. And he is one of the most decent human beings in all of American politics."

There it is—that damn decency business.

As a politician, McGovern isn't all that "decent." Republicans insist he and Shriver ran the nastiest campaign in recent history. Even in those early days, there were indications that McGovern could be something less than "decent" in attacking his enemies. For some curious reason that escapes me now, he became embroiled in a shouting match with Senator Norris Cotton, New Hampshire's leading Republican, over the qualifications of Dr. Thomas N. Bonner, president of the University of New Hampshire and a one-time legislative aide to McGovern.

McGovern said Cotton is "one of those obsolete, self-styled experts whose patriotism consists largely of cheering from the sidelines while young men die in a foolish war he helped foster."

Tough words from a politician who turned out to be tougher than any of us anticipated. So why did we think of him as the one truly decent man in American politics? Because, I suspect, he was decent to us.

I'd never known George McGovern before I spent those first few days with him in New Hampshire. But we got along famously. I think he likes newspapermen; he's able to listen to other people. He can talk about things other than polls and county leaders and legislation he has proudly authored. He remembers people's names—he caught mine that first day and never forgot it—and he even reads what people write. Later, when I would run across him, he would comment upon an article or a column. It was obvious he had actually read it. Actually, I mean.

It was flattering, and in little ways, it may have affected what I wrote and what I thought. It was in these personal relationships, I suspect, that the decency business began. Not entirely unfairly, mind you. In his personal relationships, he is, after all, a decent man. It is in his public postures and positions—his self-righteousness, perhaps— that he is vulnerable.

It points up a serious dilemma for journalists: How close should they get to the people they write about? Arm's length, I think.

Anyway, as the campaign progresses, the problem becomes moot. Nobody can get within an arm's length of a winning candidate because of the crowd around him. The man I rode with in a station wagon, early on, graduates to his own chartered jet with his own private compartment. Some reporters (and all of the electronic technicians) fly in a second airplane, called the Zoo. By then, the personal impressions we have formed of the candidate are weeks old. We are the veterans, we remember the man when, and we even begin to resent lately arrived colleagues who pretend to know something about *our* candidate.*

Political reporters do their socializing with each other—and with the candidates' aides and advisors.

George McGovern couldn't tell me anything about his organiza-

---

* Of course, there are exceptions. Celebrated columnists and television commentators—James Reston, Joseph Alsop, Rowland Evans, Thomas Braden, Joseph Kraft, Sander Vanocur, and a handful more—manage to find private time with celebrated politicians, perhaps at a dinner party, perhaps late at night in a hotel room somewhere along the campaign trail. For the life of me, though, I can't remember a single instance in which this kind of socializing added much to our common knowledge of a candidate or his campaign.

tion in New Hampshire, but Jacques Joseph Grandmaison could. Grandmaison, 28 years old in 1971, ran the New Hampshire campaign; he built the organization.

Grandmaison opened McGovern's New Hampshire headquarters on April 29, 1971—11 months before the primary—in Suite 500 of the old Sheraton-Carpenter Hotel in Manchester. And, as far as I can tell (my files are somewhat incomplete for early 1971), nobody paid much attention until October, six months after Grandmaison went to work.

The New York Times recognized McGovern's efforts in New Hampshire in a story by Christopher Lydon (his by-line was misspelled "Lyon") on October 31. "Senator George McGovern's organization, spreading like an inkblot, is forcing the early pace of New Hampshire's Presidential primary campaign, supporters and rivals here agree," he reported from Manchester.

"The McGovern cadres are built around the McCarthy workers of three years ago, but this is an essentially different campaign," Lydon said. "It is much weaker because of the popularity of Senator Muskie and because of the absence of his 1968 adversary, Lyndon B. Johnson, yet it is much stronger organizationally."

The fact that "the labor of a dozen paid workers through the summer have not appreciably broadened his support in the opinion polls, which was measured at about 6 percent of the New Hampshire electorate last spring" was evidence of the "weakness" of the McGovern effort, Lydon noted.

On October 19, David Broder wrote that "George McGovern's managers think the press is missing the boat on his candidacy for the Democratic Presidential nomination. Political reporters, they say, are underestimating McGovern as badly as they underestimated Eugene J. McCarthy's chances against Lyndon Johnson four years ago at this time."

Broder conceded that "McGovern's field organization exceeds that of anyone else in the race. But other, more important questions remain to be answered. McGovern may have organized his faction of the party, but it is not clear that the McGovern faction has expanded to the point that it is a potential majority."

McGovern has failed to establish himself as the "chief challenger to Edmund S. Muskie," Broder wrote. "Indeed, McGovern has not yet managed to monopolize the support of the Democratic left."

Broder noted that Fred Harris was "poaching" and he said that Lindsay's steady movement toward an open candidacy was "far more serious." Lindsay, Broder felt, "would hand McGovern a huge—and perhaps insurmountable—problem."

That was the conventional wisdom, which, in this instance, I am pleased to note, I did not share. *The New York Times* and the *Washington Post* both indulged in an orgy of speculation about John Lindsay and then covered the announcement of his candidacy with the urgency of the attack on Pearl Harbor.

The unkindest cut of all came a little earlier, in September, from columnist Tom Braden, whose partner, Frank Mankiewicz, had gone to work for McGovern in early May. "Idealism is an enormous force in American politics," he wrote, "but it has never sufficed to win an election." The one plus that might grow out of the McGovern campaign, he felt, was that it would "keep Ed Muskie honest."

The only serious, in-depth attention McGovern received in either *The New York Times* or the *Washington Post* during the latter half of 1971 was an article in the *Times* Sunday Magazine written by L. Clayton DuBois, a free lance. The headline, "Is He Really Serious About Becoming President? Yes," probably betrayed the skepticism of the headline writer. DuBois himself was almost prophetic. He concluded:

". . . McGovern is no conventional politician, and his staff is quick to point out some recent historical parallels where convention was wrong. Where was Gene McCarthy in the polls before New Hampshire? they ask. . . . Wait until Wisconsin, they say. That's when 1972's surprises begin." The reader assumes that DuBois shared this opinion.

Paul R. Wieck, writing in *The New Republic* on October 30, was optimistic too. McGovern, he said, must be considered a major contender for the nomination. His organization, Wieck wrote, is the best in the field "at this stage of the game." Like DuBois in the *Times* magazine, he copped out at the end with someone else's quotation. "Everybody always underestimates George," the quote read. "Don't make that mistake." Wieck, too, one assumes, shared that opinion.

Further investigation would no doubt unearth other examples of prophetic journalism. I know, for example, that the *Boston Globe*'s Martin Nolan treasures a tattered clipping of one of his own columns, in which, he says, he had nice things to say about McGovern's chances. But the examples are isolated and, sometimes, they merely reflect the wish that was father to the author's thought.

But, I suspect, the question of prophecy is not really the issue. The fact that most reporters, commentators, and columnists were unable to predict what would happen is no criticism of them, per se: because there was no way any of us could predict the outcome. We simply didn't have enough data on which to base sensible predictions. We didn't know what George Wallace would do, or what would be done to him; we had no way of knowing what kind of candidate John Lindsay would be. We wondered about Senator Henry Jackson and what kind of appeal he might make to more conservative elements in the party. And the man who emerged as the final, most important challenger, Hubert Humphrey; well, we weren't even thinking about him. Nixon's political future was closely tied to events in Vietnam and elsewhere and to what might happen to the economy at home, and we had no way of knowing how those things might turn out.

The criticism is not that reporters, commentators, and columnists were wrong; that was inevitable. The criticism is that they insisted upon playing the prophecy game at all.

What we should have done is pay more attention to the candidates themselves—introduce them, so to speak, to the voters. Perhaps if we had analyzed what McGovern was saying about amnesty, abortion, marijuana, the war, welfare, all these things, there would not have been so much confusion in the minds of the voters later on. It is ironic, perhaps, that the clearest exposition of McGovern's positions to appear in all of 1971 was published as an interview in *Playboy* magazine in August.

I think, too, that we could have described McGovern's organization at work—and left it at that. The temptation, always, was to enter caveats. Sure, we said, it's a good organization, maybe the best around, but. . . . Always the fatal but.

I plead guilty to my own charge. I did go to New Hampshire and look at the McGovern operation; I did talk at length to Joe

Grandmaison. And I wrote all about it. In October of 1971, I wrote that McGovern's volunteers began their canvassing in June. Most of them were college kids, on vacation. They were given a free room and $45 a week. By the time they were finished, they had made contact with 3,000 voters. What the canvassers found was transcribed on little index cards and coded. No. 1 voters said they wanted to help McGovern. No. 2 voters said it was still too early, but they'd like to know more about McGovern. No. 3 voters said they liked Muskie or Yorty or nobody at all.

The No. 1 and No. 2 voters were put on a McGovern mailing list. They began receiving a newsletter and they were placed on local committees and recruited for special projects.

I even talked about the awesome commitment of just one of these volunteers—Edward T. Hall, headmaster of St. Mark's School in Southboro, Massachusetts. *The* St. Mark's, of the St. Grottlesex St. Markses. Ed Hall showed up at the Manchester headquarters early in the summer and asked Grandmaison what he could do. For the rest of the summer, he worked two days a week in Manchester and three days a week in Hanover. He spent that time typing *personal* letters to all those No. 1 and No. 2 voters identified by the canvassers. He wrote 200 letters a week, and there wasn't a single form letter among them. "My God," Grandmaison told me, "that's commitment."

I talked about the trouble the McGovern people were having in getting the names of people eligible to vote. Those names appear on the "checklist" and each of the state's 302 voting districts has its own "checklist." You can't canvass the voters without the checklist.

In 1969, the state legislature had passed a law stating that these checklists must be made available at reasonable cost to anyone wanting them. Presuming the law meant what it seemed to say, Grandmaison's people sent form letters to every checklist supervisor in the state. "We are anxious to obtain information on registration dates and times from all towns and cities in New Hampshire," the letter began. It asked for more information, including where copies of the checklist might be obtained and how much they would cost.

And what was the response?

Landaff's was typical: "Dates have not been set yet," the supervisor wrote. "Too far off to worry about now."

Or Lyme: "I have just written to the secretary of state and he advises me that we supervisors of the checklists in Lyme have nothing to do in 1971."

Or New Castle: "Not for sale."

"It's all so eighteenth century," said Mrs. Jean Wallin, New Hampshire's Democratic national committeewoman and an early McGovern convert.

Well, that's the sort of work the McGovern people were doing in 1971 in New Hampshire. It was slow, tedious, undramatic, but it was moving ahead.

On that same visit, I stopped in Suite 200 at the Sheraton-Carpenter, the Muskie headquarters, just three floors below McGovern headquarters, and talked to Mrs. Maria Carrier, Grandmaison's opposite number in the front-runner's camp. She was not very happy. "We had to start work in June, in response to *them*," she said, staring in some anger at the ceiling and in the direction of the McGovern headquarters upstairs. But I could find no Ed Halls or Jean Wallins working in her headquarters.

"In all of this," I concluded, "one can see some pretty serious trouble for Ed Muskie, who's supposed to win this primary in a breeze. What if Joe Grandmaison can pull off a big surprise and turn out, say, 30 percent of the vote for George McGovern? What if Bill Loeb can dirty the waters once again, and turn out 25 percent of the vote for Sam Yorty? And what if John Lindsay enters the race, and siphons off 10 percent of the vote?

"That leaves Ed Muskie the winner with something like 35 percent of the vote and the Great Percentage Maker wouldn't think very much of that.

"For what it's worth" [not very much, as it turned out], "I don't think it will work that way. I suspect McGovern's strength is tough and vocal—and pretty narrow. I suspect that Loeb, this time, with Yorty, won't get his usual 25 percent. And I think Lindsay is too late to do much here. I think Ed Muskie is strong in New Hampshire, everywhere."

This is the sort of thing so many of us were writing. The total effect was overwhelming, and each day, somebody in New York at CBS, NBC, and ABC was storing away these clippings. It was not yet television's moment to join the battle, but that time was not far off now, and what we in the print medium had written would dictate what they soon would have to say. How could it be otherwise? After all, we were the experts and we were there first.

I might even write a scorecard for myself. I was correct in believing that McGovern was doing better than one might expect and that Muskie was having some problems. I was right in believing that, this time, Loeb wouldn't pull 25 percent of the vote. I was wrong about Lindsay; he never entered the New Hampshire primary. But candidates I didn't mention at all—Vance Hartke and Wilbur Mills—did. Perhaps I was right in October of 1971 when I wrote that Muskie was strong, everywhere. But, if that was supposed to be a prediction about what would happen on election day in March, I was wrong.

My instincts in October of 1971 told me that McGovern was the only candidate in New Hampshire who was doing very much. That was worth reporting and analyzing, but I was swayed by the siren song of Dr. Gallup's poll and, no doubt, by what my own colleagues were saying and writing.

Organization was going to count in 1972 because organization would decide who would go to the convention in Miami Beach. This time, things were going to be different.

Here, once again, we went wrong. We underestimated the vital importance of party reform. Without reform, McGovern had no real chance; with it, he won the nomination.

It is not my intention to tell the whole story of party reform here (thank God for that, you may well say), but the high points of it are worth remembering. Reform grew out of the events at Chicago in 1968, when the losers could argue, with some justification, that they'd been had.

"The 1968 Democratic National Convention in Chicago exposed profound flaws in the presidential nominating process . . . ," the report of the Commission on Party Structure and Delegate Selection begins.

The Chicago convention had directed the Democratic National Committee to establish the commission and Senator Fred Harris of Oklahoma, the national chairman, appointed its 28 members in February of 1969. McGovern was the chairman and Senator Harold Hughes of Iowa, the true father of party reform, was the vice-chairman. It was reasonably representative of the party's membership. One of its members, for example, was I. W. Abel, president of the Steelworkers, who rarely attended its working sessions. The irony of that was pointed up when he gave what was surely the angriest speech at the convention that saw the commission's work bear fruit.

In its report, the commission said:

"After a lengthy examination of the structure and processes used to select delegates to the National Convention in 1968, this is our basic conclusion: meaningful participation of voters in the choice of their presidential nominee was often difficult or costly, sometimes completely illusory, and, in not a few instances, impossible."

Delegates, the commission found, had been chosen at secret caucuses and closed slate-making sessions. ". . . widespread proxy voting—and a host of other procedural irregularities—were all too common at precinct, county, district, and state conventions."

Of the 2,622 votes cast at the convention, 970, or 38 percent, represented delegates who had been chosen prior to the year in which the convention was held. Most of these delegates, not so surprisingly, were loyal to Lyndon Johnson and to his heir at Chicago, Hubert Humphrey.

And what kind of people went to the convention? Not many were black or female or young. "Representation of blacks, women, and youth at the convention was substantially below the proportion of each group in the population," the commission found. Five percent of the voting delegates were black; 13 percent were women, and about 4 percent were under thirty.

To open the party, to make participation meaningful, the commission adopted eighteen stringent guidelines. Each state party was requested to form its own reform commission to bring each state party into compliance with the guidelines adopted by the national commission. The commission declared that its guidelines were binding on the states, subject only to review by the 1972 convention.

The unit rule was abolished at all levels; proxy voting was outlawed; discrimination of any kind, especially against women and young people, was condemned, and each party was expected to take "affirmative steps" to "encourage minority group participation, including representation of minority groups on the national convention delegation in reasonable relationship to the group's presence in the population of the state."

On that final point, the commission said, in a footnote, that "this is not to be accomplished by the mandatory imposition of quotas."

"Timeliness" was one of the key reforms; delegates had to be selected, the process itself had to start in the calendar year in which the convention would be held. As a result, 22 states and the District of Columbia scheduled delegate-selection primaries in 1972, against 16 states and the District of Columbia in 1968. Almost two-thirds of the delegates going to the 1972 convention would be elected in primaries; in 1968, fewer than half came out of primaries.

The guidelines were adopted on November 19 and 20, 1969, and from then on, through 1970 and 1971, the tedious work of bringing the state parties into compliance went forward slowly, undramatically, and almost unobtrusively.

In 1971, the only major coverage of the reform situation was given to the battle over the choice of a temporary chairman of the Credentials Committee. Reformers wanted Senator Hughes as chairman; regulars, including the national chairman, Larry O'Brien, wanted Mrs. Patricia Roberts Harris. At a meeting of the Democratic National Committee on October 14, Mrs. Harris won, 72–31. "It was," said R. W. "Johnny" Apple, Jr., of *The New York Times,* "a striking victory for [O'Brien] and for the American Federation of Labor and Congress of Industrial Relations, which had bitterly opposed the Hughes candidacy."

Senator Muskie supported Senator Hughes, in what Evans and Novak must have believed was another attempt to appease the party's lunatic left.

As things turned out, it meant little or nothing. Mrs. Harris carried out her duties efficiently and fairly. Reformers could have asked for no more.

To recapitulate, then, McGovern was doing very nicely as 1971 came to a close. His grass-roots organization in the two primary states he had targeted—New Hampshire and Wisconsin—was superb. And the reforms his own commission had written were being quietly implemented.

Our attention, meanwhile, was riveted elsewhere. We were watching John Lindsay.

5

Lindsay

In August of 1971, following Mayor John V. Lindsay's breathlessly awaited switch from the Republican to the Democratic Party, grumpy old William S. White wrote a column that almost made sense. It is a unique document.

"Talk of Lindsay as a 1972 contender for the Presidential nomination is the sheerest of moonshine," he began. "A man unable to obtain the renomination of his own party—the Republican—for municipal office and re-elected by a distinctly minority vote could hardly use the disaster area that is New York as a viable springboard to the Presidency of the United States."

From that point on, the column runs downhill. White talks about the danger Lindsay will pose to "such far-out senators" as McGovern and Harris. He even sees Lindsay lending a little help to his own specially blessed candidate, Senator Henry M. Jackson.

Initially, though, White had a point: Lindsay faced far too many obstacles.

Yet, in the final six months of 1971, Lindsay received more coverage by the press than any other person seeking, or thinking about seeking, the Democratic Presidential nomination. It was a media orgy, especially in *The New York Times,* which sometimes can display a brand of parochialism that, transplanted to Ohio, would embarrass the *Ashtabula Star-Beacon.*

It is a supreme irony that John Lindsay, supposedly the master of the media, was hoist by his own petard. The media made him and the media exploded him.

The Lindsay phenomenon boggles the mind, now that the smoke has cleared. Lindsay was not a popular mayor of New York except, perhaps, in some salons on Manhattan's Upper East Side. In Queens and the Bronx and Staten Island too, he was honestly detested. Why, he was the man who couldn't even get the snow plowed. Under Lindsay's rule, New York had become a symbol of urban hopelessness and frustration. Maybe that wasn't his fault, but it was the fact of it.

So what was so impressive about him?

In a word—terrible word—"charisma."

"Oomph," old-timers would call it. Star quality. In a field of broken-down nags, he was a Thoroughbred. He would be able to grab the ears of all our TV sets and shake us right out of our slippers.

Once again, I suppose, some of us had been reading books. Particularly Joe McGinniss's *The Selling of the President 1968:*

"The television celebrity is a vessel," McGinniss wrote. "An inoffensive container in which someone else's knowledge, insight, compassion, or wit can be presented. And we respond like the child on Christmas morning who ignores the gift to play with the wrapping paper.

"Television can be particularly useful to the politician who can be charming but lacks ideas. . . . He need be neither statesman nor crusader; he must only show up on time. . . . Style becomes substance. The medium is the message and the masseur gets the votes."

God knows John Lindsay was a TV celebrity. Thanks to countless appearances on the Johnny Carson show, he was almost as well known in Ashtabula as in Forest Hills. More importantly, the people in Ashtabula liked him. On TV, he had style.

It was McGinniss's thesis that "a group of young men attuned to the political uses of television" managed to create a "new Nixon." If he was humorless, they would feed him funny lines. If he lacked warmth, they would show his "emotional involvement" in the issues. . . .

"It was as if they were building not a President but an Astrodome, where the wind would never blow, the temperature never rise or fall, and the ball never bounce erratically on the artificial grass."

McGinniss argued that it worked. He suggested it was the principal reason explaining Nixon's defeat of poor old Hubert Humphrey who, when he was invited into our homes on television, "vomited on the rug."

Thus, if the manipulators could package "grumpy, cold, and aloof" Richard Nixon, imagine what wonders they could perform with charismatic, warm, and lovable John Lindsay?

There's a slight problem here: Nixon was *not* successfully packaged. He started the campaign at 42 percent in the polls; he ended it with 42 percent of the vote. Despite all the money spent by McGinniss's people, there was no *movement*. In fact, Nixon won because George Wallace also was running and because millions of Democrats and ticket splitters were appalled at what they had seen in Chicago.

Surely other candidates, Lindsay himself, in his second race for mayor, have been packaged with some success. *But it only works when the voters are unaware that a candidate is being packaged.* The voters must believe what they see on the tube; anything less is disaster.

And that's precisely what happened to Lindsay in 1971. The press was convinced because he was an attractive package—and they told the voters about it. Later, when TV had its fling, their reporters picked up what they had read in the magazines and newspapers. The "Report on Network News' Treatment of the 1972 Presidential Candidates," prepared by the Alternative Educational Foundation, Inc., noted that the networks "darkly hinted that there was something artificial and manipulative about a candidate who relied so heavily on television gimmickry; that such a media campaign was essentially a camouflage designed to mask (and thus overcome) serious flaws and deficiencies in the candidate himself. . . . The John Lindsay of television advertisements and campaign stunts, then, was an artfully crafted media *image* that in no way reflected the *reality* of Lindsay's candidacy."

Lindsay switched parties on August 11, announcing what he had done at a press conference in the ballroom of Gracie Mansion. The *Washington Post* said 15 TV cameras recorded the event; *The New York Times* counted 13.

"The news rated front-page treatment in newspapers in all sections and massive coverage on the national television shows," David Broder reported in his story that was spotted under a three-line, three-column head in the upper-right-hand corner of the *Washington Post.* The *Post* also carried an analysis written by Tim O'Brien and the full text of the mayor's statement transcribed by United Press International.

The *Times*'s lead piece ran under a three-line, four-column head. It was written by Martin Tolchin, the City Hall reporter. Another piece running under the same headline, reporting reaction to the mayor's decision, was written by James Naughton, whom we have met already. Still another Page One story was written by Richard Reeves. Two more major stories, one of them a profile of the mayor, appeared inside the paper. The transcript of his statement and even a photograph of the document in which he applied to change his party enrollment also formed a part of the package.

The opening paragraph of the profile, written by Maurice Carroll, is revealing: "A casting director's dream of a television-era politician. . . ."

Now that Lindsay had ended the speculation about changing parties, the next round began: Would he run for the Democratic nomination for President? Lindsay's own talkative staff was pushing him in that direction; they seemed convinced he'd be a strong candidate. Why? "There aren't any state chairmen who can't be overcome by good media and good organization," an anonymous aide told *The New York Times.*

In the three months that followed the announcement of his switch, Lindsay embarked on nine road trips—"political fishing trips" they were called, inevitably. Everywhere he went, the press traveling with him wrote about his "charisma" and the way his handlers performed their wondrous manipulative assignments.

The demonstration in Pittsburgh was "carefully staged." He "projected too much charm and not enough substance" during his visit to California. His "media-conscious advisers" always "knew just where to put the people for the 'right' television shots." His consultants picked a Tuesday night for his appearance on the Dick Cavett show; they knew Tuesday night had the biggest ratings (Cavett, on Tuesdays, follows "Marcus Welby, M.D."). Talkative aides confirmed that "Lindsay had been briefed before the show to underline one salient point during each segment between commercials."

That was one side of the coverage: Lindsay was something of a puppet in the hands of brilliant advisers. The other side was that he was not very convincing as a candidate when his advisers couldn't control the situation. Evans and Novak said Lindsay "floundered" when he was "suddenly introduced" to a crowd of steel-mill blacks "long before he should have been [introduced]." He ended his speech with "a dog-eared joke built around a lady of easy virtue called Annabelle.

" 'Good Lord,' whispered a top state party official, 'has John lost his marbles? To these cats Annabelle smacks of a racial joke.' "

Stephen Isaacs, writing in the *Washington Post,* discovered that Lindsay is "not the country's most vibrant speech reader." Isaacs said many people in one of his crowds "obviously were watching more than listening." Evans and Novak said the trouble was that Lindsay's "rhetoric was packed with clichés of Eastern-style drawing-room politics."

Still, the excitement continued to mount. On November 10, *The New York Times* reported in its lead Page One story (three-line, three-column headline) that Deputy Mayor Richard Aurelio had resigned to "set up a national network of Lindsay headquarters, ostensibly to assess the mayor's Presidential prospects." A separate Page One story said Aurelio had selected seven target states—Florida, Pennsylvania, Massachusetts, Wisconsin, Indiana, Iowa, and Arizona.

Aurelio was held in some awe by the New York press. Even though he had no experience in Presidential politics, New Yorkers believed he was the best political operative in the nation. He is good, but not that good, as events would amply demonstrate.

On December 28, at the Dupont Plaza Hotel in Miami, Florida, Lindsay made the announcement that was by now anticlimactic: He was running for President. This time *The New York Times* was restrained. There was only one story on Page One, and it was not the lead.

The most remarkable Lindsay story of the entire campaign appeared in the *Washington Post,* starting on Page One. "Lindsay Off, With an Eye to the Media" the headline read.

The theme of the story, written by Stephen Isaacs, the *Post's* New York correspondent, was manipulation.

The room in the Dupont Plaza Hotel "was packed and hot and sweaty because Lindsay's advance men wanted it that way. Larger rooms were available, but they were not used. Cooler rooms were available, but they were not used.

"Lindsay's media adviser, David Garth, is one of those campaign specialists who worries about details that can come across on television and affect a viewer's vote."

Isaacs said the small room was chosen—part of it was even closed off—"to heighten the impression that the conference was immediate and overflowing with those interested in Lindsay.

"The effect was heightened by scheduling the conference only a 10-minute walk from the hotel in which 77 reporters covering the President's talks with Willy Brandt are staying. Lindsay's press conference was scheduled at 10:30 A.M., leaving ample time for those [77] reporters to look in and still make their noon bus to Key Biscayne."

Further, Isaacs reported, the room was "papered" with students from North Miami Beach Senior High School "and a number of elderly women brought to the conference by the mother of Lindsay aide Sid Davidoff. Davidoff's mother lives in Miami."

Isaacs was warming to his theme now. "Garth," he continued, "attended to such details as moving several newspaper reporters out of a group of aisle seats so an ABC camera crew could have a better shot, and at one point personally supervised the placing of microphones on the podium so that none would obscure the cameras' view of Lindsay's face."

After the press conference, Isaacs said, Lindsay visited a shopping center that had been carefully selected by his staff "because it is perhaps the busiest in all of Florida." Shoppers came up to see Lindsay "out of curiosity," Isaacs said. Later, "Lindsay visited a home for the elderly—a stop that also had been carefully planned."

Thereafter, Isaacs began writing about what Lindsay had said— about the problems of the cities, about the problems of blacks and browns and old people and young people, about corruption in Washington, about unemployment and the war in Vietnam, about his own chances of winning the nomination.

The New York Times story by Frank Lynn failed to mention any of the manipulative details supplied so amply in the *Post* by Isaacs. Lynn's only dig was in response to Lindsay's statement that he was announcing his candidacy in Miami rather than in Washington or New York because Florida "would be the scene of his first primary campaign." Lynn retorted that "several politicians [unnamed] said that a news conference in New York might be dominated by questions about various city problems and thus possibly embarrass the mayor."

The Isaacs story in the *Post* disturbs me. Here we have John Lindsay announcing his candidacy for the Presidential nomination, setting the tone for his entire campaign, and Isaacs, writing in one of the two most influential newspapers in America, is carrying on paragraph after paragraph about the way Lindsay's appearance was stage-managed.

So the advance men carefully chose a small, sweaty room to give the event "immediacy." That's the oldest trick in the advance man's bag. So the conference was scheduled to enable 77 White House reporters to drop by. What's wrong with that? Probably it was an educational experience for them, clearly a plus. So the audience was "papered" with friends and admirers; people like that are called claquers, and the word goes back to 1837. So Garth cleared out some newspaper reporters to make way for a TV crew; we've been kicked around like that for years. So Lindsay visited a shopping center picked by his advance men because it was the busiest in Florida; better he should go to a penny candy store?

What happened at that press conference happens all the time. There was nothing unusual about it, nothing that was newsworthy. Sure, what happened should be noted; whenever it happens, which is most of the time, it should be noted. But Isaacs built his whole story around it, and it was shameful.

I suspect, but can't prove, that the routine treatment given to Lindsay's announcement in *The New York Times* reflects, once again, a parochial consideration: that Lindsay ignored the Big Apple and went to faraway Miami, a joke kind of place, to do his thing. Surely his own justification for it—that Florida was his first primary state and crucial to his prospects—was reasonable. Not only reasonable;

damn good politics. Lynn's use of those unnamed politicians to suggest another explanation is a cheap shot.

Thus, by the end of 1971, Lindsay had been fingered by the press. As *The New York Times* said, even his political foes concede his strong point is his "television charisma, a major asset in the era of electronic politics."

That was not the message John Lindsay was trying to deliver. His message was that he was a big-city mayor and he had something to contribute to the national debate. We chose to disregard that message. I know of no story, article, or commentary that analyzed in any real depth what his record as a big-city mayor was. I know of no analysis of his singular theme that the time had come "to send someone to Washington to be the President, someone who has at least lived where the people's problems are, instead of waiting for the tight, closed, and unchanged political community of Washington to send somebody out to the country."*

I don't imagine that stories and articles exploring Lindsay's record and his theme would have changed anything. Columnist White was correct: Lindsay faced far too many obstacles to be, in his word, "viable." Yet, by exposing the way he was being "packaged," we neglected to peek at what was inside. The result was devastating. Lindsay was brought down faster and farther than anyone could have anticipated.

In Massachusetts, politicians call friendly stories "good ink." Lindsay got plenty of ink but almost all of it was bad. Other candidates had a different problem: they couldn't get any ink at all, good or bad.

Especially Senator Henry M. "Scoop" Jackson of Washington, who believed that his long and important service to the party, his astounding record as a vote getter, his close connections with labor and Jewish leaders, his position in what he thought was the center of his party, would dictate otherwise.

---

* Each political reporter, I suppose, just like taxi drivers and bartenders, has a special hang-up. Lindsay is mine. I have never been impressed by his administrative abilities or his intellect. He is, I do believe, a true media candidate, more show than substance. To suggest all of this may be so is proper commentary, but there is an additional responsibility to deal with the essence of what a candidate is trying to say. I ducked that responsibility, and I'm sorry about it.

6

Jackson

The Occasional Observer, "published irregularly by the Jackson Campaign Office," asked this question:

WHO IS THE CENTRIST?

"There has been a good deal written to the effect that Senator Muskie is the 'centrist.' The schematic for such a statement, reading from left to right, goes roughly like this:

(L) McGovern—Muskie—Jackson (R)
(Center)

"Now the Occasional Observer rejects most left-right alignments these days. (Why is a stand in favor of a prudent national defense considered 'right of center'?). But, once in a while, we'll play the game also. And so do the other candidates. The Humphrey camp also lays claim to the centrist spot. Their schematic looks like this:

(L)—Muskie—Humphrey—Jackson (R)
(Center)

"So we are happy now to present here the real spectrum of the Democratic Party. Now, it may not be the spectrum that many people wish it were, but it does conform to reality. (All the men listed are, or were, elected Democratic officials and each represents an ideologically identifiable group of Democratic voters.)

(L) McGovern-Lindsay-Muskie-Humphrey-Jackson-Mills-Connally-Yorty-Wallace (R)
(Center)

"If that's so, then which candidate actually receives the political blessings of the centrist (i.e., 'he's the only man who can hold the party together . . .')?"

Jackson's people, especially Ben J. Wattenberg, coauthor of *The Real Majority,* worked desperately in an attempt to convince political reporters that their man was a "centrist" and a "moderate." Wattenberg argued that Jackson represented precisely that "center" he and Scammon talked about in their book. He alone, it seemed, offered something to the "47-year-old housewife from the outskirts of Dayton, Ohio, whose husband is a machinist."

She is the Middle Voter, they said, and "the single strategy [for victory] involves a drive toward the center of the electorate . . . to gain the vote" of that Dayton housewife. At the very least, they argued, a winning coalition must incorporate "a large piece of the attitudinal center."

The Dayton housewife, Wattenberg and Scammon said, "very likely has a somewhat different view of life and politics from that of a 24-year-old instructor of political science at Yale." But that young instructor doesn't know much about politics unless he understands what is bothering the lady in Dayton.

"To know that the lady in Dayton is afraid to walk the streets at night, to know that she has a mixed view about blacks and civil rights because before moving to the suburbs she lived in a neighborhood that became all black, to know that her brother-in-law is a policeman, to know that she does not have the money to move if her new neighborhood deteriorates, to know that she is deeply distressed that her son is going to a community junior college where LSD was found on the campus—to know all of this is the beginning of contemporary political wisdom."

By this standard, Jackson's political wisdom was contemporary. He was strong for national defense, strong in his unrelenting opposition to communism, strong for the old "bread and butter" issues so popular with labor, and strong on what Wattenberg and Scammon called the Social Issue, that amalgam of attitudes that allegedly concerned the Dayton housewife.

That, said Jackson's people, made him a moderate, and they argued he was perceived as such by the voters themselves, at least in Florida. In January of 1972, Jackson's press office released an elaborate document showing the highlights of an Oliver Quayle poll of Florida Democrats. Quayle asked the voters to position the candidates on a liberal-conservative scale. Results:

	Liberal %	Moderate %	Conservative %
Liberal			
Edward Kennedy	75	16	9
John Lindsay	56	27	17
Hubert Humphrey	55	25	20
Edmund Muskie	52	29	19
George McGovern	51	30	19
Moderate			
Reubin Askew	26	42	32
Lawton Chiles	25	50	25
HENRY JACKSON	22	56	22
Conservative Moderate			
Wilbur Mills	19	46	35
Conservative			
Richard Nixon	12	36	52
Spiro Agnew	20	27	53
George Wallace	25	12	63

According to Quayle, 27 percent of Florida's Democrats identified themselves as liberal, 38 percent said they were moderates, and 35 percent said they were conservatives. Jackson's staff was pleased that his profile dovetailed so neatly with Florida's own Senator Chiles and Governor Askew. The "approval" ratings for both of them were extremely high—74 percent for Chiles, 76 percent for Askew.

The point of this campaign was to convince the press that Jackson was a "centrist" or a "moderate." If the press believed that, then they would take Jackson more seriously. It didn't work. Most of the time in the final six months of 1971, reporters were looking elsewhere—at Lindsay, for example, and at Muskie. Editors and their reporters can only look so many directions at once; there wasn't time or broad enough range of vision to consider Jackson.

Two exceptions might be noted.

First, David Broder—surely the most highly regarded political writer in the preprimary stage—wrote a long and informative story about Jackson beginning on Page One in the *Washington Post* dated October 3. The headline read:

THE CONTROVERSIAL CANDIDATE

Scoop Jackson: Libertarian, Old Guard Favorite

". . . Jackson's campaign has a slightly schizophrenic quality," Broder said. "The candidate's speeches are determinedly in the middle of the Democratic road, but his audiences and backers seem to be drawn almost exclusively from the Old Guard of the party."*

In state after state, Jackson's supporters were Old Guard Democrats, former Governor Roger Crowley in New Hampshire, former Senator Spessard Holland in Florida, County Commissioner Leonard Staisey in western Pennsylvania.

His staff, Broder noted, "also has an Old Guard look." The campaign manager, white-haired Hyman B. Raskin, was 61; he started in politics with Adlai Stevenson. The Washington headquarters was run

---

* Broder may have been reading different speeches. In August, for example, Jackson told a state AFL–CIO convention in New York that the "absolutists on the left" were trying to take over the party. These Democrats, he said, were "indifferent or downright hostile" to the workingman.

by Paul Aiken, an assistant postmaster general in the Truman administration.

"The average age of the Jackson high command," Broder estimated, "is probably 15 years older than that of any other Democratic candidate."

Two weeks later, I wrote a column about Jackson. Its headline:

SENATOR JACKSON SHARES
APPEAL WITH GOV. WALLACE

The column began:

" 'I'm a liberal,' he likes to say, 'but I'm no damn fool.'

"One can suppose that Henry M. 'Scoop' Jackson, the 59-year-old senator from the state of Washington, is no damn fool. But is he a 'liberal'?

"Does spinach taste good?

"Of course, Jackson likes to think he's a liberal, and he likes to think that his opponents for the nomination are modern-day barn-burners. His staff professes anger at the way the press and others label him.

"But, in any consideration of Presidential politics in October of 1971, *it doesn't make any difference.* The perceptions about Jackson are frozen, solid as ice. And, in those perceptions, Jackson is no liberal. He is, in fact, the 'conservative' Democratic candidate for the nomination."

What little attention Jackson did receive in the press underlines the point, because his journalistic friends represented their trade's Old Guard. His friends were Evans and Novak, Joe Alsop, and William S. White. Evans and Novak, especially, made Jackson's campaign almost a personal crusade. Consider these headlines from their columns:

May: MEANY LIKES SEN. JACKSON.

June: SEN. JACKSON'S GAME PLAN.

August: NIXON WARY OF JACKSON.

November: JACKSON'S BOLD CHALLENGE.

But then, in December, Evans and Novak concluded the game was up. "Jackson in the Doldrums," the headline read. And ". . .

neither Jackson's mastery of the issues, adequate financing, nor skilled advisers have made the slightest dent on mass opinion," they wrote.

Of course not. First, the press neglected him. Second, when we had time for him, we wrote him off as Old Guard. We also noted he was drab and colorless.

No surprise, then, that when TV got its licks, the theme was repeated. "Henry Jackson as anachronism" was the theme of CBS's first profile, the Report on the Network News' Treatment of the 1972 Democratic Presidential Candidates concludes. ABC, the report said, was the only network "to come to grips with the more substantive aspects of the Jackson candidacy." The effort, undertaken by commentator Howard K. Smith, consisted of about 50 words.

The Network News Report somehow missed the one real breakthrough Jackson made on television. On November 14, CBS's "60 Minutes," with Mike Wallace as narrator, asked the question: "Who goes to the Washington public schools?" The answer: "Certainly not the children of Washington's liberal establishment."

Attending St. Alban's, the most exclusive private boys' school in Washington, were the sons of Tom Wicker, ultraliberal columnist for *The New York Times,* Philip Geyelin, editor of the *Washington Post*'s liberal editorial page, and Senators Birch Bayh of Indiana and Edward Kennedy of Massachusetts, Wallace reported. Muskie's children, he said, went to private Catholic schools. McGovern lived in the District of Columbia and transported his daughter across the district line to Bethesda–Chevy Chase High School in Maryland's wealthiest suburb. Kennedy, Muskie, and McGovern all were asked to appear on the show; all refused.

Wallace found one contender for the Democratic nomination who had a child attending a public school in the District of Columbia, and that senator was happy to appear on the program. Of course, he was the Old Guard candidate, Scoop Jackson. "I feel it's so important that a child's experience be an experience in diversity and that's America—kids from all walks of life," Jackson, the anachronism, said.

The producer, Barry Lando, noted, in some surprise: "This broadcast attracted more mail than anything ever done on our program."

In 1973, long after the election was over, nine-year-old Anna Marie Jackson was still attending Horace Mann elementary school and her little brother, Peter, six, had joined her.

7

The Others

Wallace, Humphrey,
Kennedy, and Bayh;
Chisholm, Harris, Hartke,
Hughes, McCarthy, Mills,
Yorty; Ashbrook and
McCloskey

When you walk up Dexter Avenue in Montgomery, Alabama, you can almost hear the muffled drums of a mighty coalition that died more than a century ago. It was up this street that the inaugural parade of Jefferson Davis marched, and a full band played "Dixie" for the first time that day. On the crest of the hill is the Capitol of Alabama, built in 1851. The Stars and Bars of the Confederacy first flew over this building; that flag flies there still.

You walk into the handsome old building and, straight ahead, in the middle of the rotunda, is a marble bust of the late Lurleen Burns Wallace, governor of Alabama, 1967–1968, victim of cancer May 7, 1968. The bust is mounted on a marble column; the column is mounted on a marble pedestal. A silver bud vase rests on the pedestal. It contains a single yellow rose. Behind the bust, taking up almost an entire wall, is a heroic portrait of Governor Lurleen. On the opposite wall is an equally heroic portrait of Governor George.

Yankee reporters know the place well, for in recent years we have repaired there to talk to the Stand Up for America candidate, the leader of a new coalition that has spread far beyond the boundaries of the 13 states of the Old Confederacy.

In 1971, George Wallace had plenty of Yankee visitors, each wanting to know what this tough, shrewd, mean, funny man was going to do. But Ol' George wasn't really talking, not about that anyway. Everything else, but not that.

It was hardly a wonder, then, that George Wallace would become the biggest surprise of the 1972 campaign . . . until May 15, when Arthur Bremer gunned him down in a shopping center within 30 minutes' drive of my office.

The one thing most of us were sure about was that Wallace would run, somehow and somewhere. That was his nature; that was the ultimate pleasure in his life. Because his third-party organization had never been broken up, we presumed he would run again in the fall of 1972 as a third-party candidate for President.

We were wrong—he decided to run in the Democratic primaries —and that threw everybody's calculations into a cocked hat. How he must have loved that, all by itself.

We knew what a difference he could make in the general election. We knew he had carried five states—46 electoral votes—in 1968 against Nixon, winning almost ten million votes, 13.2 percent of the total cast. If he ran again, he would carry those same states and maybe this time he would concentrate his efforts in the South and carry three or four more. That, in a close election, would threaten to throw the outcome into the House of Representatives. And then Ol' George would move in.

I made the pilgrimage to Montgomery early in June. Things weren't going so well for Wallace as governor; he had barely been reelected in 1970 and the legislature elected with him was rambunctious. They wouldn't appropriate the education funds he'd promised in his campaign; worse, they wouldn't pass the budget at all. The lieutenant governor, Jere Beasley, wouldn't cooperate with him, so Wallace took away his state-owned automobile.

But the real business was going on out at the edge of town, in what was once a Gulf Oil office building. That was the headquarters of the Wallace Campaign, and it was moving along nicely. Money was pouring in and the advance men were arranging what seemed to be an endless series of "appreciation dinners" across the country. The old lists of names, kept chaotically on index cards, had been cleaned out and put on computer tape. The old gang—Tom Turnipseed, Seymore Trammell, Bill Jones—were gone, and Charles S. Snyder, a mod young businessman, was the boss. This time, he promised, things would be different.

"You ought to be ready to go in '72," I said.

"Why wait so long?" he asked.

"What do you mean by that?"

"Well, there are gonna be some Southern Democratic primaries this time."

"You mean you'd run in those primaries?"

"Sure."

I couldn't believe it was possible; I hadn't thought about it. But I checked the primary laws in Florida, North Carolina, and Tennessee, and it became obvious: Wallace could run in all three. I left it at that; it was enough for one day.

The word that Wallace was thinking about running in Southern Democratic primaries spread slowly, but nobody made very much of it. William Greider wrote in the *Washington Post* in August that Wallace felt he might win the Florida primary, especially if the field was crowded with Yankees. A victory like that "would regenerate his followers, and he surely would be taken more seriously," Greider said.

James T. Wooten, in *The New York Times,* quoted Wallace as saying that the Southern primaries "will be a perfect opportunity to show the national parties just how the people feel about the important things."

"Put George Wallace in some 1972 Democratic primaries, and it would be the best political show in years," said Kevin P. Phillips in his column. "Such a campaign would tear the Democratic Party apart and leave deep, lasting scars." Wallace would "drive the fashionable Establishment nuts with his gutsy populist attacks on the left-wing media, Harvard disarmers, foundation limousine liberals, fat cat labor leaders, and the presidential candidates who cultivate them." Phillips, author of a much-debated book, *The Emerging Republican Majority,* could hardly wait.

But, as far as I can tell, nobody anticipated that George Wallace would win the Florida primary in a landslide and then head north seeking new worlds to conquer. In Florida, he destroyed poor Scoop Jackson, who had sought the same constituency, more or less, and he left Ed Muskie gasping.

Wallace was the biggest surprise of all, and everybody was fooled.

No one knew what Hubert Horatio Humphrey was going to do either, least of all Humphrey, perhaps, and he turned out to be still another surprise.

Humphrey is a little like Wallace; he's always running. It was dangerous for Muskie, and for us, to presume he wouldn't run again in 1972. Yet, it seemed logical he wouldn't. Muskie was his friend; he always boasted that one of the best things he'd done for his country was introduce Muskie to us in 1968. And then there was the war; Humphrey had been Johnson's Vice-president, and he was stigmatized too. He openly admitted he had much to be sorry for. In June, *The New York Times* began printing the Pentagon Papers, and Humphrey told me:

"There's not a single Democrat that's not going to be damaged by the disclosures of the Pentagon Papers in *The New York Times*. And, of course, the Papers hurt me more than the others."

He seemed almost morose as we talked about Vietnam. But the mood didn't last long. "I intend to be a factor to be reckoned with," he said, almost physically pulling himself together. "I'll be a factor somewhere along the line, you bet. There's still a lot of zip left in Hubert Humphrey."

I thought the Papers would remain a political issue for months. They didn't. They came like a summer storm and were gone almost as quickly. And Humphrey was back in business.

One of the quaint traditions in Washington is the background session between important people and selected members of the press. The best-known of these "backgrounders" is run by Godfrey Sperling of the *Christian Science Monitor*. Humphrey attended two of Sperling's breakfasts in 1971, and each produced an escalation of Humphrey's own intentions.

Over scrambled eggs and sausage the morning of May 27, his sixtieth birthday, Humphrey told Sperling and the other reporters:

"I've got the sails up and I'm testing the weather. I'm not salivating but I'm licking my chops."

Oh God, I thought. Humphrey again.

Most reporters, especially the veterans, are fond of Hubert. But, by 1971, he was like somebody's aging uncle, wonderful old fellow, but, you know, a bit of a bore. He had his chance in 1968, and he blew it. So why doesn't he stand aside now and let someone else have a chance?

Uncle Hubert would have none of it. He told the reporters that he probably would bypass the early primaries—they'd be inconclusive, he thought—and then "take a look" at the big ones in June, California and New York. Ultimately, he thought, it might come down to Kennedy and himself.

His predictions make the worst of us look like seers. In June, he told Johnny Apple of *The New York Times* that Birch Bayh probably would win the Indiana primary and might even win in Florida. Muskie would win New Hampshire and one or two others. McGovern would win in South Dakota and maybe Nebraska. And Humphrey was interested in Senator William Proxmire of Wisconsin: he just might be tough. All in all, he thought, nobody would emerge a clear winner and so he could move in and sweep it up in California and New York.

In September and October, Humphrey moved around the country at a pace that would have left a man half his age breathless. He wasn't a candidate, of course, just looking around. In one week in October, he traveled 15,000 miles.

Broder in the *Post* wasn't convinced it was working. On September 21, he wrote that Humphrey might not be able to play the waiting game much longer. Why? Because Muskie, more and more, was looking like a winner. That, Broder said, was the talk at the National Governors' Conference just concluded in San Juan, Puerto Rico.

On October 5, more scrambled eggs and sausage with the Sperling gang. Humphrey said he thought he might just let his name go on the ballot in Florida, which would mean that his name automatically would appear on the ballots in several other "all-candidate" primaries.

In late November, he opened a campaign office in Washington

and chose 39-year-old Jack Chestnut as his campaign manager. Nobody had to speculate about Hubert Humphrey anymore. "I do not intend to be a zilch," he had told Apple of the *Times* in June. Now, in November, he was making sure of it. So, once again, we would have Hubert Humphrey to kick around. And we would.

And then there was Edward Moore Kennedy, waiting. The terrible events at Chappaquiddick were fading, and all of us were watching Teddy out of the corner of our eye. Of all the Democrats, he was special. He was a Kennedy, and the press and the Kennedys have always had this love-hate thing.

Either you're with us, they seemed to be saying, or you're against us. Reporters who were with the Kennedys could count on an occasional invitation to Hickory Hill or perhaps to the theatre or to dinner somewhere. It was less so with Teddy, probably, than it had been with John and Bobby. But there was still this temptation: Flatter the Kennedys and you get some pretty rarefied attention.

And, dammit, he and his aides and his friends are more fun. They're the kind of people most reporters like best; they can banter with insults, dancing around a heavy subject with light steps; they like an occasional night on the town. They know what power is, and how to exercise it. It tends to rub off on people passing by.

Unlike Hubert, though, Teddy wasn't having any of it. He said he wouldn't run, and he didn't. He said he wouldn't support anyone in the primaries, and he didn't. Perhaps he knew what the press might do to him if he did run. Perhaps it was his fatalism about what others might do to him, as they had done to his brothers before. Whatever the reasons, he kept his word. To some of us, especially the skeptics and the Kennedy-haters, that was a surprise too.

Then there were all the others.

Birch Bayh was smart and ambitious. By October, he had put together an exceptional staff in Washington and in the field. Speculation centered on where his money was coming from; no one ever figured it out. But his campaign came to an abrupt end on October 12 when he withdrew to be at his wife's side. She had undergone surgery for cancer five days earlier.

Shirley Chisholm, the first black woman elected to the Congress, decided without much consultation with male black political leaders that she would run for President "to shape things up" at the national convention. The males, presumably, had other ideas, but they didn't matter. Mrs. Chisholm, very tough, very ambitious, handed them a fait accompli. She was the black candidate, and that was the end of it.

Political reporters, all white and almost all male, were wary of this candidate who was both black and female. The usual skepticism—cynicism even—that occasionally intruded in the way we reported male, white candidates was conspiculously absent. Mrs. Chisholm, when we found time to talk about her, was treated with respect. It wasn't enough; she couldn't get much attention and she couldn't raise the money she needed to organize a major campaign.

Vance Hartke, I suppose, ran for the nomination for the hell of it, or maybe for something worse. Hartke is the other senator from Indiana. Together, the two senators are known in Washington as "Bayh and Bought." When Hartke said he might run, feisty Jimmy Doyle of the *Washington Star* asked him why people said things like that. Hartke exploded in anger. None of us took him seriously.

Harold Hughes of Iowa was the year's first dropout. He had started early and gotten almost nowhere, despite the fact that he is a large, handsome man with a deep, booming voice and a reputation for toughness and honesty. Columnist Mary McGrory seized upon him early in the year as her kind of candidate, but he failed to attract many more recruits. When he admitted in an interview that he sometimes talked to his dead brother, members of his staff figured he was no longer that much interested in running.

What we thought of Eugene J. McCarthy can be gleaned from reading the headlines our editors wrote on our stories about him.

> KIND OF FLOATING AROUND IN FRONT OF THE NET
> MCCARTHY, ON TRIP, ACTS LIKE CANDIDA
> MCCARTHY'S OFF AND CONTEMPLATING
> POETICS, NOT POLITICS
> MCCARTHY "KIND OF" ANNOUNCES HE'LL RUN

Relations between the press and McCarthy in 1968 were never good. We didn't understand him (he thought), and he surely didn't think most of us were very bright. The trouble with McCarthy is that he is different. He thinks a lot and he has all these private little jokes. His ideas about politics seem alien and curious. So we became bemused by him. Perhaps McCarthy was serious about making a major effort in 1972, but we never thought so. I think I know what he had in mind: he was interested in certain positions and beliefs and he wanted to campaign for those positions and beliefs in a few, scattered places where he thought he might win. Then, later, perhaps at the convention, he would deliver his delegates to the candidate who came closest to agreeing with him. He never went out of his way to explain exactly what he had in mind. We never went out of our way to explore his thinking.

Wilbur Mills, "influential chairman of the powerful House Ways and Means Committee," was almost as puzzling as McCarthy. Mills kept saying he didn't want the nomination, he didn't expect to get it, and yet people working for him were spending a great deal of money in his behalf. Somehow, it was thought, he wanted to "influence" events in 1972. Maybe, some thought, his real aim was to be Ted Kennedy's running mate. Maybe, others thought, it was just an ego trip; he wanted more people to realize just how influential and powerful he really was. Or, maybe, he was campaigning to become Speaker of the House. Mills, himself, wouldn't say. He isn't much for sitting down with reporters and talking about his plans.

No reporter took Sam Yorty's Presidential ambitions seriously. We were impressed by one fact: Bill Loeb, publisher of the *Manchester Union Leader,* was backing him in the New Hampshire primary. That, it was suggested, guaranteed Yorty as much as 25 percent of the vote. Serious newspapermen are contemptuous of Loeb and his kind of journalism; most of us already were contemptuous of Yorty and his kind of sleazy politics. They deserved each other.

The Republicans produced two challengers to Nixon in the primaries—Paul N. "Pete" McCloskey, Jr., the California congressman who got to Washington by defeating Shirley Temple Black, and John Ashbrook, a quintessentially conservative congressman from Ohio. McCloskey would attack Nixon from the left, Ashbrook from the right. Of the two, we were more interested in McCloskey. He started earlier, worked longer. He trudged up and down New Hampshire for weeks, talking earnestly about the bombing of North Vietnam and the rest of Southeast Asia. It was a moral issue with him and his own war record—he is a decorated Marine veteran—seemed to give his candidacy a certain poignancy. I think, secretly, most of us wished him well.

There is one last Democrat we haven't mentioned—Fred Harris of Oklahoma. His slogan was "no more bullshit," borrowed, he admitted, from Norman Mailer and Jimmy Breslin. In place of the old bullshit, there would be "the new populism." He was going to get the "bums" out of government and get people like Nader's raiders in it. He would break up General Motors into five smaller companies. A new coalition of workers, students, blacks, Chicanos, and Indians (Harris's wife, the remarkable LaDonna, is a Comanche) would "turn this country around."

I was intrigued. Here, it seemed, was a candidate with a clear and distinctive program. I read Harris's book, *The Time Is Now,* I listened to him, and I talked to his people.

"There is a Populist majority in America, which can be put together if we will try," he wrote.

". . . if we will but listen, we will find that all over America people of the most disparate backgrounds—the young college student, the militant black, the suburban housewife—are saying the same thing; we want to live in a society which believes in something, which stands for something, in which there are some obvious values and ideals; and we are tired of having so little power in helping make decisions."

Harris felt he was especially qualified to lead a New Populism movement because of his rude beginnings. "As the son of a Mississippi-born Oklahoma dirt farmer and former sharecropper," he wrote, "I know that some people look down their noses at middle- and lower-income whites, in the South and elsewhere. I know that government must do better toward responding to the legitimate complaints of these Americans, as well as others."

Talk, talk, talk. I preferred Mary E. ("the Kansas Pythoness") Lease, an *old* Populist, whose famous suggestion was: "What you farmers need to do is raise less corn and more HELL."

But Harris's rhetoric—it was never much more than that—was

enough to convince many reporters that here was a truly singular candidate. Garry Wills, the most erudite of our columnists and a tough fellow with a very high sense of moral outrage, exposed Harris for the weak-kneed "Populist" he really was.

Wills wrote:

"In a recent interview, he [Harris] gave me his populist pitch: everybody would end up against him but the people. I suggested there are things even the bluntest politician just cannot say. 'That's not been true in my case. By a combination of geography and personal background, I find I can talk to just about everybody, and express what's bothering them. That's been fortunate, since I never can tell what I think, and that has worked so far.'

"I gave as an example of a politically unpopular stand the rescinding of laws against marijuana. 'I'm on record for lowering the penalties.' I argued that would have little effect, and he agreed—rescinding the laws entirely is the politically risky thing. 'That problem does not arise for me, since I believe in the marijuana laws.' Why? 'Because adolescents have a hard enough time adjusting to responsibility without adding another thing to cope with.' But the thing is added already. The laws don't keep marijuana away from the kids; they just add to the problems caused by its omnipresence. 'Well, I'm for some discipline.' I suggested the same age-limit could be kept as for legalized things like liquor and cigarettes. 'So you *do* favor some controls.' I told him almost everyone who supports legalization believes in controls—after all, this is the generation that admires Nader's approach to consumer regulations. It was news to him."

Devastating, I thought, an example of a kind of journalism we almost never see. When Harris withdrew, Wills concluded that his problem was that he failed to live up to his slogan, "No more bullshit."

"Fred Harris probably spoke no more 'b.s.' than other politicians. But he had proudly trumpeted that he would speak no 'b.s.' That is a promise no politician is likely to keep for more than 49 waking minutes. . . .

"It took Senator Harris far less than the allotted 49 minutes to hedge on such matters as abuses of union power, the persecution of the Berrigans, or the need for pot laws. This kind of waffling alienated press people who would have found real honesty refreshing, and might have supplied the exposure he lacked on other grounds."

Maybe so. But, then, maybe it wasn't much of a year for honesty. CBS's Roger Mudd was along when Harris spoke to union officials in Akron, Ohio. When the meeting was over, Mudd asked one of the officials what he thought about Harris.

"I didn't think much of him," was the reply. "All he's doing is talking about humanity, and the problem is much deeper than that."

Along with Wills, I didn't think much of Harris's "new Populism." First of all, it seemed to me, it wasn't new. The coalition he kept talking about was very much like the coalition that Bobby Kennedy was putting together rather successfully when he was killed in 1968. This time, a good many others—McGovern, Lindsay, and, in a different and more limited way, Wallace—were thinking about the same thing.

I thought Harris's campaign was poorly conceived, hastily prepared, and almost wholly unconvincing.

Harris opened his campaign on September 25. He closed it on November 11. "I am broke," he told a news conference in the Senate Office Building. And the reason this exponent of the "new Populism" was broke was that his chief financial angel, Herbert Allen, Jr., a young New York investment banker, had called it quits.

No one worried much when Harold Hughes quit. No one worried much about Shirley Chisholm's inability to bankroll her campaign. No one cared that Jackson couldn't convince the press that he had something to say.

But, curiously, some reporters cared that Harris had been forced out. It was a unique reaction.

The *Post*'s Broder said "it demonstrates how our system of campaign financing distorts the range of choice voters enjoy. Harris quit because he was flat broke. . . . If he had been able to stay in the race through the early primaries, Harris might have raised certain issues which are of concern to him, and by raising those issues, he might have forced the other Democratic contenders to respond to them.

"It is a rotten system," Broder concluded. "We all know it is rotten."

Broder makes two presumptions: One. Harris had something to say that no one else could say, or would say. I don't believe that. Two. Money guarantees that a candidate's ideas can be communicated to the voter. I don't believe that either.

Jackson, with all his fat-cat, industrial-complex money, couldn't communicate. Nor, during most of 1971, could George McGovern, with his superb organization and moderate cash flow. Nor could Lindsay, the media manipulator.

Perhaps that union official talking to Roger Mudd in Akron reflected what millions of Americans felt: they weren't prepared in 1971 to listen to talk about humanity and things like that.

Except for the true believers, the voters who are really oriented to issues (and, thankfully, I suppose, their numbers are growing), most voters don't give a damn. They are more interested in "images" —What kind of guy is he? What's he look like? How's he sound? How's he *doing?*

If that's what most voters want, that's what they got in 1971.

Funny, isn't it, but we are the true image makers. The old linear, non-McLuhan writing press.

part three
★
THE PRIMARIES

8

New Hampshire

So it is appropriate that the 1972 Presidential campaign began in a state that has only two television stations and gets most of its news, and all of its paranoia, from the most outrageous, the most scandalous, the most biased newspaper in America—William Loeb's ineffable *Manchester Union Leader.*

I first met Loeb in 1964, interviewing him in his office at the newspaper, a rare privilege because he spends most of his time at his homes in Prides Crossing, Massachusetts, and Reno, Nevada. When the interview was finished, he asked me to look inside the open middle drawer of his desk. In it was a loaded .45 caliber revolver. "I'm always ready for anything," he said.

New Hampshire is what it is today—poor, badly governed, anachronistic—because Loeb likes it that way. The state has no sales tax and no income tax; aid to local schools, higher education, and local government is fiftieth and last in the nation. Its reasonable voices are muted; decent men fear Loeb's wrath. The condition of New Hampshire is testament, in nightmare reality, to the power of the printed word.

Marshall McLuhan, meet Bill Loeb.

It is in New Hampshire, one of the three or four most unrepresentative states in the nation, that the panoplied press begins the serious work of electing a President of the United States.

It is a farce.

And yet, as it turned out, the votes of 86,000 New Hampshirites, fully 60 percent of them conditioned daily by the *Manchester Union Leader* and probably half of that number French Canadians, indicated to us that Edmund Muskie, the established front-runner, was in serious trouble and that George McGovern, the hopeless six percenter in Dr. Gallup's poll, was a serious contender.

The votes of 116,000 other New Hampshirites assured us that Richard Nixon needn't worry about challenges in his own party by Paul N. McCloskey, Jr., from the left, or John M. Ashbrook from the right.

And Endicott Peabody won 95 percent of the Democratic vote for the Vice-presidential nomination.

The New Hampshire primary is important because it is the first (22 were to follow) and because most of us can't wait to get the game started. We are also impressed by its history, so much of which is now legend. In 1952, we remember, Estes Kefauver defeated Harry Truman, and Truman withdrew as a candidate 18 days later. In 1964, write-in candidate Henry Cabot Lodge defeated both Barry Goldwater and Nelson Rockefeller. In 1968, Eugene J. McCarthy *almost* defeated write-in candidate Lyndon B. Johnson, and Johnson withdrew as a candidate 19 days later.*

New Hampshire, then, has a negative reputation, which is only fitting. Front-runners don't do well there. In 1972, that reputation would be enhanced.

The trouble is, New Hampshire is so hard to resist. The part of it that is politically unimportant, the sparsely settled lakes and mountain regions, are spectacularly beautiful. Some of the natives even talk the way they're supposed to. In January, colleagues I've campaigned with for almost a decade are on their way. It's where the

---

* McCarthy won 42.4 percent of the vote in the beauty contest; Johnson got 49.4 percent. McCarthy, because he was smarter, got 20 of the 24 delegates. Johnson ran more candidates than there were delegate spots, so his voters, confused, diffused.

action is, journalistically at least. So that's where I go too. Every evening, at the end of a day of reporting and interviewing, we meet for drinks and steaks in front of the roaring log fire at the Dunfey family's Sheraton-Wayfarer. It is part reunion, part convention, part warm-up for what's to come. And it is irresistible.

Bizarre, too.

The first week in January, I find myself, in company with the *Post*'s Broder, in a small bedroom on the fourth floor of the Sheraton-Carpenter Hotel in Manchester. We are talking to Jim White, Hillsborough County (Manchester) Democratic chairman, and now campaign manager for Senator Vance Hartke of Indiana. Hartke signed him up on a whirlwind visit to New Hampshire between Christmas and New Year's Day. White had tried, and failed, to hook on earlier to McGovern, Yorty, Lindsay, Jackson, and Bayh.

"The senator came to my home in Pelham [N.H.] and he sat there with my bride, the mother of my four sons, and he asked for my help. I told him very frankly I was not interested in him if he was just a spoiler, to cut up someone else, but by the end of the evening I was convinced he was the fresh voice the Democrats up here have been looking for."

It was "God's will" that Hartke entered the primary, he tells us.

"What a campaigner that man is! He'll whomp the feet off 'em. And that wife of his—she's a Martha Mitchell with class!"

Things are off to a good start, he says. Just the day before, 43 former supporters of the late Estes Kefauver sent him a telegram, offering to come to New Hampshire and help Hartke. "It's good to know the senator has that kind of support."

White says the reason he signed up with Hartke is . . . because Hartke wants to do something about paying off the Democratic National Committee's debt. "That fella from next door," he says, pointing in the general direction of Maine, "won't do a damn thing about it."

We're talking, just the three of us, in a bedroom. The door opens and a tall, silent man walks into the room. "Hi, Senator Leonard," Jim White says. Broder and I exchange puzzled looks. Earlier that same day, we were given a press release at the Muskie headquarters. "Top Jackson Supporter Endorses Sen. Muskie," the headline on it read. The "top Jackson supporter," of course, is Senator Richard

Leonard. "I have decided to support the best man in the race now," Senator Leonard was quoted as saying, "Sen. Ed Muskie from our neighboring state of Maine." Muskie, Leonard added in the press release, "has the integrity and leadership ability which our country needs."

And here was Senator Leonard in Hartke headquarters.

Jim White is suddenly crestfallen. "Forget you ever saw him," he tells us. "He's off the record." Without saying a word, Senator Leonard crosses the room and goes next door, where the Hartke campaign is being put together.

Minutes later, we are joined by Pat McGann, from Atlantic City, New Jersey, in town to help out his old friend, Vance Hartke. Wow, he says, isn't this some kind of crazy, mixed-up state? It's nothing like New Jersey at all. The county chairmen here in New Hampshire don't mean a damn thing, not a thing.

Jim White, the Hillsborough County chairman, starts shuffling some papers. Broder and I make our departure, still afraid to look at each other.

Another day, I'm traveling with Mayor Sam Yorty of Los Angeles. This is his eighteenth political campaign. His record is ten wins and seven losses, about what you'd expect from a pretty good relief pitcher for, say, the San Diego Padres. The other reporter with us is a young man, with a large moustache, from the *Kansas City Star.* It's his first Presidential campaign. "I think Yorty's got a chance," he's telling me. "That's why I'm here. It's really exciting, isn't it?"

Yorty is moving around the state in a limousine. We're following behind with Mrs. Yorty in the self-propelled "Yortymobile," a 31-foot-long Winnebago mobile home. "Sam's the Man" is written all over its sides and the rear end has been fixed up to resemble the platform of a whistle-stop campaign train. Each time we hit a town, Epping for example, the driver switches on the loudspeaker for another rendition of "Stars and Stripes Forever."

In Exeter we tour a bank and make a little political history: Yorty is photographed by the gentlemen from, left to right, *Time* magazine, *Foster's Daily Democrat,* and the *Rolling Stone.*

In Exeter, Yorty also stops on the street to chat for about 10 minutes with John Oswald, who says the planet is being invaded by unidentified flying objects. One appeared in Exeter on September 3, 1965. Saucers, Mayor Yorty says, don't appear to be a major political issue. We move on to Lee Bee's clothing store, where "Betts," the mayor's wife, buys a patchwork skirt.

The day ends in Dover, where the mayor tours a nursing home, whose proprietor takes us to his apartment and pours a little wine all around. Mercifully, the *Time* photographer drives me back to the Sheraton-Wayfarer.

Well, that's how it was some of the time in New Hampshire. Scholars always want to know: How do reporters decide to take one candidate seriously and to ignore another? Sometimes, it's easy.

If Yorty and Hartke were not serious candidates, at least they appeared to be serious factors in New Hampshire. Yorty, especially, because he had been anointed by Loeb and the *Manchester Union Leader.* Yorty, Loeb told Bill Kovach of *The New York Times,* "represents common sense and an unfaltering patriotic position. . . ." Loeb's laying on of hands guaranteed Yorty extensive and always flattering Page One attention in the state's only widely circulated newspaper.

The New Hampshire primary was not being watched to see who would win—we all agreed Muskie and Nixon would win; the point was to see by how much each would win.

Because Broder is so widely read and so universally admired, I suppose his first comprehensive New Hampshire story, starting on Page One of the *Post* on January 9, set the rules.

Muskie and Nixon, he said, "must not only win, but win with a large enough percentage of the vote that the press acknowledges it to be a victory. As Muskie said in Concord the other day, 'New Hampshire is important to me, in part, because you gentlemen of the press have undertaken to make it important . . . in order to test me.' "

Muskie tried to argue that "it's the guy who gets the most votes who wins," but then he temporized: "The significance of the victory may depend on the size of my vote."

And then Broder became more specific.

"As the acknowledged front-runner and a resident of the neighboring state [the propinquity factor, again], Muskie will have to win the support of at least half the New Hampshire Democrats in order to claim a victory. Mr. Nixon, by reason of his incumbency, will have to do better on the Republican side, in percentage terms, than Muskie does among the Democrats in order to preserve his prestige."

Now we have a figure for Muskie—50 percent or better. He actually got 46.4 percent—pretty close, but not nearly close enough.

Fifty percent was the magic figure. TV bought it. Said ABC: ". . . the magic figure is 50 percent." Said CBS: ". . . less than 50 percent here for Muskie against all the others is going to be interpreted by the press and politicians as a setback."

Why 50 percent? Why not, say, 45 percent, or 55 percent? It remains a mystery. That was the figure seized upon by Broder and others and that's where it stuck.

John Becker of Boston, Massachusetts, may be the real culprit. Becker is a polltaker and he was hired by the *Boston Globe* to survey the voters in New Hampshire. In January, the *Globe* ran the results: Muskie, the poll found, was leading with 65 percent of the vote.

"Mr. Muskie's most formidable foe is John Becker and his awful number," wrote the *Wall Street Journal*'s Arlen J. Large on February 18. It was one of the most perceptive articles to come out of New Hampshire.

"The number that's got to be hung on Muskie is the *Boston Globe*'s 65 percent," Gary Hart, McGovern's national campaign director, told Large. That was patent nonsense; nobody, least of all Hart, believed Muskie could get 65 percent of the vote.

"Sixty-five percent is absurd," George Mitchell, a Muskie strategist, said. "It's an impossible standard." Barry Wanger, Muskie's New Hampshire press secretary, said: "It will be virtually impossible for Muskie to get fifty percent of the Democratic vote in this state."

Large wrote:

"What Muskie men most obviously worry about is press acceptance of the *Boston Globe*'s number as the success standard for their man, and the post-mortems that will be written if he doesn't make it. 'If Ed Muskie gets 49 percent and everybody says he lost, then obviously the numbers game has hurt,' says Tony Podesta, the senator's New Hampshire campaign chief."

Podesta told Large that the struggle to get favorable press interpretation of the outcome is almost a "second election." It was nothing new, Large reported. In 1968, according to Thomas Gerber, editor of the *Concord Monitor,* an arbitrary consensus developed around 31 percent as the number needed by McCarthy to win a "moral victory" against Johnson. "I was in part responsible for it," Gerber told Large, "but I'm damned if I know where I first heard of it." McCarthy, as we have noted, got 42.4 percent of the vote and a "moral victory."

Muskie's opponents ganged up and tried to convince reporters that his figure should be very high and that their figures should be relatively low. McGovern's people tried to peddle the nonsense that 20 percent would be a moral victory. Backers of Republican Wilbur D. Mills, who spent more for radio and TV commercials than any other candidate, talked about 10 percent. The *Manchester Union Leader,* it was said, could always turn out 15 to 25 percent of the vote for anybody, which now meant Sam Yorty. Hartke, it was thought, might get 5 percent. And write-in votes were expected for Kennedy, Humphrey, Jackson, and McCarthy.

I wrote myself, in December, that 50 percent seemed out of Muskie's reach. There were simply too many other candidates, too many factors that were bizarre.

On February 14, *The New York Times,* in a Page One story by Johnny Apple, considered the numbers game for the first time. "It is an old game," he said, "but it is being played here with unusual intensity, and it puts the news media in the position of arbiters. It is they who are asked to decide, in advance, what percentage would constitute a 'real win' for Mr. Muskie.

"Robert E. Raiche, the minority leader in the New Hampshire House of Representatives, said last night that 'everyone worries about what the headlines will say March 8.'

"Mr. Raiche, a Muskie supporter, remarked that something was patently wrong in a situation where the media would choose the winner. Another local politician, not a Muskie man, told angrily of a television executive who visited the state and said, 'I'm the man who decides who wins here.' "

Apple said national news correspondents in New Hampshire "are uneasy about the game. Yet a consensus seems to be emerging around the magic 50 percent; it is cited in more and more articles and broadcasts."

The "magic number," set initially by the writing press, played perfectly into the hands of television. Somehow, the networks had to make drama out of New Hampshire, no easy task when everybody knew who the winners would be. What Muskie called his "phantom opponent"—the size of his victory—supplied that drama.

The Report on Network News' Treatment of the 1972 Democratic Presidential Candidates says:

". . . the front-runner theme as used by the network news programs did not simply provide a means of defining Muskie's position vis-à-vis the other Democratic candidates. It also provided a framework for describing the senator's campaign in an entertaining, even exciting manner. . . . While network news emphasized Muskie's early superiority, it also probed his campaign for signs of eroding strength reminded viewers that his eventual triumph was not a certainty, and, in the case of the New Hampshire primary, provided a formidable opponent (in the front-runner's 'needed' margin of victory) when none could be found among the candidates themselves. In this manner, network coverage of the Muskie campaign in the Democratic primaries became a kind of unfolding drama that focused on one question: Can Ed Muskie withstand the challenge of competing candidates and maintain his grasp on the front-runner's mantle long enough to capture the party nomination?"

That Muskie was the front-runner can hardly be in doubt. All during November and December of 1971 and January of 1972 stories appeared, in endless procession, recounting the latest convert to his candidacy. The *Times*'s Johnny Apple seemed to have the inside track for most of the major endorsements. Typical of what he was doing during these months are these headlines from his stories about the plans of Governor Gilligan of Ohio.

Nov. 22:
GILLIGAN IS EXPECTED TO ENDORSE
MUSKIE OR RUN AS FAVORITE SON

Dec. 20, on Page One:
OHIO GOVERNOR WILL BACK
MUSKIE FOR PRIMARY RACE

Dec. 23, on Page 18:

GILLIGAN BACKS MUSKIE;

MAY CARRY MOST OF OHIO'S DELEGATES

The stories, apparently, were leaked to Apple. Thereafter, Muskie would hold joint press conferences with the people endorsing him, and get attention on the network news shows. It was an interesting one-two punch that seemed to work.

Muskie's political chief, John F. English, spent most of his time during this period nailing down the endorsements. Little time was spent organizing workers for Muskie farther down the ladder. That, it turned out, was a miscalculation.

Muskie was spread impossibly thin. In New Hampshire, he was running against a "phantom," plus, as it turned out, a very real George McGovern. In Florida, Muskie was running against Wallace, Humphrey, and Jackson, all of whom would finish ahead of him and none of whom wasted any time in New Hampshire.

McGovern's organizers were much smarter—they had targeted New Hampshire for a "moral victory," and they would get it. They were pretty much writing off Florida, looking ahead to Wisconsin on April 4, where they anticipated their first victory. They had the money, the staff, and the volunteers to meet those modest goals. Except for his endorsements and his position in the polls, Muskie was outgeneraled and outnumbered.

He announced his candidacy formally on January 4 in a speech that was televised nationally (at a cost of $35,000). He taped the eight-minute broadcast in the unheated living room of his summer cottage in Kennebunk Beach, Maine. It was an obvious effort to re-create the mood of his widely acclaimed election eve broadcast in November of 1970. Most reporters I talked to were unimpressed: Muskie was frozen in a chair, perhaps literally as well as figuratively. He never smiled, never even moved. He said government can lead and government can be truthful and the nation's leaders should be straightforward. He called for "a new beginning."

James Naughton, writing about Muskie's announcement in *The New York Times,* said:

"The senator's advisers believe that his strength is his image as a calm, deliberate, and credible politician. Accordingly, they are hoping to establish him as the natural, philosophic rival to Mr. Nixon and the focal point for Democratic attempts to turn the President out of office."

Muskie, Naughton noted, "is the only Democratic contender who plans to run in all 22 state primaries."

The newspapers on January 4 carried another piece of news: Wallace had decided to enter the Florida primary and perhaps several more. Hours later, Humphrey announced, formally, that he was in the race too. Muskie's problem was that people weren't taking the front-runner status we had awarded him seriously enough: too many candidates were getting into the act. The grand strategy, it seemed, already was obsolescent.

It was also schizophrenic. While his TV commercials continued to show centrist Muskie as that essential man of decency—a man you can believe in—Muskie himself in some of his speeches, in some of his position papers, and in his choice of new advisers was moving to the left. His position on the war hardened, to the point that the Nixon Administration singled him out for very special criticism. His tax program was a chapter right out of Fred Harris's book. He went to Florida and called the space shuttle "pork barrel." Reports that Muskie was too bland and that he fudged on the issues really can't be taken seriously when this part of his campaign is examined.

Bill Loeb, when he had the time for it, gave Muskie hell. But Loeb's problem was that he was so busy—he was in a fight with Dr. Bonner, president of the University of New Hampshire; he was in a much bigger fight with Governor Walter Peterson, who was proposing an individual income tax; and he was trying to promote the candidacies of Yorty and Ashbrook.

A sampling of the *Union Leader* rhetoric:

February 4, in an unsigned editorial:

"While Senator 'Flip-Flop' Muskie, the Vietnam War hawk-dove-chicken, issues statements concerning the Vietnam War that border on incomprehensible, other presidential candidates must at least be given credit—for stating their positions in words of clarity and precision.

"Senator Muskie's position, after close analysis, is found to be virtually identical to that of the Viet Cong. . . ."

February 7, in an editorial signed by Loeb beginning on Page One. The headline reads: 'Flip-Flop Muskie Is a Phony.'

"It has been this newspaper's hope that New Hampshire voters would be perceptive enough regarding Senator Muskie's obvious phoniness that it would not be necessary to call attention to some of Senator Muskie's very definite shortcomings."

Loeb then urged his readers to read a column by Ralph de Toledano "at the top of our back page today." In that column, de Toledano took Muskie to task for his speech at the National Governors Conference in Puerto Rico. That speech was delivered after the rioting and massacre at Attica prison. Muskie had said, "We have reached the point where men would rather die than live another day in America." That, said Loeb, is "hysterical nonsense."

February 8, the next day, Loeb ran another de Toledano column at the top of Page One. In it, de Toledano attacked both Hartke and Muskie for their statements on the war.

February 11, three days later, Loeb ran a column by Holmes Alexander at the top of Page One. Its headline: "Senator Muskie and the Freaks." Alexander thought Muskie's endorsement of the April 24, 1971, antiwar demonstration deserved censure by the Senate.

February 13, a headline on Page One read: "Muskie Pulls New Copout." The thrust of the story was that Muskie had not appeared at a Jefferson-Jackson Day dinner in Bedford.

February 16, in another Page One editorial, Loeb explored an old story connecting Muskie with Fred H. Vahlsing, Jr., and a sugar-beet fiasco in Maine. The story had been examined by reporters earlier and no improper connection or relationship between Vahlsing and Muskie had been established. Loeb didn't see it that way. In capital letters, he wrote:

"FUNNY BUSINESS FOR A MAN WHO IS ALWAYS WRINGING HIS HANDS FOR PURE WATER AND ECOLOGY IN GENERAL!"

This kind of editorializing may strike outsiders as extraordinary, but it was simply standard Loeb treatment. Muskie, in fact, was getting off pretty lightly because Loeb had so many other enemies to attack and friends to promote.*

On February 24, though, Loeb scored. The headline on his Page One editorial read: 'Sen. Muskie Insults Franco-Americans.' The editorial began:

"It is always surprising to this writer that people who ought to be smarter seem to think they can get away with saying something derogatory in some other part of the nation and that it will never get back to the home-folks.

"If you never do anything else, be sure to look at the letter which we have reproduced exactly as it was received and which we run in place of our editorial cartoon today."

Turn now to Page 19, the first page of the second section, and this is what Loeb reproduced:

Feb. 17, 1972
Deerfield Beach, Fla.

Mr. Loeb —
Manchester Guardian
Manchester
New Hampshire

Dear Mr. Loeb —

I saw you on TV the other night and my friend's father gets your newspaper. We went to Ft. Lauderdale to meet Sen. Muskie—we were right beside him at seed house, when one of the men asked him what did he know about blacks—and the problems with them—he didn't have any in Maine—a man with the senator said 'no'—not blacks but we have *cannocks.*

---

* McGovern, it should be noted, escaped almost all of Loeb's wrath. McGovern was quoted in the paper saying he thought his treatment in the news columns was fair. The explanation probably stems from Loeb's underestimation of McGovern's candidacy. He may have hoped McGovern would take some radical-left, fringe votes from Muskie, allowing his man Yorty to score impressively. Loeb guessed very badly.

What did he mean? We asked—Mr. Muskie laughed, and said come to New England and see—could you write me the answer—or print it in your paper—my friend gets it from you—

Thank you
Paul Morrison
Deerfield Beach
Fla. 33064

Back to Page One. Loeb, writing now in capital letters, continues:

"IF PAUL MORRISON, THE AUTHOR OF THE LETTER, HADN'T TAKEN THE TROUBLE TO WRITE ABOUT HIS EX-PERIENCE WITH SENATOR MUSKIE IN FLORIDA, NO ONE IN NEW HAMPSHIRE WOULD KNOW OF THE DEROGA-TORY REMARKS EMANATING FROM THE MUSKIE CAMP ABOUT THE FRANCO-AMERICANS IN NEW HAMPSHIRE AND MAINE—REMARKS WHICH THE SENATOR FOUND AMUSING."

There are only two more paragraphs in the editorial:

"We must remember that this is the same Senator who had the gall to come to New Hampshire and say that the publisher of this newspaper didn't understand northern New England.

"WE HAVE ALWAYS *KNOWN* THAT SENATOR MUSKIE WAS A HYPOCRITE, BUT WE NEVER EXPECTED TO HAVE IT SO CLEARLY *REVEALED* AS IN THIS LETTER SENT TO US FROM FLORIDA."

Muskie had visited the Seed, an experimental drug-treatment center in Fort Lauderdale on February 1. But had Paul Morrison been there, and had there been any talk about "cannocks"? Loeb main-tained the letter was legitimate and he hinted he would have more to say about its authenticity later. Reporters from other newspapers tried to find "Paul Morrison" and got nowhere. No such name was listed in any phone book and no one had ever heard of him.

The only confirmation offered by Loeb was another letter from Florida, reproduced on March 4. It was from "Harold W. Eldredge" of Fort Lauderdale and he said he was the man who asked Muskie about the blacks. "Eldredge [said a] young man companion" of Muskie said Maine had "canucks." Then a young man asked what "canucks" were "and some one answered something about come to New England and see." Morrison, of course, identified that "someone" as Muskie.

On October 10, 1972, the *Washington Post,* in a lead Page One story by investigative reporters Carl Bernstein and Bob Woodward, reported that "law enforcement sources" said the Morrison letter was a fabrication, the best example of "political spying and sabotage conducted on behalf of President Nixon's re-election and directed by officials of the White House and the Committee for the Re-Election of the President."

On its own, the *Post* seemed to have pinned down the culprit. "*Washington Post* staff writer Marilyn Berger reported that Ken W. Clawson, deputy director of White House communications, told her in a conversation on September 25, 'I wrote the letter.' "

Interviewed on October 9, however, Clawson denied he wrote the letter. "I know nothing about it," he said. Loeb, interviewed at the same time, said he remained convinced the letter was "authentic," while admitting that Morrison had never been located. Loeb said he and his paper were still investigating.

Earlier, the *Post* said, B. J. McQuaid, editor in chief of Loeb's newspaper, conceded that Clawson had been "useful" in connection with the Morrison letter. Clawson said he met McQuaid briefly during the primary when he had lunch in Manchester with editors of the paper.

So, until the Watergate case is finally played out, we won't know the real truth. For now, the presumption remains strong that the letter was planted. It is no mere footnote, for it took root and, more than anything else, destroyed Ed Muskie.

The letter and Loeb's editorial appeared in the *Union Leader* on Thursday, February 24, 11 days before the primary. That day, at Muskie headquarters, something approaching panic occurred.

Franco-Americans, comprising half the Democratic vote in Manchester, which produces almost half the Democratic vote in New

Hampshire, were a key segment of the constituency Muskie was trying to build. The implication that Muskie had slandered these voters was catastrophic.

Checks by members of Muskie's staff indicated that the letter and the editorial had been widely read and almost as widely believed. Something, therefore, had to be done, and somebody, probably campaign manager Tony Podesta, figured head-on confrontation with Loeb was the course to take. After all, it was not as if Muskie had been silent about Loeb; on February 9, he had attacked him. This time, it was decided, he would go to the newspaper building and make the charge against Loeb stick, dramatically.

On Friday, the *Union Leader* ran a guest editorial that was, in fact, an item from the "Newsmakers" column in the December 27, 1971, issue of *Newsweek*. It was about Jane Muskie and it read:

"The White House could be in for a drastic change of pace if Jane Muskie becomes First Lady. Campaigning in New Hampshire last week for 'Big Daddy,' as she jokingly referred to her husband, the Maine Democrat's 44-year-old wife unleashed the kind of style that provided a field day for Women's Wear Daily reporter Kandy Stroud, who took down all the breezy quotes. 'Let's tell dirty jokes,' shouted Jane to the reporters and aides aboard her charter bus. Also: 'Pass my purse—I haven't had my morning cigarette yet.' She chewed gum, sighed that she couldn't wear a certain dress because someone else had 'the g.d. thing on' and owned up to a preference for two drinks before dinner and a creme de menthe afterward 'because the next day everything seems to work just right. But I can't mix booze and wine or I get a headache and have little dreams.' Spying Senator Ed's picture in a newspaper, his wife hooted: 'There he is. Isn't he cute?' "

And that's all there was to it, a "guest editorial" in the *Union Leader* of a *Newsweek* item that condensed a typically bitchy article from *Women's Wear Daily*.* Muskie read it on Friday, presumably

---

* Women's "society" reporting is a special substratum, and there isn't space in this book to consider it. Suffice it to say that often it is harmless and supercilious, but sometimes it is personal and very nasty. For reasons I can't explain, veteran "society" reporters are dragons, and they strike terror in the hearts of most men. A press secretary to a well-known politician says that he always returns telephone calls to society reporters at the *Washington Post* before he telephones anyone else. "You've got to," he says, "or they'll kill you." I think he means it.

for the first time, just hours before his aides had scheduled him to appear in front of the *Union Leader* and attack Loeb dispassionately. Muskie is a proud and emotional man, and, late in February, he was beleaguered. The *Post*'s Broder, borrowing a line from the late Ed Lahey, said Muskie was being "nibbled to death by ducks."

At 9:30 A.M. Saturday, Muskie began his attack on Loeb and the *Manchester Union Leader*. The snow was falling and it was cold.

Muskie said the incident in Fort Lauderdale described by "Paul Morrison" never occurred. The assertions were "lies." He said Franco-Americans are "my strongest supporters" and he produced three of them as living proof.

"I can remember when I was a boy being called a Polack," he said. "It was a term of derision and I hated it. I'd never use that kind of term with respect to any other ethnic group." (Of course, Morrison hadn't said it was Muskie who used the word, only that Muskie seemed to be amused by "a man with [him]" who had used the word.)

"I've been in politics all my life. I am no child. I know these things happen. I've got to be prepared to take them. But what really got me was this editorial attacking my wife: Big Daddy's Jane." He paused. "A good woman . . . ," he began, and then he broke down and began to cry. He recovered. "This man doesn't walk," he said, referring to Loeb, "he crawls." He broke down again. "He's talking about my wife. . . ." The pause this time was longer. "Maybe I've said all I should on it. It's fortunate for him he's not on this platform beside me. . . ." And Muskie cried again. Louis Jolbert, a French-Canadian friend from Maine, shouted "Who's for Muskie?" in an effort to give Muskie time to pull himself together.

Muskie, recovered, said, "It's an insult to the people of Manchester that you have to pick up this rotten newspaper every morning."

That's what happened. Let's see now how the press covered what happened.

At that very moment, President Nixon was in China, accompanied by dozens of reporters and cameramen and technicians. But Muskie, on February 26, 1972, was covered regularly by six reporters —Naughton of *The New York Times,* Richard Stout of *Newsweek,* Dean Fischer of *Time,* Frank Reynolds of ABC, Bruce Morton of CBS, and David Horowitz of NBC.

These "regulars" were told by traveling press secretary Dick Stewart that Muskie was going to make a speech at the *Union Leader*. The in-state press secretary, Barry Wanger, told national reporters in New Hampshire (but not assigned specifically to Muskie) about the addition to the schedule. One of those reporters was Broder; another was Bruce Winters of the *Baltimore Sun.* Wanger also alerted the two wire services, AP and UPI, neither of which had assigned a reporter to travel regularly with Muskie or any other Democratic candidate.

AP and UPI would pick up Muskie with their local reporters, as he came into their territories. That Saturday morning, AP covered Muskie with its bureau chief in Concord, Joe Zellner, and UPI countered with its bureau chief, John Milne.

"There are so many candidates that we can't staff everybody all the time," Louis Boccardi, AP's managing editor, told me after the episode occurred. At that moment, *The New York Times* was covering Muskie, McGovern, Humphrey, Jackson, and Lindsay regularly. On almost any given day in February, six or more *Times* reporters were in New Hampshire, doing God knows what.

The *Washington Post* covered New Hampshire differently; it was a zone defense, rather than man to man. Broder was assigned the New Hampshire primary, and he moved there for the duration. George Lardner, Jr., was doing the same thing in Florida. NBC was experimenting with a zone too, although in mid-February it had assigned correspondents to the leading contenders (but not, it should be noted, film crews). Its New Hampshire correspondent was Douglas Kiker. Attached to him—TV reporters travel with a retinue, like an American army—was a researcher, a field producer, and a three-man crew. Kiker was given "carte blanche" in deciding what stories to cover and what stories to ignore. "It's a calculated risk," Irwin "Bud" Lewis, NBC's director of election operations, told me. That Saturday morning, when Muskie cried, NBC had taken its calculated risk, and it had no film crew at the *Union Leader.*

ABC and CBS were both there with film crews; that evening ABC had a minute of film on its news show and CBS had a minute and 20 seconds. NBC reported the story, without film.

"What did we lose?" Wallace Westfeldt, producer of NBC's evening news, asked. "Muskie yelling at Loeb? Hell, people have been doing that for years." Anyway, Westfeldt said, he watched other networks' film "and I didn't get the feeling Muskie was choked up. I didn't see any tears."

But Broder, who was there, did. As soon as the speech was concluded, he called his office in Washington and told his editors what he had. That afternoon, at the regular news conference, his story was scheduled for Sunday's newspaper. Also attending that conference was an editor of the joint news syndicate operated by the *Post* and the *Los Angeles Times;* the syndicate serves more than two hundred clients. It was decided to move Broder's story on that wire.

The AP's bureau chief, Joe Zellner, listened to the speech and then filed a story that went on the AP's state wire—meaning it went to AP clients in New Hampshire. His story began moving to those clients about 11 A.M.

But it wasn't until about 5 P.M.—six hours later—that Zellner's story reached the "A" wire that goes to clients all over the country. The AP says it did move a story earlier, perhaps about noon, on its "B" wire, a secondary national wire that goes to most AP clients. The "B" wire is not always closely watched by editors receiving it.

"We moved the Muskie story on the 'B' wire so the copy we were moving for Sunday morning papers—mostly our China file—wouldn't get held up," an AP editor in New York explained.

The irony is delicious; if the "canuck" letter was indeed a plant by Republican saboteurs, Nixon's trip to China was knocking it off the "A" wire. Nixon was sabotaging the saboteurs.

AP's intransigence didn't end there either. Its stories mentioned only in passing, deep into the seventeenth paragraph on the "A" wire, that Muskie cried.

The UPI did better. Its story moved on the "A" wire at 11:05 A.M. But that story never mentioned, even by passing reference, that Muskie had cried. It simply said, in the eighth paragraph of a brief and routine story, that Muskie was "visibly shaken."

Broder's story ran on Page One. It began:

"With tears streaming down his face and his voice choked with emotion . . ."

Winters of the *Sun* struck almost the same note. His second paragraph reads: "Overwhelmed by emotion, the Maine Democrat wept openly as he defended his wife, Jane."

The New York Times ran the Muskie story on its special election page, which turned out to be Page 54 on Sunday. However, the *Times* did use a photograph of Muskie speaking in New Hampshire on Page One. The *Times*'s Naughton reported in the sixth paragraph that Muskie "broke into tears."

A curiosity is that the *Los Angeles Times,* the *Post*'s partner in the wire syndicate, ran Zellner's AP story. On Page 3.

On February 29, three days after Muskie's appearance at the *Union Leader,* the *Post*'s Broder was on Page One again. The headline: "Support for Muskie Wavers in New Hampshire." In the questionnaire I mailed to political reporters just prior to the New Hampshire primary, I asked this question: "Is there any story written by *someone else* (that comes to mind quickly) that you wish you had written?" Broder's February 29 story is the winner, by a mile. More importantly, perhaps, it is the favorite of the reporters who should know most about good reporting in their own field. It is the favorite, in other words, of the inner-circle regulars.

It is the favorite because it is perceived as the first story suggesting that Muskie "appears to be in trouble in New Hampshire," which was Broder's lead. Others wrote the same thing about the same time (Gannett's Jack Germond, for example, wrote his story the same time Broder was writing; but Germond's story was published a day later), but Broder called the shot. To us, spotting a trend like this about one of them is crucial.

The *Post* story was based on "lengthy interviews in the homes of 75 voters in three wards of Manchester and the towns of Somersworth and Newport." Assisting Broder were Don Oberdorfer and Mary Russell.

The first reason cited by Broder for the "erosion in the presumed front-runner's strength that could leave the Maine senator with an embarrassingly low percentage of the vote in the March 7 Democratic primary he has counted on to send his presidential campaign off on a flying start" was:

"His failure to match either the personal campaign effort of such rivals as Sen. Vance Hartke and Los Angeles Mayor Sam Yorty, or the television spending for write-in candidate Wilbur Mills or the precinct work of the organization backing Sen. George McGovern."

Hartke got 2.7 percent of the vote; Yorty got 6.1 percent (half the minimum most of us had anticipated), and Mills got 4.1 percent. McGovern, listed last, got 37.1 percent.

Thereafter, the reasons were:

"The voter perception of him as a man who is wrong on some issues and vague on a good many more.

"The almost daily attacks of the state's largest paper, the *Manchester Union Leader,* and the mixed reaction to Muskie's emotional response Saturday to the newspaper's publisher, William Loeb.

"And an apparent inability so far to capitalize on his being a neighbor from Maine or to present himself as the national Democrat likeliest to defeat Richard Nixon."

That same day—February 29—Broder wrote a column on the *Post*'s "op-ed" page. It seems to me the column makes a lot more sense than the story based on those 75 lengthy interviews. Muskie's "trouble," he said, is that he has failed "to solve the problem of how a rational man should behave in an irrational situation."

New Hampshire, he continued, has frustrated and unnerved Muskie, whose "prime asset throughout his political career has been his reasonableness, and the sense of calm good judgment that he conveys." He is frustrated and unnerved because he is "struggling somewhat desperately to protect his home base against the likes of George McGovern, Vance Hartke, Sam Yorty, and Wilbur Mills."

McGovern, Broder says, is "a serious, capable opponent, who has waged an excellent campaign here, but he has no natural base in New Hampshire, as Muskie does, and he has only the dimmest chance of being the Democratic presidential nominee."

So, Muskie is seen as fighting off minor, no-chance candidates with one hand and Bill Loeb and the *Union Leader* with the other. Broder ends with his own prescription for solving Muskie's ills: he must exploit the "argument that he is, by every reckoning, the man who is likeliest to unite the party and return the White House to Democratic control."

It didn't take TV long to pick up what Broder and the rest of the print reporters were writing. Consider this report on ABC the night of March 2. Note, especially, the similarity of language.

"There are indications of an erosion of Muskie's support in this state." Broder had said: ". . . an erosion in the presumed front-runner's strength." The ABC report continues:

"Perhaps that would happen inevitably to everybody [sic] who has been out in front for so long and who is the sole target of a collection of well-financed and hard-working opponents."

The New York Times came up with its own survey on March 3. The story, written by Johnny Apple, appeared on the special election page. It is more honest, more accurate, and more objective than the *Post*'s.

More honest because Apple concedes that "the sample was not scientifically drawn and not large enough to justify any assertion that Mr. Muskie is in serious trouble. . . ." Yet, Apple and other *Times* reporters interviewed 120 persons in six parts of the state, possibly a larger effort than the *Post* undertook.

More accurate because Apple and his reporters determined that it was a "Muskie-McGovern contest" and that Hartke, Mills, and Yorty "are attracting only fragmentary support." Apple wrote that Muskie "has a sizable following, but it constituted less than half of those interviewed." Apple also found that McGovern "has won the commitment of most students, most antiwar liberals and—surprisingly—many blue-collar workers."

All in all, the *Times* survey is a model of its kind. Only one problem: it was three days behind the *Post*'s, and coming in first is what counts with us.

And if that's the kind of game we play, I'd like to put in a word for myself. Why not: If I don't, who will? Late in January I went to Florida and discovered that Muskie had failed to build an effective grass-roots organization there. When I got back, I thought Anne Wexler, executive director of National Citizens for Muskie, might have something worthwhile to say, so I tape-recorded an interview with her that ran in the *Observer* on February 8.

"We're way behind," she told me. "I just started [organizing for Muskie in the nonprimary states] and nothing, literally, has been done . . . in terms of beginning to try to pull the people together who are for Muskie, aside from the politicians." She said the much-publicized endorsements from leading Democrats eventually would be "counterproductive" and she said the way the Muskie campaign was being run in Florida—with volunteers calling *all* Democrats and asking them to vote for Muskie—was "folly" and "stupid." Ms. Wexler's analysis was as profound as it was prophetic.

Back to New Hampshire.

The *Boston Globe* weighed in on March 5 with its final New Hampshire survey, conducted once again by John Becker. The first survey in January, remember, showed Muskie with an improbable 65 percent of the vote. This one gave him 42 percent, off 23 points. McGovern was second with 26; Yorty, 4; Mills, 2; Hartke, 2, and others, 4. Becker found 20 percent of the voters still undecided, suspiciously high.

The campaign drew to a close Sunday night when Muskie, McGovern, Yorty, Hartke, and Edward T. Coll, a 32-year-old social worker from Connecticut, who was on the ballot, debated the "issues" on the national educational TV network. McGovern argued that Muskie had not disclosed all his campaign contributions. Muskie said he grew up only 25 miles from the studio. Hartke said he wanted import quotas for shoes. Yorty denounced the "left-liberal" bloc in the Senate. Coll pulled a rubber rat out of his pocket and waved it at the cameras. "This is the problem," he said.

It was comical.

On Tuesday, 86,000 New Hampshirites went to the polls to vote in the Democratic primary, which in itself is surprising. Most observers had been anticipating a Democratic vote of 60,000. Where those extra 26,000 votes came from has never been satisfactorily explained.

Newspaper and TV reports the next day gave Muskie 48 percent of the vote and McGovern, 37 percent. But those were incomplete figures. In final returns, never published to my knowledge, Muskie won 46.4 percent of the vote and McGovern, 37.1. That's a drop of 1.6 points for Muskie; the real figures, in fact, were worse for him than the ones we based our conclusions upon.

Given all that had gone before, the reaction was predictable. Senator Muskie won "in the face of a strong challenge" by McGovern, the *Times* said. The "surprising strength" of McGovern kept Muskie from getting the 50 percent of the vote "that would give momentum to his nomination drive," the *Post* said.

Adding to Muskie's woes was the fact that he managed to win only fifteen of New Hampshire's twenty delegates to the national convention in separate balloting. McGovern got the rest.

Muskie tried to argue that the important thing was that he had won. But then he explained he could have done better if he'd just had the time and the resources to make a "maximum showing." He reminded us that he was running in Florida and Illinois and Wisconsin, too, and time and resources had to be invested there.

An elated McGovern boasted he had won a "moral victory" and he and his staff were especially pleased at the size of his blue-collar vote in Manchester, home of the *Union Leader*. They could thank Bill Loeb for that.

Maria Carrier, Muskie's in-state campaign manager, looked at the returns and said: "It's heartbreaking—but it's New Hampshire."

And crotchety Joe Alsop, still burning at the way the press interpreted Lyndon Johnson's performance in New Hampshire four years earlier, wrote:

"At the moment, it seems to be obligatory to say something about the New Hampshire primary. The only thing to say is: 'Abolish it.'

". . . In sum," he said, "this has been an expensive charade. . . . Most people of the media believe what they tell one another, and most politicians believe what the media tell them. So Sen. Muskie will probably be hurt a bit, by failing to roll up more than 48 percent of the vote."

The real test, Alsop said, parroting just what the "people of the media" had been telling each other, would be Florida, a "vastly more important primary."

New Hampshire was a farce. Surely Florida would be an improvement.

9

Florida

The fact that "Peter Sheridan," self-styled original ranking Boohoo of the Neo-American Church, was aboard Senator Edmund Muskie's "Sunshine Special" when it rolled into Miami on February 19 was entirely the fault of Hunter S. Thompson, political correspondent for *Rolling Stone* magazine.

Recognizing the Boohoo as an "obvious aristocrat of the Freak Kingdom" and "a serious, king-hell crazy," Thompson graciously gave him his press credentials somewhere along about 6 A.M. And the Boohoo managed to climb aboard the whistle-stop train two hours later to begin a full day of drinking raw gin out of a bottle he swiped from the bar. Thompson overslept in his room at the Ramada Inn in West Palm Beach (he insists Muskie's aides intentionally erased his name from the wake-up list) and missed the whole thing.

What happened at the station in Miami, Thompson learned from a friend, "was that the Boohoo reached up from the track and got hold of Muskie's pants-leg—waving an empty glass through the bars around the caboose platform with his other hand and screaming: 'Get your lying ass back inside and make me another drink, you worthless old fart!' "

Welcome to Florida, Ed Muskie, the state that, because of its size and variety, will begin to tell us something *meaningful* about 1972.

The good folks of Florida had decided to hold a real Presidential primary for the first time because they thought it would be good publicity for the Sunshine State in the growing, changing New South.

In an August 16, 1971, memo to "political correspondents, pundits, and grubby reporters," George Hanna, press secretary for the state's Democratic Executive Committee, noted that "the candidates will be campaigning in January and February, which is an ideal time to do some depth analyses and interpretives in Florida. Why should it just be those baseball writers who get to winter in Florida?"

The committee's publication, *Florida Democrat,* argued that "Florida's diverse population makes the state more representative [than New Hampshire], so the primary figures to be an important test of candidate strength."

That was before most of us guessed George Wallace from neighboring Alabama would run in it. What that might mean was forecast in an October 8 story by Alan L. Otten of the *Wall Street Journal.*

"In a crowded field, with the middle and left split 10 ways to breakfast, George could easily sweep across the Northern Panhandle and do well enough in other parts of the state to rack up a win," a Florida officeholder told him. "Then, instead of the nice sophisticated image we hoped to get from the primary, we end up with a big, black eye, a bunch of bigoted rednecks."

Over the years, the *Journal's* Otten has been one of Washington's two or three most highly regarded political writers; in 1972, though, he was relatively inactive because of his duties as the new chief of his bureau. Yet, when he did find time to escape Washington and do some reporting, important people listened. His October 8 story set the rules for Florida, just as his friend Broder's story in the *Post* had set the rules for New Hampshire.

Florida, Otten said, was "crucial" to Henry Jackson, because it was his kind of state—heavily laden with defense and space industry, cluttered with friendly labor leaders, bursting in the Miami area with Jews who knew and applauded Jackson's pro-Israel stance.

But, of course, if Wallace did run, he would "cut deeply into Sen. Jackson's conservative support and, many politicians believe, would doom the Senator's Florida chances."

Muskie, as the front-runner, "must do very well to keep his candidacy moving—a win or a very strong second showing. Anything less and he might be disastrously damaged." Otten thought—in October 1971—that Muskie could do very well, although he was perceptive enough to record complaints that Muskie's "pace is too cautious, firm direction from Washington is lacking, the candidate doesn't spark real enthusiasm."

An uncommitted state senator said: "He's perfectly acceptable to most Democrats, everybody's second choice. That may be good in a convention, but in a primary you need to be people's first choice, to have them really committed."

McGovern, Otten said, can't expect to carry the state. "But he does need to score high in some of the university areas and in Miami, where he is concentrating his efforts. Despite lack of charisma, he is arousing here, as in other states, considerable ideological commitment."

Otten thought Bayh had the best organization in the state and might surprise people. Harris was unknown, and had lots of work to do. Humphrey would have to campaign hard, and even that might not work because "most of his former rank-and-file workers have become committed to some other candidate."

Next to Wallace, "probably the biggest unknown factor" is Mayor Lindsay. Anonymous Muskie and McGovern aides told Otten that Lindsay could hurt them. (When Lindsay's decision to campaign in Florida was made, a secondary plot was written: Lindsay would have to finish ahead of McGovern, and vice versa. The two liberals were assigned a contest of their own.)

So, the question in Florida was not, as it had been in New Hampshire, the size of Muskie's victory; it was the order of finish of several candidates who were perceived as important nationally. Muskie, in fact, got a break: he could survive by coming in second to George Wallace.

Wallace made a shambles of the primary, and our expectations of what it might prove, by running so far ahead of everyone else. He got as many votes as Humphrey, Muskie, and Jackson combined. It really should have been no surprise, because, we said, the issues were his. And some of us even came to believe that this was a "respectable" George Wallace campaigning in Florida.

This is really an astonishing turnabout: I know of nothing quite like it in modern political journalism. Consider:

Writing January 2 in *The New York Times* Sunday magazine, Stephan Lesher, an Atlanta-based correspondent for *Newsweek,* said:

"For the last decade, George Corley Wallace has been America's poltergeist, a bumptious bogeyman personifying the cholesterol in the nation's bloodstream.*

"But times and men change, and George Wallace, the 52-year-old suzerain of Alabama, has gone respectable. There is even the satisfying suspicion that Wallace—the man who vowed 'segregation forever,' who postured in the schoolhouse door like a counterfeit Lee surrendering his sword at Appomattox, whose brutal minions spilled innocent blood at Selma and Birmingham—has been negated as a force for evil in America's body politic and, oddly, may even have become a force for good. He is the hard-hat's cathartic, playing Santa Claus instead of Satan by passing out beribboned nostrums for the shadowy cholers afflicting middle America."

Wow.

Or the *Washington Post's* Ken Ringle, writing almost as gothically 12 days later:

"Once looked upon as simply a dark knight of the Southern soul, posturing in the schoolhouse door and calling for 'segregation now . . . segregation forever,' he now basks in a wider spotlight as the nation's first and foremost prophet of the 'social issue': that tangle of racial and physical fears summed up by the words 'law and order' and 'busing.'

"The same political and social scientists who once dismissed him as a regional freak, are newly convinced of the 'social issue's' potency

---

* When a news magazine reporter gets a chance to step out under his own by-line, he can almost be excused for stumbling. But "cholesterol in the nation's bloodstream?"

among the electorate and now peer nervously down from above the Mason-Dixon line, analyzing his every action and awaiting his every word."

Ringle didn't have the generosity to credit our old friends Scammon and Wattenberg for coining the "social issue." But Lesher did, and he quoted advice from their book at some length. ("Do *not* say, 'Crime is a complicated sociological phenomenon and we'll never be able to solve the problem unless we get at the root causes of poverty and racism.' *Do* say, 'I am going to make our neighborhoods safe again for decent citizens of every color . . .' Vintage Wallace," Lesher concluded.)

What is remarkable is that Wallace hadn't changed, except for a charming new wife, a new wardrobe, a new haircut, a new staff, and some computers. Sure, he didn't talk about "niggers" very often anymore. He didn't need to; who, by now, didn't know where he stood? Deep down, he was the same wily, ambitious, angry demagogue we had known for a decade.

We had changed. We had read Scammon and Wattenberg; maybe we'd even listened to Joe Kraft talking about "Middle America." Perhaps we'd heeded Richard Nixon and Spiro Agnew. At the least, we had come to believe that white, working-class Americans had some real grievances. Hell, so did we. We worried about our kids and drugs. We worried about schools that didn't teach and colleges we couldn't afford. Takin' our little children and busin' 'em from here to kingdom come didn't make much sense to us either.

I said we saw Wallace as a "respectable" candidate in Florida. That needs more defining. "Fit to be seen" is one of the dictionary's definitions, and that's about right. Not "respectable" in the sense of "decent or correct in character or behavior." He was still a demagogue, still dangerous, and we believed that. But he was now "respectable" because his constituency, we had come to realize, possessed legitimate grievances and we couldn't blame them for being deceived by this angry little man.

Columnist Garry Wills, the toughest of all political commentators, described Wallace best, I think. Writing in *New York* magazine on March 6, he said:

"It is often said that Wallace is just a charming scoundrel in the classic Southern mold, a 'good ole boy.' But the essence of a good ole boy is complaisance. He'll hang you a nigger in no time, but he don't *mean* nothin' by it—he was just bein' sociable. (It is this that makes of Southerners such engaging rogues.) But Wallace is never very sociable; his life has a sour and joyless air to it, reflected in the glum company he keeps, his teetotaling pointless austerity, the aimless air he has when he gets away from politics—and the very limited definition he has given to his 'politickin'.' Public malevolence is his lifeblood. Without it he would not know what to do with himself. He is a good hater, which good ole boys never were. They were good forgetters; and George remembers—a slight on Air Force One, just as much as an attack on his table manners. And, with pugnacity he remembers the attack by persisting in the bad manners. He won't 'climb,' at least not thet-away. He's cold-sober serious on this point. (Southern politicians often can't handle their booze, but without it they'd be unbearable.)"

"Wallace," Wills concluded, "has such great talent as a demagogue, it is lucky for us that he lacks all human graces. That makes him incapable of our politicians' smoother deceits."

We agreed more or less with that: Wallace was a demagogue but he wasn't smooth enough to win the Democratic Party's nomination or to be elected President on his own third-party ticket. Spoil things, yes; win, no.

To spoil things, he didn't have to do very much. For George Wallace, there was no need of polltakers or volunteers or even advance men. He simply materializes and begins campaigning, which means The Rally, over and over again. It is always the same; even the words are virtually the same, year after year.

And that's one of the reasons it's so hard to cover Wallace (but not his constituency, for that, of course, is another matter). We can (and we did) write about his new wife and his new double-knit suits and the way his hair was cut. We can (and we did) note that his voice seemed a little lower now, but he had the best explanation for that.

"I don't really think I've changed so much," he told the *Post*'s

Ringle. "It's just that I don't have to yell as loud now as when I was first elected. . . . Like the old story about the farmer who had to knock the mule down to get his attention. . . . Now you all listen to what I say so I can talk a little softer."

In Florida, there were just five things he wanted to talk about, and Wills in his article in *New York* magazine summed them up:

"(1) Defense: 'We gotta get off this unilateral disarmament jag . . . I'm not going to gamble on it. We ought to be Number One.'

"(2) Taxes: 'My own church owns a printing plant that prints books with four-letter words in them and sells them for profit.' Soak the rich institutions, for the little guy.

"(3) Foreign Aid: 'We spent billions of dollars, and most of that went down the drain.' In more raucous mood, he says down a rat-hole. 'I'm against helping people ten thousand miles away who just spit on us in the U.N. The U.N.'s a kind of Playboy Club, with a bunch of folks who don't know what to do with themselves.'

"(4) Law and Order: 'There were 127 policemen killed last year, more than any year in our history. The Federal judges have just about destroyed the law. . . . And what's so sacro*sawnkt* about a judge? He don't hang his britches on the wall and run and jump in 'em in the morning.'

"(5) Busing: The big one last—'All five of the Senators running for President down here voted for busing. I got the records right here.' "

Busing, of course, was the big one. The crowds just waited for it; they knew, he knew, we all knew it was coming.

"Busin'," he'd say, spitting it out. "It's the most atrocious, callous, cruel, asinine thing you can do for little children. Fifty years from now, the American people will look back and say, 'how cold and callous were those in our Government who brought it about,' and those who bring it about, where do they live? They don't live in Washington, they live over in Maryland, or Virginia and they've got their children in a private school. They're more pluperfect hypocrites. . . ."

And then his voice would be swallowed in the bull-throated roar of the crowd.

"Send Them a Message" was Wallace's slogan and it seemed "them" included Richard Nixon and almost all the other Democratic candidates. Nixon, getting the message, told members of Congress trampling over each other in a rush to file amendments to the Constitution that he would not "leave the situation as it is." He announced he would decide on a course of action after he returned from China on March 1.

Among the Democrats, Jackson was listening best. He proposed a Constitutional amendment prohibiting what Wallace called "forced" busing and he was telling his Florida crowds that he was "opposed to this business of busing people all over the place."

Muskie and McGovern both argued that busing is one of several tools that could and should be used to eliminate segregation. But the real problem, both added, was building good neighborhoods and providing good jobs. Shirley Chisholm, the only black in the race, took substantially the same position.

Only Lindsay defended busing on moral grounds. ". . . when we debate busing now," he said, "we are debating what this country stands for."

Thus, for the first time, a legitimate issue was born—and Wallace was responsible for it. That the issue should surface in Florida was a measure of Wallace's political instincts.

It is my own suspicion that "busing" in Florida, Michigan, and elsewhere was a code word for a great many things, some of them not really connected with racism at all. McGovern's polltaker, Patrick H. Caddell, who was reared and first worked in Florida, insisted that busing, as a practical matter, was not an issue. The real issue, he argued, was a pervading sense of frustration and alienation shared by millions of Americans that could be capitalized upon by either a McGovern or a Wallace.

"Our surveys," he told me, "indicate that 50 to 60 percent of the people feel the country is in trouble. In that category is a hard core of 33 percent to 40 percent of the voters who are hard-core in their feelings of alienation.

"That's a tremendous amount of people. These are the people

who hold the balance in any election, and—unlike most alienated voters in the past—they are turning out to vote, making their minds up how to vote at the last minute."

These voters, Caddell said, "believe that government at all levels doesn't care about them. They believe that voting doesn't make a whole lot of difference. They believe things are much too complicated. They have a sense of loss and isolation. They have a real feeling they're being taken."

McGovern, Caddell thought, was getting through to these people, even if they didn't agree with him on some specific positions. "People think he is anti-Establishment and pro-change. And that is good."

Caddell was on to something. Millions of Americans were (and remain) alienated and frustrated, and for a while McGovern took advantage of it. But, surely, he was not pure, as Caddell himself admitted. Of all the candidates, Wallace was consistent, simplistic, unchanging.

He had no programs (except, once, in Wisconsin, I heard him say he would soon reveal "white papers," and his face blanched—"as they call 'em," he added, apologetically—about, I think, taxes and agriculture. No one ever heard about them again).

Other candidates did have programs. The trouble was, nobody paid any of them much attention. On January 12, for example, McGovern offered what his press release called "a broad program of tax and welfare reform, coupled with a proposal for a 'redistribution of income' which could bring as much as $92 billion in additional revenues to the Treasury, reduce local property taxes, and provide every American with a guaranteed annual income 'to replace the present welfare mess.' "

On January 31, Muskie (according to his press release) "proposed broad reform of the property tax system and a housing security system to insure decent homes for low income elderly citizens."

Hubert Humphrey supported "a major tax reform proposal 'to close the loopholes that protect the super-rich and to make available some $16 billion a year for property tax relief. . . .' "

McGovern's proposal, to become so highly controversial later and finally to be abandoned, received 16 paragraphs of routine attention in *The New York Times,* and no mention was made of the

$1,000 demogrant. I can't find any mention of the proposal in the *Washington Post.*

With a handful of clichés and absurd rhetoric, Wallace was able to win acceptance as a true populist, even as he went on "Issues and Answers" to say he saw nothing wrong with big corporations getting bigger.

It is still more evidence of a theme that recurs: the press is more interested in the mechanics of politics than it is in the substance of whatever ideas politicians may have—until, at least, the substance begins to affect the mechanics.

Curiously, though, the TV networks didn't pick up the "respectable" Wallace theme until after he had won the primary. I can offer no reasonable explanation, except for the possibility that papers like the *Times, Post,* and *Wall Street Journal* weren't as available in Florida as they had been in New Hampshire. I am reminded of a wonderful incident related by Robin MacNeil in his revealing book, *The People Machine.*

"In 1963," MacNeil wrote, "when Governor George Wallace tried to prevent the integration of Alabama's schools with his 'stand in the school-house door,' NBC correspondent Tom Pettit, covering the story there, phoned a producer in New York, who started telling Pettit how to handle the story.

" 'There's a good story in the New York Times this morning,' he said.
" 'We don't get the New York Times down here,' Pettit said.
" 'Well, the night lead of the AP says—'
" 'We don't have the AP.'
" 'Never mind. UP's got a pretty good angle on it—'
" 'We don't have UP either,' Pettit said.
" The producer said, 'You don't have the UP?'
" 'No.'
" 'You don't have the AP?'
" 'No.'
" 'You don't have the New York Times?'
" 'No.'
" 'Then how do you guys know what's going on down there?' "

And then MacNeil, who covered the 1972 campaign, in tandem with Sander Vanocur, for public broadcasting, concluded:

"Television news is not set up to cover or gather the news routinely but to disseminate news that other organizations gather. The greatest proportion of the material is supplied by the wire services. Camera crews and reporters are assigned to cover some headline stories, and there are a handful of reporters on permanent beats like the White House and the State Department. With those exceptions, the network news operation is largely reactive: it goes out to cover the stories which the wires, the newspapers and the magazines have developed through original reporting."

MacNeil makes this further point:

"The chief difference between television and newspaper journalism lies in their respective attitudes to the function of the reporter. Television news has not found a central role for the reporter. Preoccupation with the logistical problems of getting 'pictures' have made the reporter secondary, while show business economics have replaced the reporter in the studio with a 'commentator' or front man."

It is a valid observation by a man who should know. MacNeil and Pettit are two of the best "reporters" television has ever known. The networks have never quite figured out what to do with either of them.

I would quibble with MacNeil only in the way he lumps the wires and *The New York Times* together. The wires do supply the fast-breaking information the networks need to deploy their troops. But *The New York Times* and the *Washington Post* and other papers and magazines supply the themes—the points of view—that TV will underline when they get to the places the wires have directed them.

Another point made by MacNeil is worth noting too. The more famous a television reporter becomes, the harder it is for him to function as a reporter.

"Occasionally," MacNeil says, "correspondents do go out to cover a story, but their fame often attracts more public attention than do the events themselves. During the 1964 campaign, David Brinkley went to a shopping center in California to watch Nelson Rockefeller on the stump. There was a sizable crowd around Rockefeller but, when Brinkley was spotted, it melted and re-formed around the bigger attraction, the TV commentator."

A "commentator" can't avoid it. I traveled with CBS's Roger Mudd for a day or two in the 1972 campaign. In Madison, Wisconsin, as we walked along the street to meet a politician for lunch, a young man raced across the street, narrowly avoiding several speeding cars, grabbed Mudd by the elbow, and said: "You're the greatest journalist who ever lived." It took us three blocks to shake him off.

Until Wallace won the Florida primary with 42 percent of the vote, television news portrayed him "as a regional, one-issue candidate who effectively translated the largely racial fears of white Americans into political support, and who, in appealing to the elemental passions of voters, sowed violence and discord wherever he went," according to the "Report on Network News' Treatment of the 1972 Democratic Presidential Candidates."

NBC, according to the report, viewed busing as an artificial issue devised by Wallace himself. CBS's coverage was "less unfavorable" because it viewed busing as a real issue. And ABC "was ambiguous on the precise relationship between Wallace and the busing issue in Florida."

Most newspapermen covering the Florida primary became convinced that Wallace would win big, and some of them offered the kinds of explanations we have already noted to explain that it was more than just an old-fashioned racial appeal that would gain him that crushing victory.

But, the evening of March 14, television news had to backtrack rapidly and explain how a one-issue, regional candidate had swept to victory in every part of Florida, including heavily urbanized, polyglot Dade County. CBS's explanation was typical:

"Send them a message, George Wallace urged Floridians, and, overwhelmingly, they did. The message is that Wallace is real, as real as white Americans' pent-up resentment over school buses, big government, and taxes that pinch. Wallace won big, leaving the rest of the field mired in a Florida swamp. He got more votes than Humphrey, Jackson, and Muskie put together, and became a serious contender in places like Wisconsin and Michigan. . . . George Wallace's lopsided victory here means that he, too, is off and running as a national Democratic candidate, to be taken seriously by the politicians and the voters in the primaries ahead."

And by CBS news, the commentator might have added. For the record, the results in Florida were:

> Wallace: 41.5 percent.
> Humphrey: 18.6.
> Jackson: 13.5.
> Muskie: 8.8.
> Lindsay: 6.5.
> McGovern: 6.1.
> Chisholm: 3.6.

Receiving a handful of votes were McCarthy, Mills, Hartke, and Yorty.

Let's look at those returns in the light of the rules set down weeks earlier. Otten had said (and so had we all) that Jackson had to carry Florida; it was his kind of state. But what Otten had forecast— a strong Wallace race, cutting into Jackson's expectations—came to be. Jackson, as a result, was destroyed. Muskie was supposed to come in first or second. He came in a sorry fourth; he was a big loser. In the separate battle between McGovern and Lindsay, both fared so poorly and came so close to each other that neither could boast of very much. Lindsay was the biggest loser, we said, because he had tried the hardest. Humphrey, by finishing second, did himself no harm.

Once again, Muskie appeared overemotional. In his statement to supporters election night, he said:

". . . what disturbs me most about this campaign and this election is that it reveals to a greater extent than I had imagined some of the worst instincts of which humans are capable. . . . The George Wallace victory in Florida is a threat to the unity of this country. It's a threat to the underlying values of humanism and decency and progress. . . ."

McGovern wouldn't agree. The vote for Wallace, he said—mindful, one supposes, of his interest in winning some of the Wallace vote in his key state, Wisconsin—was not "entirely a racist vote." For many people, it was "a way to register a protest against things as they are." In Wisconsin a few days later, he would say Wallace's victory in Florida was "an angry cry from the guts of ordinary Americans against a system which doesn't give a damn about what's really bothering people in the country today."

Moreover, McGovern said, "People got the impression that he [Muskie] was crying again instead of responding to a problem that we've got to do something about."

The *Times*'s Tom Wicker, that paper's most liberal voice (except when Anthony Lewis was writing about the war), wondered how Muskie, if he won the nomination, would appeal "next fall to those Florida Wallace voters—and the millions like them in other states—that he so vigorously denounced? His attack may have given him a tougher image for the primary campaign; but it did not enhance his ultimate chance to be President and it did not provide the Democrats with the kind of leadership they will need to handle the Wallace problem."

What Wicker didn't say is that Muskie's outburst played into the open arms of Nixon and Agnew, for all along it had been the Republican strategy to add the Wallace vote to their own (about which we will have more to say later).

Muskie, we discovered in New Hampshire and Florida (and again in Wisconsin and Pennsylvania and Massachusetts), was not much of a politician. The reasons for his deficiencies are perhaps best left to a psychologist, but it seemed to us he lacked self-discipline and self-control. A successful politician needs steel in his spine and bile in his blood: he must learn how to cope and how to survive.

The *Rolling Stone*'s Hunter Thompson may lack self-discipline and self-control but there's bile aplenty in his blood. He had the final word.

Muskie's problem, he told his readers without a blush, was the Ibogaine Effect. That's what caused "Muskie's tearful breakdown on the flatbed truck in New Hampshire [and] the delusions and altered thinking that characterized his campaign in Florida."

According to Thompson, who should know, ibogaine comes from the roots of Tabernanthe iboga, "a shrub indigenous to West Africa. . . . It has been used for centuries by natives of Africa, Asia, and South America in conjunction with fetishistic and mythical ceremonies."

When a person chews large quantities of T. I. roots, "his nerves get tense in an extraordinary way, an epileptic-like madness comes over him, during which he becomes unconscious and pronounces words which are interpreted by older members of the group as having a prophetic meaning and to prove that the fetish has entered him."

Well, Thompson explained, a doctor from Brazil had mysteriously joined the Muskie entourage, and that was the key to it. "The Man from Maine had turned to massive doses of Ibogaine as a last resort."

Humphrey, at the same time (Thompson said), "was using an exotic brand of speed known as 'Wallot,' " which wasn't causing much controversy because Humphrey "has always campaigned like a rat in heat."

Compassion is hardly Thompson's strong suit, but he did have a lukewarm feeling for George McGovern, whose moment had now arrived.

10

Wisconsin

George McGovern's advisors knew that Wisconsin should not be an important primary. They also knew, as early as June of 1970, that Wisconsin would be their principal battleground. Why? Because they knew that the press, like generals fighting the last war, would make Wisconsin crucial.

They were right, and it was one of the most brilliant, even Machiavellian judgments of the campaign.

The McGovern strategists knew Wisconsin probably could not be a legitimate expression of *Democratic* inclinations because Republicans would be permitted to vote in it. With an incumbent President, little action could be expected on the Republican side, so crossovers surely would be a major factor.

And they were. Hubert Humphrey actually won the Democratic primary; George McGovern got the most votes. One-third of the McGovern vote, it was later conceded by the McGovern camp, came from Republicans.

We credited McGovern with a mighty victory. It was, in fact, no such thing, and the McGovern people, secretly, knew it wasn't.

The difference is in what really happened—and in what the press thought had happened. McGovern, thanks to us, won, and he was well started on the way to the nomination because of it.

Of all the candidates, the McGovern people knew their press best. They knew that the press would flock to New Hampshire because the New Hampshire primary is traditional and legendary. They knew the press would flock to Wisconsin for the very same reason; after all, in 1960, John F. Kennedy had won a very famous victory there, when poor Hubert Humphrey was the loser for the first time. Twelve years later, he was going to catch it in Wisconsin again, and there was almost nothing he could do about it.

Worse for Hubert, once again we had the propinquity factor. Humphrey came from next door in Minnesota, and he was even called Wisconsin's "third senator." Propinquity did him no more good than it had done Muskie in New Hampshire.

In hustling from Florida to Wisconsin, most of us skipped right past Illinois, which had its primary on March 21. Muskie won the "beauty contest," defeating Eugene J. McCarthy, who was making his first serious run of the year (and last), by a margin of about five to three. We wrote that off, because no one took McCarthy seriously this time. Except that in Illinois, he was spending heavily in the media and campaigning in an energetic way hardly anyone could remember his doing before.

More important, really, was the battle for delegates in which George McGovern made a serious and extensive effort—and lost. Muskie won 59 delegates, McGovern 14, about half of what his Illinois managers had anticipated. The rest of Illinois's delegates were uncommitted, except to Chicago Mayor Richard Daley, who ended up in control of about 80 of them.

Muskie had changed his strategy after Florida, and in Illinois it seemed to be paying off. On March 17, Muskie told the *Times*'s Johnny Apple that he hadn't been clear enough or tough enough on the issues and that his own "subliminal" television ads had compounded his problem. Now, he said, he was hitting hard on two or three issues, "his voice louder, harsher, almost rasping," according to Apple. "His eyes looked intense and angry; his wattles shook as he jerked his head for emphasis. The pedagogical style was gone."

Who is the real Muskie? The avuncular pedagogue or the man

with the rasping voice and the jerking wattles? Who knows? I can only say that I preferred the former because, in his latter transfiguration, Muskie sometimes looked and sounded like a . . . madman. It was, even if not chemically induced, Thompson's Ibogaine Effect. It was, we said, the "new Muskie," apparently abandoning forever his centrist style and his centrist position, battling Humphrey now for the party's legitimate left. Where, after all, was the party's center? No one, yet, had seen a single sign of it.

There are, it turned out, two warring factions in the Democratic Party. Call one the "new politics" of George McGovern. Call the other the "old politics" of George Meany and Henry Jackson and Hubert Humphrey. It is not so much a battle of issues, but of institutions. What was beginning to occur now was not only a battle for the nomination, but a battle for the party itself. Ultimately, it would be fought out between George McGovern and Hubert Humphrey. Muskie's problem was that he was caught in the open, in no-man's-land, and there was nobody there with him.

If the war was to begin, McGovern had to win at least one skirmish, and Wisconsin—foolish, irrelevant Wisconsin—would be it.

So we settled in at the Pfister Hotel in Milwaukee—the war correspondents—and said Hubert Humphrey was doing nicely. Muskie's Wisconsin's chairman, Harold Ickes, Jr., had sent a long memo off to headquarters, detailing everything about Wisconsin, and he never mentioned George McGovern's name. Some of us did better than that, but not much.

Here, I think, we can see why national political writers can be misled so easily. Say a reporter arrives in Wisconsin, a strange state, on Monday and has to start writing on Thursday. Two or three days at best to settle down and begin talking to people.

And who are the people to talk to? The institutional people, obviously, because they are the people everybody knows. Officeholders and labor officials, local newspaper writers and editors. Essentially, in fact, we begin talking to the "old politics" people of Hubert Humphrey and, to some extent, Edmund Muskie. Nobody's ever heard of George McGovern's "new politics" people, and it takes a while to find out who they are. By then, we've been briefed and maybe even brainwashed by the regulars.

That, at least, is what happened to me on my first trip to Wisconsin. Nobody seemed to really know what was happening, and then I met John W. Schmitt, the tough, earthy president of the state's AFL-CIO. I told Schmitt I was impressed by the McGovern organization and the registration efforts I'd watched the day before in Madison, home of the University of Wisconsin.

"Look," he told me, "with the trouble we've had at Madison, it's a liability being the kids' candidate. He [McGovern] talks about the war. Well, Nixon's going to take that right away from us anyhow. And then there's amnesty and abortions. They don't cut with us. I get the women coming in right in this room. They want free abortions. Hell, I say to them, I've got thirty pieces of legislation I want first. Education, for example. Get all these poor people educated and they'll use the pill, just like you do. And then we won't need abortions."

There are 306,000 AFL-CIO members in Wisconsin, plus 120,-000 other workers belonging to the Auto Workers, the Teamsters, and smaller independents, and most of them, I concluded, felt like John Schmitt.

McGovern was out of it, except in the congressional district surrounding the state university. Wallace wasn't going to do very much, but just to make sure Schmitt's office had sent 2,000 anti-Wallace pamphlets to labor leaders around the state. "Wallace Tried to Fool Us Once," the headline said. Muskie wasn't going anywhere because Humphrey had moved in. Humphrey would win, Schmitt told me—and it seemed reasonable. This, after all, was the first person I'd met in Wisconsin who seemed to make much sense.

People would vote for Humphrey "out of loyalty. He's an old friend. And when ya listen to Hubie, he'll take ya. He'll move ya along. He's the best speaker we got, and Wallace is second."

I went campaigning with Humphrey the next night in black neighborhoods in Milwaukee, and Hubie, indeed, was moving them along. It was the old civil-rights champion Humphrey, not the candidate whose radio commercial in Florida had said, "Humphrey will stop the flow of your tax dollars to lazy welfare chiselers." Why, there wasn't a lazy welfare chiseler in all of Milwaukee. And now too, here in Wisconsin, Humphrey discovered that he didn't agree with Nixon's proposals to limit school busing after all. Earlier, Humphrey had said: "Thank goodness that at long last the President has been able to get his finger up in the air and sense what's going on and has decided that he would say amen to some of the things that some of the rest of us have been trying to do." But Humphrey had been reading the "fine print" of the President's message and that had "tarnished" his thoughts about the proposal.

That night, we went to the Turning Point and the Top Hat, black nightclubs, where Humphrey's Secret Service bodyguards were joined by silent Black Panthers. At the Top Hat, the master of ceremonies said, "These people here, they're just chicks and dudes right off the street." Humphrey gave them his standard, arm-waving, high-decibel civil-rights speech. He was going to fight the President's busing plan, he said, and he was flat out in favor of "commonsense busing." "That's right! That's right!" Even some of the hookers cheered.

In almost every speech he gave, Humphrey went all the way back to his election as mayor of Minneapolis in 1945, and moved forward, month by painful month, it sometimes seemed. But he never mentioned the four years he served as Lyndon Johnson's Vice-president. "Don't look where we've been," he would say, perhaps in reference to that time, "but where we're going." In those black nightclubs in Milwaukee, there wasn't any reference either to where he had been on school busing in Florida and what he had thought there about welfare chiselers.

The *Wall Street Journal*'s Norman C. "Mike" Miller wrote about Humphrey's Wisconsin campaign on March 28. The headline:

PROMISES, PROMISES
Now the Front-Runner,
Sen. Humphrey Pledges
Something for Everyone

In Little Chute, Wisconsin, Miller discovered Humphrey telling three hundred school kids in Village Hall that he really didn't lose the 1960 Wisconsin Presidential primary to John Kennedy, even if he did come up on the short end of the vote. Rather, Humphrey said, "My victory was to gain John Kennedy's friendship. . . . My victory was to become his legislative lieutenant for the thousand days of his administration." Little Chute is in the Fox River Valley, heavily Roman Catholic, and strongly pro-Kennedy in 1960.

I am convinced that dozens of reporters turned away from Humphrey, in disgust, during the Wisconsin primary. We are not necessarily idealists—though we are more idealistic than we care to admit—but we do have some sense of decency. Humphrey's performance, it struck me, was simply indecent, and what he did and said in Wisconsin affected all my attitudes about him through California and the convention. It affects them now.

John Lindsay's performance in Wisconsin is harder to describe. Bizarre may be the word. Strapped now for money to blitz the tube, Lindsay strategists turned to gimmicks to get their man on television, free; not just the usual gimmicks, like going to black night clubs, but big-time gimmicks that may become legendary. John Lindsay slept on Arthur Young's couch. ". . . there is no safe place for the average citizen to hide," Myra MacPherson wrote in the *Post*. "A guy puts down his beer in a bowling alley, and a candidate picks it up for the TV cameras."

But sleeping on somebody's couch? It was Jerry Bruno's idea. Bruno is the most famous advance man who ever lived, and he was thought to be (by Broder and others) Lindsay's secret weapon. Bruno dropped by Mr. and Mrs. Young's house three days before the sleep-in occurred. Mrs. Young told Ms. MacPherson that "he wanted to know how much Art made [$112 take-home from Maynard Electric Steel Casting Co.]. They were looking for someone that makes less than $6,000 a year. . . . when this Bruno came around, I just couldn't believe it."

On Sunday, Lindsay pulled up at the Youngs' in his limousine, the press bus right behind him. Lindsay, the reporters, and the camera crews tramped into the house to record the greatest pseudoevent of 1972. One of the neighbors got drunk and had to be thrown out, but otherwise it went off as Bruno had scheduled it. Lindsay, sitting in an aluminum chair in the kitchen, talked about emergency relief for property-tax payers. Under his proposal, the Youngs would have gotten $100 of the $500 they pay on their $16,000 duplex back.

The next morning, Lindsay got on the bus to go to work with Art Young. They were going to tour the plant together (with TV recording that too) but the famous Lindsay advance team apparently hadn't advanced very well, because the guard at the gate wouldn't let Lindsay in.

After it was all over, the Lindsay organization sent Mr. and Mrs. Young and their eight children a basket of fruit. Days after that, the kids would come home and ask, "Did the mayor call?" No, the mayor hadn't called. And Arthur Young is still working more than a month each year just to pay his property taxes.

That John Lindsay came in sixth in Wisconsin (in a field of 12) and dropped out of the race is only justice. Maybe now, the *Village Voice* speculated, the mayor will find time to go out to troubled Forest Hills and drink some beer and spend a night in the home of somebody like Arthur Young there.

Campaigning brings out the worst in some of us, and it brought out the very worst, we thought, in Hubert Humphrey and John Lindsay.

But what in God's name were we to make of George McGovern? Dr. Gallup completed another of his famous polls on the eve of the Wisconsin primary and it put Humphrey in first place, with 31 percent of the Democratic vote, Muskie next with 22 percent, and Wallace third with 18 percent. McGovern, following his "moral victory" in New Hampshire, stood at 5 percent, a *loss* of one point since the preceding Gallup poll.

Yet, in Wisconsin, everybody said McGovern was doing pretty well. And Wisconsin is a populous northern state (4,500,000 people) with considerable diversity—425,000 union members, 100,000 blacks in Milwaukee's ghettos, a heavy Polish population on Milwaukee's south side, some 30,000 students at Madison. By any measure, Wisconsin had to be more representative of the nation than either New Hampshire or Florida.

Writing in the *Post* on March 27, Broder looked at the Wisconsin primary from the perspective of the Seventh Congressional District, and he determined it was a three-way race between Humphrey, McGovern, and Muskie. In other parts of the state, he said, Jackson figured importantly. But Lindsay and Wallace didn't have much chance. ". . . if either man captures a state-wide plurality or wins any of the district delegates, it's going to be regarded as a major upset," he concluded.

The *Times*'s Johnny Apple, reporting four days later, went to Kiel, a small town in the Sixth Congressional District which, he had learned, was something of a bellwether in Wisconsin. The race, he said, was between McGovern, Humphrey, and Wallace, in that order. He found "little support" for Muskie.

Valentine E. Siehs, a shopkeeper, told Apple that "you can trust him [McGovern]. He isn't like old Triple-H, taking a different position every state he goes to, or wishy-washy, like Muskie." Donald Drum, an insurance salesman, said: "I'd never vote for that windbag Humphrey. I'm for McGovern. He seems pretty honest and calm, he doesn't spend all his time running people down."

But *why* was McGovern doing so well?

Part of the reason, James Doyle, writing in the *Washington Star,* suggested, was organization. He got there first. Gene Pokorny, McGovern's 25-year-old campaign manager, "spent months traveling around Wisconsin, meeting people, sizing them up, and asking the ones he thought could produce to sign on for the South Dakota Democrat as local organizers."

It is a point we tended to overlook. There is an essential ingredient to campaign success: an early start. When the *Observer* began checking out delegate strength, our delegate counter, Bruce Biossat, discovered that only two Democrats, McGovern and Muskie, were visible in all 50 states; McGovern setting up grass-roots organizations; Muskie getting his endorsements and setting up high-level committees. Humphrey's greatest mistake, his campaign manager, Jack Chestnut, has conceded, was his late start. It was Wallace's problem too. It wasn't until January of 1972 that he decided to enter the Florida primary, and it was even later when he decided to head north. After he won the Florida primary, he went home to Alabama for an entire week. It was a very serious mistake; when he got to Wisconsin, it was too late. Even more important to remember is the fact that Nixon and his managers began planning their campaign in late 1970; by early 1971, the outline was completed, right down to the "attack" strategy we will explore later. There is nothing in politics—nothing—as important as an early start, especially when the thinking that goes into it makes some sense (as McGovern's did, as Muskie's did not).

That's why the Gallup poll was so deceptive. In most states, nobody knew who George McGovern was; that's why he came out so low. But, first in New Hampshire and now in Wisconsin, early starts meant that most voters had been contacted by McGovern volunteers. If a voter was uncertain, the volunteer would go back to headquarters, write him (or her) a personal letter and enclose a leaflet about an issue the voter had indicated interest in. The McGovern volunteers in Wisconsin, by the time they were through, rang one million door-bells. The people in Wisconsin, unlike people responding to the Gallup poll elsewhere, knew about George McGovern. And enough of them—just enough—were willing to vote for him.

The McGovern strategy, laid out in 1970, worked. A good show-ing in New Hampshire, then a victory in Wisconsin. And then the momentum—and the press—would begin to roll, right down to Cali-fornia, for the final shoot-out with Humphrey on what should be friendly ground.

In a sense, the McGovern campaign in Wisconsin was over before we even got there.

Not very much of this was reported because most reporters still tended to discount McGovern as a serious candidate. "It is fair to say," Doyle wrote in the *Star* on March 29, "that a large portion of the national reporters who trail candidates around the country don't be-lieve George McGovern can win the Democratic nomination."

McGovern won because he started so early, and so well. He got the sizable antiwar vote and he got most of the youth vote. According to a survey by *The New York Times* and Daniel Yankelovich, Inc., he also won conservative and liberal votes because of his positions on tax reform, inflation, high property taxes, and unemployment.

McGovern's campaign managers trumpeted that he "carried the vote of working men and women, the so-called 'ethnic' vote, farmers, upper-income areas. . . . Only McGovern can stop the strong Wallace candidacy because of his appeal to the same kind of disaffected, alien-ated voters upset with the status quo. And he can appeal not by play-ing on their fears, but with positive and detailed programs to solve the problems."

The results:

McGovern: 29.6 percent
Wallace: 22.0
Humphrey: 20.7
Muskie: 10.2
Jackson: 7.8
Lindsay: 6.9

The rest of the vote was scattered among McCarthy, Chisholm, Yorty, Patsy Mink, Hartke, Mills, and "none of the above," who, surprisingly, got only 0.1 percent of the vote.

It wasn't hard from all of this to conclude that 52 percent of the vote was anti-Establishment and pro-change. McGovern and Wallace were both sending them a message. Television, especially, took this line.

Noted NBC:

"The message from Wisconsin is that 52 percent of the voters . . . voted against the political establishment. And the fact that many Republicans voted with Democrats means that the result here is a warning, not only for the Democratic Party, but for Richard Nixon."

Said CBS:

"It is the two least Establishment candidates—George McGovern and George Wallace—who leave this state as winners."

Wrong, pretty much, on all counts. Wrong, for sure, that Wisconsin indicated real trouble for Richard Nixon. His strategists, in fact, may have pulled their low-key campaign out of Wisconsin (Ashbrook and McCloskey were on the ballot, but McCloskey was out of the race, supporting Lindsay, and Ashbrook never came to Wisconsin) just to encourage crossover voting for Wallace.

And later studies indicate that the Wallace vote and the McGovern vote, in Wisconsin and elsewhere, were not the same. The *Times* and Daniel Yankelovich, Inc., examined data from Florida, Wisconsin, and Pennsylvania and concluded that "the typical Wallace and McGovern voters have almost nothing in common."

The McGovern voters, it was found, were impatient with the political establishment and sought change. But the Wallace voters were content with the political establishment, and two-thirds of them approved Nixon and his policies. Two-thirds of the McGovern voters disliked Nixon.

"The only area in which the concerns of the two camps overlap involves their shared and sharp criticism of current economic conditions," Jack Rosenthal, summarizing the findings, wrote in the *Times*.

The situation in Wisconsin was knocked entirely out of shape because 30 percent of McGovern's 332,298 votes and 50 percent of Wallace's 248,191 votes were Republican. Louis H. Bean, the election statistician, figured out that if the Republican votes were eliminated, the order of finish would have looked like this:

Humphrey: 21 percent
McGovern, 20
Wallace, 11
Muskie, 11

If we had known that, maybe we would have interpreted the Wisconsin primary just a little differently. But, of course, we didn't and McGovern nailed us, just as his strategists had planned so many months before.

I would hate to leave Wisconsin with the suggestion that it is only the press who misinterpret events. Scholars can be just as mistaken, and Nelson W. Polsby, professor of political science at the University of California at Berkeley and coauthor of *Presidential Elections,* deserves mention.

Writing in the *Washington Post* on April 9, he said two propositions—both of them "conventional wisdom"—cannot stand close examination. "The first is that the Democrats are tearing themselves apart and that President Nixon's chances of re-election have been enhanced. The second is that the primaries are destroying the chances for nomination of Senator Edmund Muskie, whose candidacy is now generally regarded as on the ropes."

Professor . . . welcome to the club.

11

Pennsylvania Through Oregon

Massachusetts, Indiana, Ohio, Alabama, District of Columbia, Tennessee, North Carolina, Nebraska, West Virginia, Michigan, Maryland, Rhode Island

It was 6:02 P.M. Wednesday, April 26, when Billy Alfond, a student at Colby College, in Waterville, Maine, walked up to me at National Airport in Washington and said: "I'm sorry but we won't be flying to Toledo tonight. The senator will have a press conference at ten tomorrow morning."

I looked out the window. The *Josephine,* Edmund S. Muskie's chartered Electra, was parked on the ramp, forlorn. Crew members began unloading 40 steak dinners, and I don't know what happened to them. Or to the *Josephine,* named for Muskie's mother. It was sent away, I suppose, to the place where old airplanes go.

Billy Alfond was depressed. He'd come all the way from Maine to make his first campaign trip. "I guess I won't get the chance now," he said.

"I have made my decision . . . to withdraw from active participation in the remaining Presidential primaries," Muskie said at his press conference the next morning. "I do so with regret, but I have no other choice. I do not have the money to continue."

Muskie had thought of dropping out after the Florida primary and again after the Wisconsin primary, but he had pushed on to Pennsylvania and Massachusetts, only to lose again—to Humphrey in Pennsylvania, to McGovern in Massachusetts.

Sleazy, fading old Pennsylvania was Muskie's final indignity: he should have won most of the delegates because Governor Milton J. Shapp and the party organization in Philadelphia were on his side. I was there when he opened his campaign headquarters on South Broad Street, just a block or two from the crenellated City Hall where I once worked for three years. The Polish-American String Band turned out to greet him and so did Eddie "Scoop" Lieberman, publicity man for the Democratic City Committee. When I knew "Scoop," he wrote a gossip column for a beer-and-whiskey weekly. Faces I hadn't seen in 10 years lined the streets, hangers-on and the committeemen who had turned from Republicans to Democrats so easily when Joe Clark and Dick Dilworth took the city over. This was all that was left for Ed Muskie, and it was as poignant as it was pathetic.

The situation, then, as we pictured it, was a final do-or-die stand by Muskie against Humphrey, who was supported enthusiastically by the state's labor barons, who remembered him when.

In Massachusetts, the fight was between Muskie, the candidate, in *Newsweek*'s words, of the "top brass," and George McGovern, the candidate of the kids and the antiwar people.

I haven't said much about *Time* and *Newsweek,* because I don't believe there is very much that can be said. Except for the impact of a cover story—important to Muskie back in September of 1971—and except for well-argued columns in *Newsweek* by Stewart Alsop, most newsmagazine reporting tends to be an echo chamber to what others, especially *The New York Times* and the *Washington Post,* have already said. The reporting by *Time* and *Newsweek* is important only because it is so widely read, but it is not very original or, I think, very perceptive. It may well be that *Time*'s political reporting was much more influential in the days of Henry Luce when it was so patently unfair. In 1972, though, *Time* was about as fair as anyone else, with even a slight bias to the left. Thus, in positioning itself ideologically with the *Times* and the *Post,* it may well have seriously undermined its own powers of persuasion. I suspect that, in years to come, both of these magazines will head more in the direction of by-lined journalism; when what happens, each will become more influential in affecting the attitudes of readers and other journalists.

As of now, production-line newsmagazine journalism produces copy that sometimes should be recalled. I can't resist mentioning an article in *Newsweek* in the issue dated April 24, the day before the Pennsylvania and Massachusetts primaries. It said:

"Muskie will probably emerge with a slight majority of Massachusetts' 102 delegates, and he may well hold his own in Pennsylvania's delegate count. . . ."

McGovern, of course, won all of Massachusetts' 102 delegates and Muskie trailed both Humphrey and McGovern in winning delegates in Pennsylvania. So much for that.

The predicting business, I've noted (and noted and noted) already, is dangerous and foolhardy. I might point out now that I directed a project for my own publication that might seem dangerous and foolhardy too. Beginning after the New Hampshire and Florida primaries, the *Observer* ran a series of state-by-state delegates counts, awarding candidates votes that, in many instances, they hadn't yet won. Thus, in March, we gave Muskie 1,282½ votes, which represented the estimate of what he would get if all the delegates were being chosen at the time our delegate counter, Bruce Biossat, was conducting his survey. Biossat talks to dozens of people in all 50 states to get a sense of what's happening. If, for example, his sources in Texas agree that Humphrey is the favorite, trailed by Muskie and the rest, Biossat breaks it down into actual votes per candidate. CBS and *Newsweek,* it should be noted, perform similar speculative enterprises.

I think—and it's strictly a personal opinion—that Biossat, who has a computerlike mind, does this sort of thing better than anyone else. Yet, in retrospect, I think the results may be misleading—because so many people fail to understand that the counts do not represent a projection of what will happen at the convention. Like polls, these counts are simply a photograph of a moment in time; moreover, they are not scientifically as valid as some polls.

If I had the chance to do it over, I think I would eliminate specific figures in those states where delegates were still to be chosen. And I think I'd run some kind of warning with the count: CAUTION: THIS IS NOT A PREDICTION.

For the three weeks between the Wisconsin primary on April 4 and the Massachusetts and Pennsylvania primaries on April 25, the thrust of almost all the reporting was scorekeeping: who's ahead? who's gaining? who's fading? with a little of the whys and wherefores included.

My files turn up just three issues-related stories about Pennsylvania and Massachusetts. In one, in the *Times,* McGovern's visit to the Massachusetts Correctional Institution at Concord was described by Walter Rugaber. The visit, he wrote, was "an effort to establish the nation's penal programs as a serious issue." A five-paragraph story in the *Post* on April 19 dealt with McGovern's allegation, in a Boston speech, that the public was being "blackmailed" by the oil-import quota. On April 23, in a story by Broder in the *Post,* McGovern charged that a secret government report shows that "anticompetitive or monopoly pricing" by 100 major firms costs the consumer "more than $15 billion a year" in excess prices. A brief story in the *Times* on April 16, written by Bill Kovach, pointed out that the economy— the job issue—was the most important in Massachusetts. The story, 16 paragraphs long, was overshadowed by other stories on the same page dealing with the role of black voters in Pennsylvania and a decision by Humphrey to enter seven more primaries.

And that's all I found.

A handful of other stories suggest that McGovern was seeking the blue-collar vote in Massachusetts. The *Baltimore Sun,* for example, in a Page One story by Arnold R. Isaacs, noted that McGovern's volunteer canvassers "spent Friday tramping up and down the stairs of what New Englanders call the 'tripledecker' houses of East Boston —an old, largely Italian-American neighborhood. . . ." Kovach, in the *Times,* made the same point. McGovern's campaign, he wrote, "is focusing in on blue-collar communities where he hopes to prove the broad appeal of his candidacy." After the fourth paragraph, though, the story moved on to other matters.

There was almost no attempt to explore what McGovern was saying or what his literature was emphasizing in this crucial effort to establish himself as a candidate with "broad appeal."

The polls, apparently, were more important, and more interesting, especially the *Boston Globe*'s Becker survey that we first encountered in New Hampshire. On April 16, Broder noted on Page One that McGovern was leading Muskie 38 to 27 in a soon-to-be-published Becker poll. On April 23, on Page One again, Broder pointed out that McGovern's lead over Muskie had climbed to 43 to 19.

But the polls don't answer the key questions: Was McGovern making inroads with blue-collar voters, and on what terms? The size of his victory in Massachusetts indicates that he must have had some success, but we have no firm evidence. In Pennsylvania, where Mc-Govern's effort was limited (and not directed at blue-collar workers), *The New York Times,* working again with Daniel Yankelovich, Inc., came up the day after the election with some interesting data.

McGovern, the survey of 414 registered Democrats showed, did best in the suburbs and small towns, among liberals, women, and young first-time voters and those concerned over issues, notably the war in Vietnam and business influence on government. Humphrey did best in the cities, among more conservative Democrats and among blacks, older adults, blue-collar workers, and voters impressed by his experience in government.

The Yankelovich data indicate that the lines were forming for the ultimate showdown between McGovern and Humphrey.

And it is at this precise moment that we began writing about McGovern's move toward the center. Interesting, because if Yankelovich is correct, the perceptions about both McGovern and Humphrey already had been formed.

It requires a very special kind of savvy to know when the time is precisely right for a major interview with a major figure. Broder has that kind of savvy, and his interview with McGovern that appeared on Page One of the *Post,* April 28—the day Muskie withdrew—is a fine example. McGovern, Broder wrote, "has rejected the advice of those he calls 'the more rigid purists in my camp' and has decided to go after the support of Old Guard party and labor officials whose help could bring him the Democratic Presidential nomination."

McGovern conceded to Broder that there might be unhappiness "with his conciliation policy by some supporters who have considered him the point-man in an offensive to overthrow the entire political establishment." But, McGovern said, "they're just going to have to take me on my own terms."

The interview goes to the nub of some of the problems—rarely mentioned until now—that would soon plague McGovern. The attitude of George Meany and other AFL-CIO leaders, for example.

Relations between McGovern and labor's leaders "have been sour since 1966, when he voted against cloture to cut off the filibuster preventing Senate action on repeal of Section 14-B of the Taft-Hartley Act. . . ." Broder noted.

McGovern said that really wasn't the problem. "I think that's the symbol they use to express their animosity to my views on the war and my challenge to Lyndon Johnson and Hubert Humphrey in 1968. . . . The main thing is to talk with them, and indicate I would seek labor's counsel and input on major decisions."

And, as another example, McGovern's little-publicized proposal for a phased $32 billion reduction in the Defense budget. "They [the labor leaders] want to be reassured that I'm not going to jeopardize the defense of the country. . . . If I sit down with a labor leader and go through that defense budget of mine, I can show him that it actually means more jobs without any real sacrifice of defense capability. I'm confident of that."

Broder then asked if a reconciliation with Meany "would not require the AFL-CIO chief virtually to admit that he had been wrong in his hard-line foreign policy views for 20 years." McGovern said, "Yes, it does, and he has been wrong. His support for the Cold War and Vietnam has been a mistake. I can't compromise with him on that. I'm willing to admit with him I made a mistake on 14-B. If I can admit a mistake, maybe he can."

Fascinating. After reading that, can anybody believe that reconciliation would ever be possible? I think not. McGovern's move to the center was not going to be all that easy, and Hubert Humphrey, by attacking that defense budget and McGovern's demogrant proposal, would soon make it all the harder.

Now, only three candidates were left—McGovern, Humphrey, and Wallace. Practically, only two—McGovern and Humphrey, because Wallace's planning had been so tardy and was so incomplete that there was no way he could collect enough delegates to win the nomination. In Massachusetts, he had no delegates on the ballot; in Pennsylvania, only four, and in California he would have none.

"We never understood how important the reforms really were," Billy Joe Camp, Wallace's press secretary, has said. "We really thought that we could just win some primaries and the votes would fall in line. Well, it didn't work that way."

From Pennsylvania and Massachusetts, Humphrey moved on to both Indiana and Ohio, each of which he was to win, barely. McGovern campaigned only in Ohio, Wallace only in Indiana.

And it was in Ohio, of all places, that the question of just where George McGovern stood on the issues was finally raised, compliments of Henry M. Jackson, who had won just 3 percent of the vote in Pennsylvania and who was, by now, we thought, desperate. Jackson dredged up the fact that McGovern supported Henry Wallace for President in 1948; Wallace, he reminded his audiences, was the candidate of "Communist appeasement." McGovern, at a press conference, responded that he ultimately abandoned Wallace and voted for Harry Truman.

Jackson had more to say. McGovern was "out in left field" with his stands in favor of busing schoolchildren, slashing the defense budget, granting amnesty to draft dodgers, legalizing marijuana, pulling abruptly out of Vietnam, and leaving our allies at the mercy of communism.

"Senator Jackson's comments are an indication of how badly his own campaign is going," McGovern replied. But the attack was beginning to bite; McGovern, for example, issued a press release denying he favored the legalization of marijuana.

According to the *Washington Post*'s Richard M. Cohen, some of McGovern's young advisors were convinced Humphrey was behind it. Jackson said no; he was doing it on his own because he really felt McGovern was a left-wing extremist whose nomination would lead in the fall to a Goldwater-type debacle.

Some newspapers began investigating just what McGovern really stood for. One of the best analyses appeared April 27 in the *Wall Street Journal* under the headline "McGovern's Program: Strong Stuff." Norman C. "Mike" Miller, the author, noted that McGovern "is a great deal more than the one-issue antiwar candidate he was depicted to be for so long. To a degree unmatched by any major-party candidate in modern times, the South Dakotan has spelled out in great detail how he proposes to fundamentally change the entire 'system.' Because his candidacy seemed quixotic for so long, his program hasn't received the close examination it deserves. Its breadth and potential impact are breathtaking."

Miller went on to say that the tax rate for corporations would rise from 48 percent to 52 percent (in the *Journal,* first things first, please), depletion allowances for oil and minerals would be phased out, and, all in all, corporations would be paying an additional $17 billion in income taxes in the fiscal year beginning July 1.

The 439,568 taxpayers with incomes over $50,000 would have to pay 75 percent of the stated rates in the tax tables, increasing their payments by $6 billion a year. Along with that would go sharply higher estate and gift taxes. The entire welfare system would be scrapped and the $750 personal income-tax exemption would be repealed. Every man, woman, and child in the country would receive from the Government a "minimum income grant" of about $1,000. Under the plan, 20 percent of the taxpayers would pay more, 80 percent would pay less. "This," Miller wrote, "would result in a massive shift of income from higher-income persons to those below the poverty line—about $14.1 billion a year, according to Senator McGovern."

Tax reform would raise an additional $28 billion to help finance "a host of new and expanded social programs, including $10 billion to produce 2,600,000 new public-service jobs and a five-fold increase, to $15 billion, in Federal aid to elementary and secondary schools."

Yet, even $28 billion wouldn't be enough to pay for the new programs. The rest would come from a $32 billion cut in the Defense budget over three years, involving cancellation of development of the B-1 bomber, deployment of Safeguard and Minuteman missiles, and conversion of most Polaris submarines to the Poseidon missile system. McGovern's program also involved a pullback of all American troops in Southeast Asia and most American troops elsewhere in the world. Nine navy aircraft carriers would be scrapped or mothballed, and military manpower would be reduced from 2,505,000 to 1,735,000.

And that was only part of it.

Miller concluded with a reference to a Louis Harris finding that 40 to 52 percent of the voters "hadn't focused their attention on him [McGovern] and thus were unsure of their opinions.

"The evidence indicates, then, that the senator's general views are still an unknown to a large segment of the public. Furthermore, it is reasonable to suppose that his specific proposals for sweeping change aren't known in detail even to many of those who have formed a general opinion about him.

"Thus, the McGovern campaign, while it has made striking progress, has yet to be tested on the basic question: Do people really want the fundamental and far-reaching changes the senator advocates? Whatever the ultimate answer, the debate promises be be mighty interesting."

Miller was prescient: the debate was about to begin, and it was going to be mighty interesting.

But, in Ohio, McGovern almost was the winner. In an election marred by a breakdown of voting machines and people,* Humphrey won 41.4 percent of the vote to McGovern's 39.3. Jackson, for all his trouble, got 8.1 percent, a decimal or two below Muskie, who had dropped out. Jackson dropped out too.

In Indiana, Humphrey edged out Wallace 46.8 percent to 41.6 percent. Humphrey won the most delegates in both states.

In Alabama, Wallace beat back a challenge by "national Democrats" and won at least 23 of his state's 29 votes. In the District of Columbia, favorite-son Walter E. Fauntroy won easily, in defiance of the spirit of party reform.

By now, primaries were coming so hot and heavy that hardly any of us had time to think very deeply about any of them, much less make sense of what was happening. Consider this progression:

April 25: Pennsylvania and Massachusetts
May 2: Indiana, Ohio, Alabama, and District of Columbia
May 4: Tennessee
May 6: North Carolina
May 9: Nebraska and West Virginia
May 16: Michigan and Maryland

* "I goofed," said George Plagman, supervisor of the voting machines in Cuyahoga County (Cleveland), a landmark for candor in the campaign. McGovern aides remain convinced they won Ohio.

May 23: Rhode Island and Oregon
June 6: California, New Mexico, South Dakota, and New Jersey
June 20: New York

If that wasn't enough, it was during this period that thousands of Democrats were meeting in caucus and convention in the nonprimary states to choose delegates to the national convention. For the McGovern forces, especially, these nonprimary states were extraordinarily important, because this is where grass-roots organization really counted, and this is where McGovern was nickeling-and-diming the rest of the field to death. For example, I went to tiny Vermont late in April to attend the caucuses there. The McGovern forces were led by two sophomores at Middlebury College, Nathaniel Forbes and Prentiss Smith; the state headquarters was a third-floor dormitory with two telephones. The budget for the entire state was $900. Muskie was supported by every prominent Democrat in the state—but, apparently, by no one else. At the caucus I attended in Burlington, the vote was McGovern, 331, and Muskie, 138. "I tried," Bennett Greene, chairman of Ward 4, told me, "but we turned out zilch for Muskie." McGovern swept Vermont and the delegates it sent to Miami Beach were loyalists who wanted McGovern and no one else. With this kind of people, compromise would not be possible; what was true in Vermont was true in a dozen or more other states. It was one of the great under-told stories of the campaign.

Wallace, predictably, won Tennessee on May 4; he had no orgaized opposition and busing, once again, was an important issue. He won again two days later in North Carolina in a close contest with former Governor Terry Sanford. Sanford picked up 27 of the state's 64 delegates.

For Humphrey, West Virginia—a sentimental state; it was there he lost it all to John Kennedy in 1960—was supposed to be a showdown with George Wallace. It never turned out that way, though, because both Humphrey and Wallace spent most of their time campaigning in Michigan. Humphrey won easily, with 68 percent of the vote.

Nebraska was a hard-fought contest between Humphrey and Mc-

Govern; it was a state McGovern was supposed to win fairly easily, but the attacks on him that began with Jackson in Ohio accelerated in conservative Nebraska.

Nebraska was interesting for a number of reasons. It marked the midpoint in the primary season; it was the thirteenth of 23 primaries, and it was the first primary in which McGovern was labeled by the press as the front-runner. His position in Nebraska, Don Oberdorfer wrote in the *Post,* was much the same as Muskie's in New Hampshire, even to the proposition that McGovern came from a neighboring state; the old propinquity factor again.

A front-running position is a defensive position; it was for Muskie in New Hampshire; it was now for McGovern in Nebraska. He was assaulted because of his alleged "triple-A" beliefs—acid, abortion, and amnesty.

It began, perhaps, with a column written by Evans and Novak that appeared in the *Washington Post* on April 27. Humphrey, the two columnists wrote, was in a "sudden surge" because Democratic politicians saw him as the only "visible alternative" to McGovern. The regulars, they said, "fear McGovern as the Democratic Party's Barry Goldwater." And then they added this paragraph:

"The reason is given by one liberal senator, whose voting record differs little from McGovern's. He feels McGovern's surging popularity depends on public ignorance of his acknowledged public positions. 'The people don't know McGovern is for amnesty, abortion and legalization of pot.' he told us. 'Once middle America—Catholic middle America, in particular—finds this out, he's dead.' "

Tom Braden, in a column appearing in the *Post* on May 9, responded to the allegations of the anonymous senator quoted by Evans and Novak. Braden's mistake was to keep the names of the columnists anonymous too. Anyway, Braden said that the column was "being passed out all over Nebraska and a large advertisement in *The True Voice,* a statewide Catholic weekly, makes it the basis for this question: 'How do you stand? Are you for legalization of marijuana. . . ? Amnesty for deserters . . . ? This is the McGovern record.' "

Braden said that the statements of Evans and Novak's "liberal senator" were not true. Braden said McGovern had never advocated federal legislation on abortion, had never advocated legalization of marijuana, and had never favored amnesty for deserters.

McGovern's problem was proving it to the voters of Nebraska. The *Times*'s Warren Weaver, Jr., summed up McGovern's response in this lead paragraph, written from Wilber on May 7:

"Senator George McGovern is campaigning through conservative, close-mouthed Nebraska on the coattails of Calvin Coolidge."

Coolidge, it seems—according to McGovern, and never as far as I can tell, adequately proved or flatly denied by anyone—granted amnesty to draft resisters (but not to deserters) after World War I. And so, it was said, did Lincoln and Andrew Johnson. "It would be a break with precedent if it wasn't done this time," he said.

In the final hours before election day, McGovern whistle-stopped across Nebraska, reversing the route Robert F. Kennedy had taken in his whistle-stop tour in 1968. He "repeatedly stated his positions on abortion, marijuana, and amnesty while continuing to emphasize his three standard campaign issues, credibility, the war, and taxes," Oberdorfer reported in the *Post*. McGovern also condemned "the scarecrows that have been trotted out in the closing days of the campaign by a political opposition that is cowardly and does not want to address the real issues." He did not identify what "cowardly opposition" he had in mind but he did say that the source of his difficulties was the "scare tactics" and "distortions" raised by Senator Jackson in Ohio.

McGovern took former Governor Frank Morrison with him to dispel the allegations. According to Tom Braden, "Morrison, a towering man with gray hair and a large plain farmer's face," would say:

" 'Harry Truman and Calvin Coolidge granted amnesty. Do you think Calvin Coolidge was a left-winger? Do you think Harry Truman was a left-winger? Do you think Frank Morrison would come to Huntington and tell you to vote for a left-winger?' "

The effort, which included a 30-minute television broadcast taped at dawn the Saturday before the election, seemed to work for McGovern. He defeated Humphrey in the popularity contest, 41 percent to 35 percent. Wallace was a distant third at 12.5 percent. But McGovern won only 15 of the state's 24 delegates; Humphrey won 7, and the preference of the remaining 2 wasn't known.

A week later, George Wallace won the Michigan and Maryland primaries in the high-water mark of his campaign. But, the day before, on May 15, he was gunned down in a shopping center in Laurel, Maryland. The would-be assassin was Arthur Herman Bremer, 21 years old. A bullet lodged in Wallace's spine, and on May 17 the nation knew he would never walk again.

June 12, 1963: Medgar Evers
Nov. 22, 1963: John F. Kennedy
Feb. 21, 1965: Malcolm X
Aug. 25, 1967: George Lincoln Rockwell
April 4, 1968: Rev. Dr. Martin Luther King, Jr.
June 5, 1968: Robert F. Kennedy
May 15, 1972: George C. Wallace

Six out of seven died, testament to the marksmanship of the madmen in our midst. For those of us who travel with politicians, it is the thing that haunts us: the bursting of a balloon; the backfire of an automobile; the sudden surge of a Secret Service agent.

We are an armed camp. Civilians in this country own thirty-five million rifles, twenty-four million handguns, and thirty-one million shotguns. We are obsessed with weapons and we are destroyed by them and we can't ever seem to do anything about it. It is a national tragedy and a national disgrace.

But it is not part of this story. If there was any doubt that the battle for the Democratic nomination was a two-way race, the shootout in Laurel, Maryland, resolved it. Wallace had won four state primaries and he had collected 210 delegates to the national convention. He would win no more.

It was back to business as usual. On May 23, McGovern won 41.1 percent of the preference vote in Rhode Island and all 22 of the state's delegates. He had made no campaign appearances in the state. The same day, he won 50.3 percent of the preference vote in Oregon and all of its 34 votes at the convention. Wallace was second.

And then it was on to California, the climactic struggle for the Democratic nomination, between Hubert Humphrey and George McGovern. Months earlier, Gary Hart told us it would come to this. We didn't believe him then; we believed him now.

12

California

"**F**ace the Nation," from CBS Television City in Hollywood, "a one-hour spontaneous and unrehearsed news interview with the two leading contenders in California's June 6 Democratic Presidential primary, Senator Hubert Humphrey of Minnesota and Senator George McGovern of South Dakota," had hardly begun on Sunday, May 28, when the sparks began to fly.

". . . I believe that Senator McGovern, while having a very catchy phrase, where he says right from the start with McGovern, or McGovern right from the start—that there are many times that you will find that it was not right from the start, but wrong from the start. We were both wrong on Vietnam."

McGovern looked startled, and Humphrey plunged on.

"Senator McGovern is wrong on Israel. Senator McGovern has been wrong on unemployment compensation. Senator McGovern has been wrong on labor law, and on the three great issues here in California, on his massive, unrealistic, and I think rather outside welfare program, he's wrong. On taxation, he's contradictory and inconsistent, he's wrong. And on defense cuts, I believe they cut into the muscle in the very fiber of our national security. So I believe that when people have a chance to weigh the issues, they'll find out that there are differences, and that those differences will add up into a nomination."

Senator McGovern said later he wasn't startled so much at the content of Humphrey's attack—but at its vehemence. Humphrey, in fact, press reports about the debate noted, was "shrill."

However, McGovern wasn't so startled he couldn't make a response. "Here is a senator," he said of himself, "who has spoken out against the war more consistently over a longer period of time than any other person in the United States Senate. Now I think it's fair to say that Senator Humphrey, during all the time he was Vice-president of this country, and was making statements on Vietnam, and even when he became the standard-bearer of our party in 1968, no one could have been any more enthusiastic for the course that we were following in Vietnam. Let me just cite one quote, and I'm not going to belabor the record, but as late as October 1967, several years after I had referred to Vietnam as the worst moral and political disaster in our history, Senator Humphrey was saying Vietnam is our greatest adventure and a wonderful one it is."

McGovern added that there was no "essential difference" between his and Humphrey's position on Israel and he said he would discuss in the course of the program his positions on welfare, taxation, and defense.

Humphrey was not on very solid ground with his attack on McGovern's Vietnam record, and he was fortunate that the subject was soon dropped. The debate turned to McGovern's proposals on welfare/tax reform and defense, where Humphrey held the advantage.

McGovern, remember, made his original proposals for "tax reform and redistribution of income" in a speech at Iowa State University, Ames, Iowa, on January 13; no one paid much attention.

Why? First, because no one thought then that McGovern was a serious candidate for the nomination. Second, because political reporters don't know much about economics and probably didn't understand it.

One of the earliest analyses of the McGovern program ("Strong Stuff," the headline said) appeared, as we have noted, in the *Wall Street Journal* on April 27. On May 7, the *Washington Post*'s financial editor, Hobart Rowen, had a go at it. "Strong Medicine," that headline read. Rowen conceded that "the exact arithmetic is still vague and even contradictory," but he applauded the "over-all thrust and objective" of the program. In May also, *National Review* carefully analyzed the McGovern proposals, and deplored them.

By then, the business community—if not the press—was murmuring. So, on May 22, a group called Business and Professional People for McGovern paid an estimated $21,000 for a full-page advertisement in the *Wall Street Journal*. It was in the form of a letter from McGovern to Belmont Towbin, an investment banker and contributor to McGovern's campaign. Towbin had written earlier to McGovern. "What bothers me," he said, "is the impression that perhaps your naivete about business will lead you as President down a path that could have serious repercussions for this country."

In essence, McGovern replied: Don't worry about it.

First, he said, his proposals had been incompletely or even erroneously described. Second, "I am well aware that under our system, only the Congress initiates tax measures. The suggestions which I have developed in this field should, therefore, be regarded always as suggestions for consideration by the Congress." In other words, even if my proposals are dangerous, Wilbur Mills will save me from myself. It was not the proudest moment of the McGovern campaign.

As Richard Reeves said in his column in *New York* magazine: "The Prairie Populist came to Wall Street last week, and it looks as if the bears and the bulls will survive."

As things turned out, it wasn't so much the nature of McGovern's program itself—it was the inability of McGovern's advisers, and finally McGovern himself, to put any kind of price tag on it. That's the first thing reporters want to know: How much is it going to cost? And McGovern couldn't say.

Thus, in that first debate, we have this exchange:

David Schoumacher, CBS news correspondent: "Senator McGovern, as you know, reporters covering you have been trying for quite some time to get a price tag on your welfare bill. Yesterday there was even a special session for us, and we heard numbers from $20 to $30 to $60 billion. Can you tell us today how much it will cost?"

Senator McGovern: "There's no way, Mr. Schoumacher, that you can make an exact estimate on this proposal, because what I have said, number one, is that I want to get rid of the present program entirely. I want to scrap the existing welfare mess—"

Schoumacher: "But you're asking us to accept a program that you can't tell us how much it's going to cost?"

McGovern: "That's exactly right. There is no way to estimate the cost of this program other than to say there's no net cost to the Treasury at all. . . ."

The day before, as Schoumacher noted, McGovern's economic advisors had met with the press in an attempt to explain the tax and welfare program. The session in the Wilshire Hyatt House Hotel lasted two hours and when it was over reporters were still confused about many of the details. The problem, it seemed, was that economists Ben Okner and Edwin Kuh were somewhat uncertain too. As McGovern campaign managers Frank Mankiewicz and Gary Hart prowled the room (demonstrating the importance the staff attached to the session), reporters kept peppering the advisors with questions about the troublesome details. As an exercise in enlightenment, the meeting was a failure.

Following the California primary, it was back to the old drawing board. Or back to the computer, as it turned out. Millionaire Max Palevsky, cochairman of McGovern's fund-raising committee, announced new computer studies would be made and that a panel of experts would be convened to take it from there. William Greider, in the *Washington Post,* said "the McGovern campaign ran its own calculations of the much-criticized proposal and discovered, as a number of critics have claimed, that the suggested numbers do not add up —that a $40 billion gap exists between what McGovern has proposed and how he has said he would pay for it." Palevsky and others denied the report.

And Gordon Weil, the most persistent critic of the press in the McGovern entourage, said the controversy was largely of the press's own making, because they hadn't been able to get the program "straight." Weil insisted that McGovern never had proposed a $1,000 demogrant. "He suggested it as one possibility." Mankiewicz, on the other hand, conceded that the plan had to be "clarified" or McGovern would be vulnerable to a Republican attack in the fall. "It has not been one of the strong points of the campaign," he said, in exquisite understatement.

In the weeks that followed, the McGovern campaign moved slowly away from the program, ultimately abandoning the controversial aspects of it. In California, though, it remained a major issue—and voters everywhere would always remember that George McGovern was that crazy fellow who wanted to give every man, woman, and child in America a check for $1,000. It became, in Roman fashion, the "M" factor—$1,000, to be joined soon by 1,000%.

And, by golly, Hubert did it all by himself, even raising a phony issue in the debate, which confused everybody. If it wasn't trouble enough that McGovern had been playing around with the demogrant idea, well, he had also introduced a bill for the National Welfare Rights Organization that would have paid a family of four a minimum of $6,500 a year. That, said Humphrey, would cost $72 billion a year and put 104,000,000 Americans on welfare. That was not McGovern's program; it was, as he said, just a bill he had introduced "on request."

In the debate, Humphrey also attacked McGovern's defense proposals, also unveiled four months earlier (and barely noticed at the time, although the document is some 70 pages long). McGovern's proposed cuts—he planned to "phase down" the defense budget to $54.8 billion by fiscal 1975—would rip the fiber of the nation's defense, Humphrey argued. But, as Schoumacher pointed out, Humphrey himself, in a column he wrote in 1970, suggested the budget could be trimmed to $50 billion. "Why was your $50 billion not jeopardizing security and his $58 [sic] billion is?" Schoumacher asked. Because, Humphrey said, his was predicated "on our being out of Vietnam [so, of course, was McGovern's]." Later, he argued, inflation explained the difference. Later, too, he was almost trapped into saying the Russians are no longer intent on dominating the world. But, oh no, he hadn't meant that. I don't say they're not. . . . I say they're perfectly capable of . . . I'm not about ready to let the Russians make America into a second-class power. . . .

It was not a salubrious performance by Humphrey, but he probably got his points across: McGovern had some dangerous ideas about taxes, welfare, and national defense. In Ronald Reagan's state, where the aerospace industry is king, thousands of voters must have been interested.

Just how and why Humphrey came to his decision to, in the words of a number of observers, "take his gloves off" in California is almost anyone's guess. On May 15, Evans and Novak reported "a backstage decision" was "hammered out at a secret Humphrey strategy meeting in Los Angeles Friday afternoon." San Francisco's Mayor Joseph Alioto, the columnists said, was a key figure in organizing the "anti-campaign." On May 28, the columnists had a different explanation. "Two hard-boiled Humphreyites—William Connell, Humphrey's former top aide, and Eugene Wyman, his chief fund-raiser, met in Los Angeles. . . . Consequently, a memorandum written by Wyman and Connell argued that Humphrey was a certain loser unless he—and he alone—stripped bare McGovern's extreme positions, particularly on defense spending cuts." Clayton Fritchey, in his June 3 column, had still another explanation. It was Dr. Edgar Berman, Humphrey's crony and sometime personal physician, "who persuaded a reluctant Humphrey that the only way to take off the nomination was to take off the gloves and rip into McGovern. . . ." The rest of the column is an assault on Dr. Berman for his views about women's liberation.

Despite Humphrey's decision (however it may have been reached) to "take off the gloves," McGovern continued to get most of the space in newspapers and television. One of the reasons, surely, was still another poll—the California Poll, under the supervision of Mervin D. Field and a regular feature in the *Los Angeles Times*. Early in May, the California Poll showed Humphrey leading McGovern 35 percent to 31. The sample was 466 registered Democrats, interviewed between April 26 and May 1. In February, Humphrey had 23 percent, McGovern, 7 percent, and Muskie, 28 percent.

The final California Poll was published on June 1. In it, McGovern led Humphrey 46 percent to 26 percent, a staggering twenty-point lead. "Senator George McGovern appears to be heading for a remarkable victory in Tuesday's primary election," Field said. The final survey was based on telephone interviews with 857 persons who said they were certain to vote in the Democratic primary. "California

Poll Indicates a Sweep for McGovern," the headline on *The New York Times* Page One story said.

Humphrey, on June 2, said the poll was "way off the mark." Even McGovern was skeptical. "I certainly wouldn't predict a 20-point spread." Humphrey's advisors were especially doubtful about poll results that showed McGovern leading by margins of 3 to 2 and better among blacks and Chicanos. "I can't believe they are a unique breed" in California, Humphrey remarked.

According to the "Report on Network News' Treatment of the 1972 Democratic Presidential Candidates," Humphrey's situation in the final days of the California primary was portrayed as "desperate."

". . . the Humphrey campaign had been faltering even before the survey came out," NBC reported June 2.

". . . Humphrey is drawing the smaller crowds, spending less money, has fewer volunteers," CBS said. "And even if the Field poll were 10 points off, it would leave McGovern an easy winner."

The theme of much of the television coverage of Humphrey centered on his role as "the veteran political warrior who was returning from his 1968 defeat to make a comeback bid in presidential politics, the aged candidate who was hoping to piece together—for one last great effort—the familiar coalition that had provided so much of his strength in the past," according to the report.

Thus, Humphrey's attack on McGovern's positions was the desperate response of an ancient warrior in the final, and probably losing, battle of his life. We all wrote that, because we all believed it. What we may have missed is that Humphrey's fight was bigger than Humphrey himself. Gary Hart, McGovern's campaign manager, insists that California was a colossal and historic struggle between the "old" and the "new" and that the future of the Democratic Party and even of the nation itself was at stake. Humphrey, in this view, merely served as the vehicle for all those forces that resisted, and still resist, fundamental change in the party and in the nation.

There is considerable truth in what Hart says. All we have to do is examine what happened after McGovern won the primary; then, all the forces of tradition coalesced in a final, truly desperate effort to stop McGovern's nomination. McGovern himself was surprised and deeply troubled by the reaction to a victory he felt he had deserved and had won fairly, in the traditional party pattern. I suspect he never realized, until long after the California primary, just how fundamentally his candidacy had threatened important elements in his own party.

I began a column with an anecdote that underlines the point. It went this way:

"Joe Mazzola, a tough little labor leader, is putting it straight to a joint meeting of the Contra Costa Labor Council and the Building Trades Council, here [in Walnut Creek] at the Saranap Inn.

"Syntax is a stranger to him, but he's with friends and they know what he means.

" 'This man's had 20 years of dedication to the labor movement,' he growls. 'He's been a friend of labor and the things he says he can go on and talk and say for 10 hours. Men and ladies, we're in debt—from our philosophy, from the standpoint of Gompers. And here's a man that's deserving. All of us, we ought to get behind one man and give him our respect.

" 'Hubert H—for California!' "

The crowd, I said, went wild, and Humphrey gave them what they wanted. Then I wrote.

"Humphrey is 61 years old now, fighting what may be the last great battle of his political career. Fighting for his life, here in California. This is all there is, these last few days. . . . Maybe Humphrey will lose. I suppose he really will. Yet, 'Hubert H' is going down with all the old flags flying. He's a one-man broadside."

If Hart is right (and I think he is at least partly right), I was wrong, or at least my own analysis was incomplete. Joe Mazzola and that audience at Walnut Creek represented the traditional Democratic Party, and Humphrey was a part of it. The lesson, I think, is that political writers tend to personalize situations that really are institutional. This was not just Humphrey's final battle; this was a desperate struggle, which, it turns out, was not final, for the Democratic Party. I believe that now.

It would have been easier to see what was at stake if most of us had not believed that McGovern's constituency was rapidly broadening. After all, he had won traditional Democratic votes in New Hampshire, Florida, Ohio, and Massachusetts. In California, he was fighting hard to win even more of those votes. The success he had had, and the success we anticipated, blurred what, in hindsight, we can now see clearly.

Political reporters, like most journalists, tend to be faddists, I think. Of all the reporters covering the California primary, only *Newsweek*'s John Lindsay—as far as I know—believed that George McGovern was a fad. Lindsay called McGovern "the hula hoop," in memory of an earlier phenomenon. No doubt he overstated his case, but his was a healthy skepticism.

It was in California that we encountered the "beautiful people" who had attached themselves, like bloodsuckers, to the McGovern campaign. We left the reporting of it mostly to our "society" reporters, and probably that was a mistake too.

I first encountered a skirmish line of the beautiful people in New Hampshire, where Shirley MacLaine, Marlo Thomas, and the actor who used to limp in the TV show "Gunsmoke" warmed up audiences for McGovern. McCloskey had Paul Newman. I remember a long night in the press room at Howard Johnson's when Miss MacLaine filibustered about her commitment to McGovern and the reasons why it was important for people like her to work for people like McGovern. It was very serious stuff—and dull as hell. A Hearst reporter in a corner of the room finally knocked back his last drink, got up, and said: "Cut the bullshit, Shirley, and tell us about Dean Martin and Frank Sinatra." Shirley was not amused. A little later, after we'd all gone to bed, the press room caught fire. It was that kind of night.

Shirley MacLaine, at least, is serious about her causes, and we can admire her for that. We can even understand why plain George McGovern should be so easily flattered by the attentions given to him by such famous people. The Kennedys always surrounded themselves with beautiful people. The difference, I suspect, is that the Kennedys used them, and McGovern was used.

What I have in mind is a situation described in the *Washington Post* by Sally Quinn, that paper's top cat.

"Los Angeles—Rolls Royces, Bentleys, Mercedes, Jaguars. They lined the winding Angelo Drive in Beverly Hills up to actress Marlo Thomas' English-style mansion and gardens.

"Inside the gates, more than 500 beautiful people, carefully underdressed, stood on the fake grass by the pool and checked each other out.

"Over at a small table sat Groucho Marx, Jack Nicholson, and Carl Reiner, chatting quietly. Nobody noticed.

"Then Marlo of TV's 'That Girl,' in a navy jersey and white pants, stood up by the pool and addressed her guests.

" 'When George McGovern first began running for President. . . . ,' she said.

" ('That's right,' whispered a bronze god standing next to the bar, 'this is a party for George McGovern, I'd forgotten.')

" '. . . people would say, my God, he's so honest, so decent, how could he ever get to be President . . . but when McGovern gets to the White House, he's not going to owe ITT or anybody else. He's going to owe we the people,' Marlo said."

Shirley, Marlo, Warren Beatty, and all the rest raised hundreds of thousands of dollars for the McGovern campaign, and that was a help. Yet, yet. . . . What is McGovern doing with these people? Where's Joe Mazzola? When we finally got to Miami Beach, we could ask the same questions.

Against McGovern's regiments of famous people, Humphrey had only Lorne Greene, star of TV's "Bonanza," and Greene is a Canadian citizen. Nixon, all along, has had Billy Graham, Art Linkletter, Bob Hope, Sammy Davis, Jr., and Frank Sinatra.* We have reached the point where we might be able to learn more about a politician by looking at his famous friends.

When your famous friends, earning a million or more a year, run around in blue jeans or bib overalls, shouting "right on!" and you're a Democrat looking for working-class support, you may have a problem. I think McGovern's beautiful friends may have added to the problems he would soon face.

---

* Sinatra distinguished himself at Nixon's inaugural by calling the *Post*'s Maxine Cheshire a $2 whore and dropping two $1 bills in her empty glass. Beautiful?

Thanks to the polls, to his beautiful people, to his uncharacteristic position as front-runner, McGovern dominated the coverage in newspapers and on television.

The New York Times, in a survey of the state's four largest media markets, reported on June 6 that "McGovern was getting about a third more space in the newspapers" and "more than half again as much free television time on newscasts." He also had about twice as much money to spend for paid commercials on television and radio.

The reasons explaining it, the *Times* suggested, were:

"Senator McGovern, a very distant dark horse to most campaign analysts only three months ago, has made his startling rise to front-runner the most newsworthy political story of 1972.

"With more money and a much larger staff, the McGovern organization has been able to organize a smooth publicity operation that assists both newspaper and television reporters in getting and filing timely stories."

In the period May 29 through June 2, "McGovern got 980 inches of newspaper space during the five weekdays compared with 744 for his rival from Minnesota, or 32 percent more. On television newscasts, the South Dakotan's advantage was 109 minutes to 70, or 56 percent."

My files indicate that the imbalance in stories carried by the national press was even more striking. The most widely syndicated columnists were writing almost exclusively about McGovern.

Is that bias? I suppose, in a way, it is. But we are under no mandate, legal or moral, to balance coverage on some kind of fifty-fifty basis. The exciting story in California was McGovern's remarkable climb from obscurity to front-runner, and that's what we wrote about. We would have written more about Humphrey, I think, if we had perceived the institutional nature of his challenge. We weren't biased, though; we were obtuse.

An outfit in Washington called the American Institute for Political Communication monitored the news shows of the three networks between June 1 and 14 and judged that 33 of the "episodes" were biased.

The methodology was to choose five young people, teach them a little about "alleged bias or 'staging' derived from congressional committee reports and media sources," and turn them loose in front of TV screens. They were given forms to fill out that included a "seven-position measurement scale" to rate the degree of bias. An episode was biased if a majority of the youthful monitors said it was biased.

ABC was tagged with seven biased episodes. They included: June 1, "ABC Poll shows McGovern far ahead"; June 2, "McGovern warns of overconfidence"; June 7, "McGovern wins California primary, 3 others"; June 8, "McGovern bandwagon going; Muskie will withdraw."

NBC and CBS were each guilty of 13 biased episodes. NBC was biased in McGovern's favor when it reported June 1 that "Humphrey has campaign troubles; lacks funds." It was biased for McGovern again on June 2 when "Humphrey admits he is behind—depends on free TV."

I say this is spinach, and to hell with it. Sitting five monkeys down in front of the screens, with or without typewriters, would have been equally useful. The institute's defense that there is no way to define bias—it is in the eye of the beholder—and thus the definition of bias arrived at by these five young people is as valid as anyone else's is spinach too, and I say to hell with that. If the point is to be proved that TV news is biased, we will have to do better than this.

Biased or not, McGovern's coverage had been good—for him. The high-water mark of his candidacy may have occurred on the eve of his first California debate: Saturday, May 27, 1972.

On that day, it was all coming true, just as Hart, Mankiewicz, and polltaker Caddell had said it would. McGovern was a "new politician" and people thought he was honest and forthright. His own volunteers saw him as a Eugene McCarthy with fire in his belly. He *was* building a coalition that others had only talked about building: young people, intellectuals, frustrated workers, suburban housewives. Maybe, it seemed, it wasn't a dream after all.

It would have worked if those threatened by it had let it work. Humphrey, on "Face the Nation" May 28, indicated that McGovern would not be permitted to get away with it. The time had come to cut McGovern down.

McGovern himself sensed that some trouble awaited him, because, on June 5, he flew from California to Houston in what the

Post's Richard M. Cohen and David Broder called "a sudden effort to calm the fears of Democratic governors that his nomination for President may plunge the party into a lopsided defeat." The nation's governors, including 25 Democrats, were attending the National Governors Conference at the Shamrock Hilton Hotel. Of those 25 Democrats, only three—Lucey of Wisconsin, Kneip of South Dakota, and Exon of Nebraska—were supporting him.

The meeting with the Democratic governors began at midnight —behind closed doors—and lasted for two hours. The governors opposing McGovern asked for clarification of his positions on such subjects as welfare, taxes, and national defense.

Before he left the West Coast for Houston, according to Warren Weaver, Jr., in *The New York Times,* McGovern said, "The Houston visit was one of a series of planned missionary efforts to persuade governors, senators, representatives, and party leaders that they'll have communication with me if I become the nominee. I think some of the governors possibly have the notion that I'll be difficult to approach because we've built our campaign not on their support but on the support of rank-and-file citizens. We want them to understand they'll have access to me without trouble, either as nominee or President."

That was not exactly what some of the governors had in mind. Led by Jimmy Carter of Georgia, a small bloc was trying to find a way to deny McGovern the nomination. The trouble was, the governors couldn't agree on a candidate to line up behind. As the *Times*'s Johnny Apple wrote on June 4, "the governors' effort appeared likely to be no more successful than the attempt by Republican governors in 1964 to draft Gov. William W. Scranton, the governor of Pennsylvania, to stop Senator Barry Goldwater of Arizona. That effort was also launched at a governors' conference."

Whatever his intention, McGovern hardly stampeded the governors. ". . . his flying visit failed to produce any fresh show of enthusiasm for the prospect of his carrying the Democratic standard against President Nixon this fall," Broder concluded. Many of the governors "remained openly skeptical that his promises to 'clarify' his positions on the issues and to restrain 'disruptive tactics' by his youthful supporters would improve what they regard as his dim prospects of uniting the Democrats for a winning campaign against Mr. Nixon."

Just how many of the Southern governors—and they were the ones leading the stop-McGovern movement—actually thought that the Democrats had a decent chance to win in the fall in the South is seriously open to question. One suspects that they weren't so much worried about that as they were worried by the "disruptive tactics" of McGovern's youthful supporters. Those tactics, it must have seemed to them, threatened their own leadership in the party. If McGovern won, they wouldn't be going to Miami Beach. They knew the threat McGovern posed to the traditional leadership of the party.

Even if we didn't.

To be sure, there were columnists and commentators who were now saying that McGovern would be another Goldwater. But these people, in our way of thinking, were the neanderthals who *hoped* McGovern would be a Goldwater. Most of us, I suppose, would agree with John Kenneth Galbraith's invention, Grump's Fourth Law of Politics: "If both Alsops say it is so, it can't be so."*

This time, though, it was so. That was almost the worst part of Nixon's landslide victory: it made William S. White, the Alsops, and Evans and Novak look good. In fairness, I should add too that Evans and Novak looked pretty good in a column that appeared in the *Post* on May 29. They wrote: ". . . Humphrey's eleventh-hour tactics dropped the veils from a deep schism within the party that assuredly will survive the California primary, the Democratic National Convention, and perhaps much beyond that." Exactly.

On June 6, McGovern won 44.3 percent of California's Demo-

* In that same article, in *New York* magazine, Galbraith wrote: ". . . nearly all of our political comment originates in Washington. Washington politicians, after talking things over with each other, relay misinformation to Washington journalists who, after further intramural discussion, print it where it is thoughtfully read by the same politicians. It is the only completely successful closed system for the recycling of garbage that has yet been devised." Writing in the July 1 *Saturday Review of Society,* under the headline, "The Case for George McGovern," Professor Galbraith concluded: "Speaking twelve weeks ago in Wisconsin, before the primary, I offered a scenario—not, I then said, as 'an exercise in political euphoria but as a decent prediction.' With even more than normal pleasure I now quote myself. 'McGovern will carry Massachusetts and Nebraska next month. He will carry Oregon. He will take California and New York. . . . Will the convention deny the nomination to a man with his record? I think not.' Nor, I am now convinced, will the country reject George McGovern in November." Garbage, professor? Euphoria, professor? To you too, welcome to the club.

cratic vote; Humphrey won 39.2 percent. Because it was (we thought) a winner-take-all primary, McGovern received all of California's 271 convention votes. No one ever thought the losers would challenge the outcome. Humphrey, himself, when he was interviewed by CBS's Walter Cronkite prior to the voting, said it would take a "spoilsport" to do that. "I don't believe in that kind of politics," he said.

That same day, McGovern won primaries in New Jersey, picking up 74 votes; New Mexico, 10, and South Dakota, 17. Four for four. It should have been McGovern's biggest day, but it was clouded because we were surprised by the narrowness of his victory in California. The Field Poll, on June 1, said he was 20 points ahead. He won by 5. The *Post* and the *Times* analyzed the California returns, almost instantly.

Haynes Johnson, basing his *Post* article on a Hart Research Associates survey of 847 voters in 26 counties, credited McGovern with emerging for the first time "as the candidate with the most broadly based constituency." McGovern, he said, "ran significantly better among voters who previously had been the strongest supporters of . . . Hubert Humphrey"—blacks, the poor, urban dwellers, blue-collar workers, and ethnics. They "deserted" Humphrey in large numbers.

A key finding in the Hart survey, buried deep in the story, was that "almost half of those who voted for Humphrey said they would support Mr. Nixon if McGovern is the Democratic nominee in November." Two out of three of McGovern's supporters said they would vote for Humphrey, if he were the nominee.

"Implicit in these findings," Johnson wrote, "is a potentially perilous situation facing the Democratic Party. They raise the prospect of a party so badly divided that the Republicans could be returned to office as a result."

Yet, curiously, trial heats between McGovern and Nixon and Humphrey and Nixon showed both scoring substantial victories, Humphrey by 68 to 21 and McGovern by 66 to 28. "Simply put," wrote Johnson, "this means that the President has problems in California."

Simply put, these apparently contradictory findings are puzzling.

The *Times*, with the assistance of Daniel Yankelovich, Inc., interviewed 570 voters in 11 counties, and came up with a similar finding: ". . . about 40 perecnt of Humphrey voters said they would defect to the President in a Nixon-McGovern race." The *Times,* in a story by Jack Rosenthal, led with that information.

"The high Humphrey defection rate mirrored a series of signs of relative conservatism among the Minnesota senator's supporters," the *Times* said. "The survey indicated they were less concerned about the Vietnam war and more sympathetic to Gov. George C. Wallace of Alabama than McGovern voters. And, the survey indicated Senator Humphrey's comparatively conservative positions won him growing support as the California campaign drew to a close. . . . Humphrey had cut into a potentially large McGovern victory margin with his attacks. These were made, notably, in three nationally televised debates prior to the election. . . . The rise from primary to primary in the number of Humphrey voters who would not support Senator McGovern parallels the increasing attention paid to the South Dakotan's proposals."*

The *Los Angeles Times,* in a masterful analysis by Robert A. Jones, pinpointed McGovern's area of weakness—"the Los Angeles media area." Wrote Jones on June 18:

"The discovery has worried the McGovern people considerably, for it seems to indicate that the South Dakota senator is far more vulnerable to attacks on his economic and welfare policies than they had believed possible. 'As soon as you get outside that L.A. media area, the vote goes back consistently for us,' said Pat Caddell, McGovern's principal pollster."

Los Angeles is different, Jones explained, because of "the pro-

* Edwin Diamond, writing in [*More*], notes that the Yankelovich analysis published on June 7 "credited McGovern with making inroads in all the major [voting] blocs. But in the *Times* of June 8, with all the returns in and the news reflecting the smaller McGovern margin, the Yankelovich analysis stressed that 'voter displeasure with McGovern's defense and welfare stands cut deeply into his margin of victory.' These were, of course, the same voters from the same Yankelovich polls of the day before; the second time around, however, the *Times* men were going through the data from the perspective of a McGovern 'squeaker' rather than a landslide. 'It was a beautiful case of selective perception,' says a rival public opinion analyst. . . ." There was nothing wrong with the poll, Diamond says; the problem was in interpretation.

fusion of newspapers and television stations in the Los Angeles basin which 'saturated' the final days of the campaign with charges by Humphrey that McGovern's aerospace cuts would cost thousands of jobs and that his welfare program would be enormously expensive. Campaign coverage in other areas of the state was not nearly so detailed, nor were there so many overlapping boundaries of communications media that often produced repetition in the Los Angeles area." In addition, the Humphrey campaign put what little cash it had into the purchase of TV spots in the Los Angeles area.

In the Los Angeles area, Jones's demographic analysis showed, Humphrey won the blue-collar vote and he split the Chicano and black vote with McGovern. In Jewish districts, McGovern was trounced. Yet, in the great central valley, a conservative part of the state, McGovern won by margins of two to one and three to one. There, the communications message wasn't nearly so strong and its impact was offset by a brilliantly organized door-to-door campaign for McGovern.

Finally, the *Times*'s analysis showed, "young voters attending institutions of higher learning" voted monolithically for McGovern. In a San Diego precinct comprised almost entirely of students, McGovern won 309 to 11. McGovern's victory in both Santa Barbara and San Diego counties seemed to stem from this kind of support by students. In counties with somewhat similar adult populations—and not many students—McGovern lost. Ventura was an example.

A McGovern strategist told Jones:

"Look at it this way. We won in nearly every section of the state, but then we had almost no organized opposition. In Los Angeles, the one place where the media could offset some of our organization by publicizing Humphrey's attacks, we were hurt badly. And we were hurt by an attack on the issues, which is supposed to be our strong point."

Jones's analysis, based on sophisticated reading of the returns, buttressed by interviews with voters and with campaign strategists, is a unique document. I can find no evidence that anyone else, after any other primary, attempted this kind of exercise. Credit the *Times* and the *Post* with good sense in hiring Yankelovich and Hart, but note what a sensible reporter can do at much less expense.

In the aftermath of the California primary, the press stressed two themes: Could McGovern wrap it up on the first ballot? Could Mc-Govern move toward the center and unify the party?

My own newspaper, continuing its series of delegate counts, gave McGovern 1,382½ votes on June 12, just 126½ short of the 1,509 that would be needed to win the nomination. That count presumed he would win almost all of New York's delegates on June 20; not very presumptuous, because Humphrey was making no challenge for the biggest delegation of all. We said it was just about all over.

Others didn't agree. Don Oberdorfer and William Chapman, writing in the *Post* on June 8, said McGovern's "margin of victory Tuesday, particularly in the crucial California primary, failed to generate the political and psychological momentum to sweep away the hurdles and easily close the remaining delegate gap." All McGovern had done, after all, was pick up 372 votes in one day. Never mind that, though: Muskie, said the *Post,* sitting on his 162 committed delegates, was the key.

So, attention quickly shifted to Humphrey and Muskie. Would they pull out and support McGovern? McGovern himself, in a rare display of chutzpah, had urged just such a course on both of them even before Californians had voted. Now, his agents went to work on the two rivals with the arithmetic on their side.

Humphrey wouldn't budge, even if he had lost seven primaries in a row. His people explained that away by saying he had entered the race so late and needed more time to catch up. "Hell," Joseph Napolitan, a party veteran, told the *Times's* Christopher Lydon, "Hubert knew when the election was."

Muskie was another matter. On June 9, the *Post's* Chapman and Oberdorfer wrote that Muskie was conferring with his principal rivals and key aides and supporters "amid indications he will announce his support for McGovern at a National Press Club luncheon today." They didn't know their Ed Muskie. On June 10, Oberdorfer (Chapman bowed out of this story) wrote that Muskie had decided to stay in the race. Oberdorfer now reports for the *Post* from Japan.

"Party unity is not achieved with the magic wand of the king-maker," Muskie said. "No man can hand George McGovern a united party, and I would do him a grave disservice to pretend that I could do so." McGovern, one hardly needs to add, wasn't asking for instant unity; he was asking for votes—and the nomination.

Reporters who had packed the press club to hear Muskie's endorsement were nonplussed. McGovern's aides who had come to hear the good news were stunned. Muskie, *Newsweek* said, had made five hundred telephone calls and even met with his staff until 4 A.M. in grappling with his decision.*

That just meant McGovern would have to work a little harder to pick up the final votes for the nomination. Almost no one doubted he could do it, especially after June 20, when he nailed down 255 of New York's 278 convention delegates.

Not quite so fast, though. Most of us missed the significance of an intriguing bit of news June 10, the day the headlines blazed with Muskie's decision to stay in the race. On June 9, delegates for four of the losing candidates in California—Humphrey, Jackson, Muskie, and Chisholm—formally protested to the Democratic Credentials Committee that winner-take-all was a "grossly inequitable" system that "totally disenfranchised" the 1,850,000 voters, or 55 percent of the total, who cast their ballots in California for McGovern's opponents.

George Lardner, Jr., in a brief, almost routine story in the *Post,* said "the challengers demanded that the Credentials Committee assign seats in proportion to the votes cast for each Presidential candidate in Tuesday's primary. As an added fillip, they invited McGovern to join the challenge 'to demonstrate his commitment to party reform.'"

The issue came to a vote at a meeting of the Credentials Committee in Washington on June 29. Committee members voted 72 to 66 to divide California's delegation proportionally. That way, McGovern, the winner, would get 120 votes, Humphrey, 106, Wallace, 16, Chisholm, 12, Muskie, 6, Yorty, 4, Eugene McCarthy, 3, Jackson, 2, and Lindsay, 2.

The outcome was a surprise; most of us presumed McGovern had the votes to turn back the challenge. "One of Humphrey's closest associates, William Connell, said they had decided only two days ago they had a chance to win the California challenge," William Chapman reported in the *Post.*

The reform commission had considered the winner-take-all pri-

---

* Muskie's inability to make up his mind became a joke with reporters. At a session at Harvard long after the campaign was over, entitled "Decision-Making in the 1972 Election," a reporter spotted a Muskie advisor and asked, "What's a Muskie man doing at a meeting like this?"

mary and had decided, by a one-vote margin, to permit it. The principal reason for that, Lou Cannon wrote in the *Post,* was that party leaders in California "insisted on keeping the winner-take-all provision as a condition for California's support of the reform guidelines."

That had seemed to settle it. Humphrey himself, in his early campaigning, acknowledged that "it all came down to California." If the California primary had been proportional, Cannon theorized, Humphrey and McGovern never would have poured such heavy resources into the state and the first meaningful debate on the issues never would have occurred.

All true. The vote was plainly a steal. More than anything else, though, it underscored the desperation of the traditional elements in the party. They were willing to risk almost anything to stop McGovern and maintain their own influence within the party. The fact that the bizarre coalition—ranging from forces supporting Chisholm to forces supporting Wallace—was directed by Bob Keefe, a wily, street-smart consultant to the AFL-CIO, tells us something.

Broder, writing June 30, said:

"The Democrats, it turned out, could not bear to wait for Miami Beach to blow their convention and their party sky-high. . . . The broader consequence, many Democrats agreed last night, was to inflame the deep wounds within their party and reduce the likelihood of anyone leading it to victory over Richard M. Nixon in the fall."

McGovern himself, Muskie-like, was incensed—and emotional. Interviewed in an anteroom off the Senate floor, he described the ruling by the Credentials Committee as "corrupt," "cynical," "an incredible, rotten, stinking political steal," "spiteful," "smelly," and "rigged." He didn't like it. In an interview with Bob Clark of ABC, who asked if he lost at the convention, after Humphrey's California delegates were seated, "will you support the nominee of the convention?"

"I'm not going to support anybody who is elected by crooked and unethical procedures of the kind that were used in this committee room today."

The credentials battle came just at the time that McGovern and his advisors were trying to unify the party. The battle came just as columnists and commentators were speculating on whether he could unify the party. The answer that came out of the Credentials Committee was loud and clear. The next day, forces supporting McGovern voted to unseat Mayor Richard Daley and 58 of his followers from Illinois. McGovern's advisors had hoped to avoid that, but—given what had happened with California—there was no holding the purists back.

It was not a very happy Democratic Party that opened its Thirty-sixth quadrennial convention in Miami Beach on July 10.

13

McGovern

J. Anthony Lukas, contributing editor to *More: A Journalism Review,* wrote in August that ". . . the conventions are more than news events; they are newsmen's events, probably the quintessential newsmen's events. At any American newspaper, magazine, or television network, they are the most eagerly sought of all assignments."

National political conventions, Lukas said, are not only "the most prestigious political gatherings, but the most prestigious journalistic gatherings too—the quadrennial preening of the press. Reporters want to go because other reporters will be going, and because a convention pass has become the most visible sign of their status. . . . And when they get there, most reporters exhibit priorities not all that different from politicians. They do what reporting they can, battling their colleagues for the few scraps of legitimate news. But they spend much of their time hopping from bureau to bureau seeing old friends; jockeying for a glimpse of their own superstars, Cronkite, Wicker, Mailer; trading rumors—usually about journalistic, rather than convention politics; drinking in hotel bars, hospitality suites, upstairs in somebody's room. . . . Not to be there would be unthinkable."

Lukas was writing about the *Democratic* convention and it occurred to me, as I read his vivid description of what we'd done there, that he hadn't been at the same convention I went to. In fact, he hadn't. An italic panel at the end of his story noted that Lukas watched the convention, at home, on television. "Reporting from Miami," the panel noted, "was provided by William Woodward, [*More*'s] publisher, and numerous other journalists on the scene." So much for ethics in a publication dedicated to improving them.

God knows, reporters take a drink at conventions; reporters renew old friendships. A few, in fact, do almost nothing else. Most of us, though, work pretty hard, and some of us at the Democratic convention worked almost all day and all night. Consider, for example, Walter Mears, the AP's writing machine. His editor estimates he churned out thirty thousand words—most of them making sense—between July 5 and July 14.

Mears would start work about 10 A.M., reading all the wire copy that had moved in his absence, including the thousands of words sent out on the regional wires. He would then write his first roundup about 1 P.M., aimed for morning newspapers. As the day progressed and important events occurred, he would "top" that original story again and again. One day that began at 10 A.M. ended the next day at 3:36 A.M.; another ended at 4:16 A.M.

Mears can type 100 words a minute—and sustain a running conversation at the same time. He can write faster than the AP teletype machine can print, which, at Miami Beach, was 60 words a minute. During that convention, at moments of high drama, the "A" wire was cleared for Mears's copy, moving out of his typewriter in "takes" of one or two paragraphs into the hands of an editor and straight to the wire-machine puncher.

Mears wrote just for the "A.M. cycle"—for morning newspapers. His colleague Carl Leubsdorf wrote for the "P.M. cycle"—for afternoon papers. Much the same thing occurred inside the UPI's working space in the basement of the Fontainebleau Hotel. Bob Andrews, Mears's UPI counterpart, wrote for the "A.M. cycle"; Steve Gerstel, Leubsdorf's counterpart, wrote for the "P.M. cycle." A political convention is one of the few times when the two wire services are in direct competition; newspapers subscribing to both services really look at what they're getting, and they go with the service that's first or—maybe—best. AP tends to win these battles; it won in Miami Beach.

Major newspapers and newspaper chains try to compete with the wires too, and a few of them succeed. Probably the most thorough coverage the two Miami Beach conventions received was published in the *Miami Herald,* a member of the Knight chain. For the *Herald,* of course, it was a local story, which is not to downgrade its considerable achievement. Jack Germond, Washington bureau chief for the Gannett newspapers, wrote for *both* the A.M. and the P.M. cycles, an astonishing feat.

Hundreds of reporters, employed by dozens of newspapers, worked thousands of hours to reproduce, essentially, what they were already getting from the Associated Press and United Press International. Why? Some papers and some chains think their own people can do a better job. *The New York Times,* I'm sure, *knows* it can do a better job. Other papers may be looking for more analytical material than the wire services are prepared to deliver. Still others may want to squeeze in locally oriented material. In essence, though, most newspapers expend all this time, energy, and money as a matter of pride. Journalism these days needs all the pride it can summon, but, in this instance, it seems to me, pride is more stubborn than logical. It would make more sense if most papers let the wire services handle the main, running story and deploy their own reporters to catch the mood and the true significance of the convention.

One can quibble about the strategy of newspapers and reporters, but one can hardly deprecate the work that's involved. It would be wise, then, not to talk to Mears or Andrews or Germond about preening.

But there is still a larger question: Do very many people really care what the wire service and the newspapers report from a political convention? Sure, I care; you care. Most of the readers of *The New York Times* care. Several million Americans care.

Millions more, though—maybe as many as 80,000,000—depend on television for convention coverage. For more than that, really: millions participate in these conventions, vicariously, through television.

In fact, a pencil reporter at a national convention is like a eunuch in a pasha's harem: he can watch, but he can't touch. A political convention is a television convention.

The explanation is obvious enough. For the first and last time, the entire cast is on a single stage and the cameras can see and record everything—well, practically everything. The camera can go almost anywhere a reporter can go, and some places a reporter can't go.

The drama of a convention (when there is drama) is almost matched by the drama of the three networks struggling for the plaudits of the critics and the judgment of the ratings. Can Walter Cronkite do it one more time? "His hearing's going and his vision's gone, but he's going to do nothing but rest for two weeks before this one and he'll come on like a tiger," a "CBS power" told New York magazine's Richard Reeves, who wrote the most complete report about the networks' convention coverage. Can NBC's new team of floor reporters, Douglas Kiker, Garrick Utley, Tom Pettit, and Cassie Mackin, meet the standards set by that network's famous Four Horsemen, Sander Vanocur, John Chancellor, Edwin Newman, and Frank McGee? Is David Brinkley, at 52, really over the hill? Will ABC cut into both NBC and CBS by running just 90 minutes of highlights each night, devoting the rest of its prime time to situation comedies and old Western reruns?

"There's confusion at NBC," CBS's Bob Wussler told his troops (according to Reeves). "We'll beat the ass off them!" "CBS is Pepsodent smiles and this time we're political animals who'll find a story if it's there. If it is, we'll beat the ass off them," NBC's Dick Wald told his troops. "We abandoned gavel-to-gavel coverage as an economic necessity in 1968," ABC's Walter Pfister explained. "But we found out that having little time gave us perspective. We're the wave of the future."

NBC's Doug Kiker told New York magazine's Jane O'Reilly that "we were so psyched up for the first night, we hit the floor like those little toy cars you wind up and they buzz around bumping into things."

What the networks do at a convention is not really reporting. It is a kind of happening in words and pictures, live, in color, moving, moving, moving. Keep it moving, fast. The TV picture spins from the podium to the street to a hotel and back to the floor. The viewer sees, in bewildering detail, everything, everywhere. Question: Is he seeing the convention or is he seeing a drama written extemporaneously by the men with their fingers on the switch buttons? Surely what the audience sees at home is a lot more exciting and a lot different from what an alternate delegate from Wyoming sees from her vantage point behind the latticework of the towers built to hold the TV cameras.

The convention TV gives us is news without nuance, fact without detail, event without theme. To be sure, the anchormen and the specialists sitting with them, like Teddy White, try to bring things into some kind of perspective, but there simply isn't time. Anyway, the producers want action, not talk.

It is hardly any wonder, then, that the networks get news on the air that a print reporter, upon contemplation, would reject. In 1968, for example, Sander Vanocur and John Chancellor, almost single-handedly, began a Kennedy-for-President boom that swept the floor like a brush fire. Hours earlier, it turned out, Kennedy had passed the word he was not available.

Sometimes, the networks don't get the real news on the air— because they don't know what it is. On Monday night, July 10, 1972, the networks, especially CBS, blew the first big story of the convention —the South Carolina credentials challenge.

It is a very long and very complicated story (told adequately, I might note, only in an article by Hunter S. Thompson in *Rolling Stone* that must run to 10,000 words), and I won't go into all of the subterranean details. Suffice it to say that the key question of seating all of McGovern's California delegates depended upon parliamentary maneuvering over the challenge in South Carolina, which was the first to come to the convention's attention. The challenge was based on an allegation that there weren't enough women in that delegation. The McGovern people wanted to avoid a showdown on South Carolina; that meant the vote could not fall inside what was called the "twilight zone," or between 1,496 and 1,509 votes.

The McGovern strategists, working in their trailer outside the hall, were perfectly willing to abandon the women if, as the voting progressed, there seemed to be any chance that the final count would fall within the deadly zone. When it began to look as if that might happen, the orders went out to put the fix in: selected McGovern delegates were instructed to throw their votes.

What was happening shouldn't have been any secret. *The New York Times's* Johnny Apple spelled it out in a story that appeared before the convention began. From my perch in the press gallery, I could see McGovern floor leaders—Bill Dougherty and Pierre Salinger, most memorably—rushing from delegation to delegation making hand signals. I telephoned two or three friends in delegations where the fix had been put in—a sophisticated closed-circuit system allowed that—and asked them if what I thought was happening was, in fact, happening. They confirmed my suspicions.

Down on the floor, though, McGovern leaders like Hart and Mankiewicz couldn't tell the precise truth, because they didn't want to alarm all the women in the hall who wouldn't care to know they were being played with. So, when floor reporters asked Hart and Mankiewicz what was happening, they lied, or fudged.

Up in the CBS booth, Walter Cronkite kept talking about a McGovern defeat. *New York's* Reeves wrote:

"The fix was in. The convention, for all practical purposes, was over at 10:30 the first night—McGovern was in complete control.

"You could not have known that if you were watching television, especially if you were watching CBS where Cronkite kept talking about a victory for the sloppy anti-McGovern coalition. . . . He even chuckled about the repeated 'passes' by Ohio chairman Frank King, who was actually stalling to try to switch Humphrey votes to get the total between 1,496 and 1,509.

"There was plenty of chuckling in McGovern's suite as the second-level Machiavellian drama unfolded. One of the senator's men described it this way, with dots representing laughter escalating from giggles to gasping roars.

" 'Cronkite is saying the anti-McGovern forces are gaining . . . and there's Billy Dougherty whispering in Frank Morrison's ear . . . telling him to change . . . to change Nebraska's vote. . . . And Walter is going on. . . . Then Abe switches in Connecticut. . . . We're pulling all the strings. . . . Dan Rather is interviewing Humphrey's manager and calls him 'a very happy man.' . . . He's a dead man. Mike Wallace asks Gary Hart if he's disappointed. . . . Cronkite says it's obvious that Hart's 'just a bit shaken by that vote.' . . . He's shaking trying to keep from laughing.' "

What none of us knew, until months after the convention, was that the anti-McGovern forces could have made their parliamentary challenge after the vote was completed and before it was announced. The convention parliamentarian, Representative James G. O'Hara, waited expectantly, looking in the direction of Ohio's Frank King, who had been instructed by the coalition to make the challenge. But he didn't rise. He just couldn't do it because his friend, Governor John C. West of South Carolina, dancing in the aisle next to him, would have been stunned. Because Frank King couldn't offend the sensibilities of a friend, the last chance to stop McGovern was lost.

The old pros didn't know what they were doing—or couldn't do what they had to do. It was the green amateurs working for McGovern who had the brains, the discipline, and the toughness to win the decisive battle.

Almost 90 percent of the delegates were first-timers, products of the reform movement that grew out of the disaster at Chicago in 1968. This time, it was ordained, the delegates would be representative of the Democratic Party. Everybody would have a shot at getting to Miami Beach.

How did it work?

Haynes Johnson, in an illuminating article in the *Post* on July 8, said there were more women, more blacks and other minorities, and more young people. But more representative?

"To some extent they are. But in other important respects the delegates who are gathering here . . . represent what can only be described as an American elite." The delegates, a *Post* survey found, were better educated and made more money than the population at large. An incredible 39 percent held postgraduate degrees. Thirty-one percent had family incomes of more than $25,000 a year. Forty percent of the black delegates had taken postgraduate work and 19 percent of them earned more than $25,000 a year.

"In the past," Johnson wrote, "convention delegates traditionally have represented the economic and educational elite. Four years ago in

Chicago, 40 percent of the delegates had incomes over $20,000 and four years before that the median income of the delegates was three times the national norm.

"New politics notwithstanding, the 1972 Democratic delegate still represents the old economic and educational class background. If the survey responses are an indication, where he seems to differ most is in his own state of mind. The self-portrait of today's delegate shows he thinks he is in the vanguard of a new political era."

Missing, especially among the McGovern delegates, were those Democrats *Newsweek*'s John Lindsay calls "Augie" and "Leo"—the working stiffs, the party hacks, the labor skates. Missing too were the likes of W. Averell Harriman, the party's grand old dragon, who ran for delegate against a long-haired kid, and lost. The old man was incensed. In 1976, it can be said with some certainty, "Augie" and "Leo" will be back and so will some of the old dragons. Even the reformers agree that ways must be found to permit some of these people, at least, to participate.

With McGovern's California delegation seated (and with Daley's Chicago 59 kicked out), speculation about the identity of the nominee finally ended: it would be McGovern. On Tuesday, Humphrey ended his 12-year quest for the Presidency and released the delegates pledged to vote for him. Before facing the press, Chris Lydon wrote in *The New York Times,* Humphrey instructed "more than 100 under-30 advance men, researchers, baggage handlers, and all-purpose aides of the last six months" to show their faces to the reporters who had written he was the conservative candidate of the "old hacks" in the party.

At his news conference, Humphrey declared, "This has been a good fight. We've waged a good battle. We've done it within the rules of the game." He did not mention the man Lydon called his "friend and onetime protégé from South Dakota," George McGovern.

Muskie waited until Humphrey made his move, and then—at last —he made his. He had, it will be remembered, withdrawn from the primaries on April 27; on June 9, he stunned reporters in Washington, who had expected his withdrawal, with his announcement that he was still in the race. On the opening day of the convention, he held another press conference from which great things were again expected.

Instead, he proposed a compromise on credentials that satisfied no one.

"Where the rest of us see only glass," one of his aides told *The New York Times,* "he sees mica—and feels the need to peel back one layer at a time."

This time, though, it was final. "It is now apparent to all of us that Senator George McGovern is this convention's choice as the Presidential nominee of our party. . . . I have concluded that my continued candidacy would benefit neither my supporters nor my party. My name will not be placed in nomination. I offer Senator McGovern and his campaign staff my congratulations on an impressive victory, achieved against enormous odds, by skill, perseverance, dedication and plain hard work." Once again, at the very end, Muskie showed a touch of class.

With Humphrey and Muskie gone, only Jackson, Wallace, and Chisholm remained. Jackson, now the last, desperate hope of the anti-McGovern elements in the party, never relented. On "Meet the Press" Sunday, he said:

"Whenever three Democrats get together . . . they are talking about losing the House, the Senate. . . . Wherever you get together with a group here at the convention they're all scared to death. Labor, the majority of the leadership, certainly will not endorse him. He's in trouble in the Jewish community. . . . When we have other basic elements in what has always been a winning Democratic coalition raising Cain, I think you've got problems."

McGovern, speaking earlier on the same program, said:

"I'm not where I am as a serious candidate for the Presidency because I have a narrow base. . . . I believe I have the best and broadest grass-roots organization ever built in American politics. That organization is going to be at the service of every Democrat running for office in 1972 from the courthouse right on up to the Congress and the White House. I believe that many people who are now fearful of my candidacy are going to hail it as one of the great steps forward for our party when they feel its impact."

If McGovern was right, if he did indeed have the "best and broadest grass-roots organization ever built in American politics," that was hardly consoling to regular party types. McGovern's organization was not a party organization, perhaps it might even be an antiparty organization. Maybe McGovern didn't understand, but he and his organization were a threat to all those other Democrats.

Regular Democrats could see these McGovern people, finally. They were in Miami Beach—not out in the streets, demonstrating (those people, Tim Crouse of *Rolling Stone* said, were the "dregs of the counter-culture")—but inside the hall, seated as delegates. One old-timer, after he had his first glimpse of the Massachusetts delegation, said: "It looks like the cast of *Hair*." The enemy was inside the tent; the barbarians had breached the walls.

The *Wall Street Journal's* Norman C. Miller caught the true meaning of this convention best in a story he wrote before it even began. Miller nailed down the institutional nature of the battle that escaped most of us in our earlier reporting of the California primary.

"Not one but two Democratic parties will meet in Miami Beach next week," he said, "and the all-out war they seem certain to wage could finally tear apart the coalition that has been winning elections since the New Deal."

Wall Street Journal "leaders"—those two stories that appear left and right on its front page five times a week—contain some of the best reporting in American journalism. The writing tends to follow a formula that includes what Vermont Royster, the stylish curmudgeon of the editorial page, calls a "caveat" paragraph. It often begins with the phrase, "to be sure." As in: "To be sure, some say all of this will never happen." Miller's story came complete with a caveat paragraph. "To be sure," he wrote, "the nominee undoubtedly will bend every effort to unite the factions. And once again the Democrats may display their remarkable ability to submerge differences and make common cause against the Republican enemy."

But Miller didn't believe it, not for a minute. The *Journal* formula calls for a cosmic paragraph to follow the caveat paragraph. Miller's read:

"Yet the unity effort will be much more difficult—and perhaps impossible—this time. For the issue that divides the Democrats runs much deeper than mere personal attachments to George McGovern or Hubert Humphrey or other candidates. Rather, it goes to the fundamental power alignment within the 40-year-old Democratic coalition."

The formula now requires fuller explanation. Here it is:

"On the one hand, the 'traditional party' forces—the AFL-CIO, many members of Congress, the white Southern and border-state politicians, most statehouse and city hall leaders like Chicago Mayor Richard Daley—are determined to keep the power that has made a string of Democratic Presidents beholden to their interests. Since the days of FDR it is largely these forces that have delivered the Democrats' vital constituencies in election after election; the blue-collar workers and Catholics in the key industrial states, the white South, liberal Jews, the solid black bloc.

"On the other hand, the 'new party' forces—the young, the issue-inspired activists of all ages, the affluent liberals, the militantly disaffected young blacks and Chicanos—are determined to seize dominant power for themselves. It was this group, galvanized by its intense opposition to the Vietnam war, that bitterly fought and lost to the old-line forces at the nearly disastrous 1968 convention. This time, their candidate, George McGovern, is within reach of bringing them to power, which would inevitably occur at the expense of the traditional forces."

Now, quickly, start spicing it up with some good quotes: Such as:

"One McGovern operative, who has tried peacemaking with the AFL-CIO, worries: 'The one thing the AFL-CIO can't forgive McGovern for is the one thing he can't do anything about: If he's nominated, he won't owe them anything."

And:

" 'The Daleys and the labor bosses feel McGovern is a threat to their power, and there's no way they're ever going to accept him,' says Matthew Troy, the maverick leader of the Queens County, N.Y., organization. "That's why we might as well fight them [at the convention] and bolster our own people.' "

And:

"An AFL-CIO operative, who disagrees himself with the federation's hard-line anti-McGovern stand, nevertheless shares the apprehension about the South Dakotan's electability. Typical of the rank and file, he says, is this reaction of a Nebraska union official. 'I just couldn't vote for him. . . . I'd have to sit it out. I can't vote for a man who favors killing babies. He wants wide-open abortion so they can kill babies.' "

One could argue that Mike Miller's story is biased—against McGovern. Except for the caveat paragraph, this is an exposition of the theme that the party is split, and that a McGovern campaign will split it even more. It has a strong point of view, just as TV reporting has a theme and a point of view. But this story, unlike TV's split-second efforts, is complete; it's documented. This is what Mike Miller thinks, based on his expertise and the expertise of the Washington bureau of the *Wall Street Journal*. This, I think, is what Miller and the rest of the national political writers are paid to do. They should look long and hard at what's happening, talk to people, investigate, bring it into perspective, think and ponder, and then let the readers in on what they've learned. What we're talking about is news analysis (as contrasted with straight news reporting and opinion), and perhaps analytical stories should be plainly labeled to make sure no one is confused about what we're doing. The line between straight news, analysis, and opinion is wavy and controversial. All three, it seems to me, have their place in newspapers and magazines and on television, but somewhere a very tough editor should have the responsibility to make sure that the paper (and its reporters) and the network (and its correspondents) keep the distinctions in mind. If we would only be candid about what we're doing, a lot of the criticism we've received would disappear. My idea of a great newspaper is one that's packed with news and analysis and opinion, including the outrageous. A great newspaper should be a celebration of life, full of action and ideas. Everybody's action; everybody's ideas. It should be a babble of voices, and every reader should know that behind it all is a spirit of justice and fairness.

We don't have many papers like that. My offhand impression, traveling around the country, reading lots of newspapers, is that we have fewer of them every year. Journalistic mausoleums; the country is full of them.

As I was saying, before I interrupted myself, Miller's article in the *Journal* is a first-class example of solid analytical reporting. What followed in the *Journal*'s coverage of the convention was not quite as solid, it seemed to me.* News analysis became a trifle dyspeptic, perhaps because the convention (on the surface, anyway) didn't turn out to be as riotous as Miller's scene-setter might have suggested it would be. For example, Arlen J. Large, normally one of the most solid political reporters around, led his story on July tenth with a quotation from an anonymous party functionary who said "the folks" gathering in Miami Beach "look like a bunch of people standing around before they jump off a cliff." A highly selective quote, that, and not even very accurate, I thought. Large went on to conclude: "When the business is over next Thursday, the Democratic Party may lie shattered in ruins for years to come. Or, less disastrously, it may build new inner strength to rebound after a loss this year. Conceivably, of course, it might instead be moving toward a miraculous victory over President Nixon in November." Is a political "miracle" . . . "conceivable"? I think not.

In the dyspepsia derby, though, no one can match Joe Alsop. On July 5, he reported: "By all the signs, the Democratic convention . . . will be a scene of fratricidal carnage. . . . It is hard to see how massive bloodshed can be avoided." He was speaking in the figurative sense, I think. Even as he grumbled about the performance of his rented chef at his rented Miami Beach mansion, Alsop grumbled that the "McGovern movement is a profoundly elitist movement. Make no mistake about that."

Dyspepsia or euphoria?

Most of us, I think, tended to move in one or the other of those directions. Question: Was the ticket, a Democratic Goldwater joke, doomed? Or was there a chance that the ticket, supported by the "new party" professionals, could put together a winning coalition that Meany and Daley and Joe Mazzola and the grand old dragons would have to join?

---

* I'm talking here about the reporters from the Washington bureau, not the writers and columnists working for the editorial page in New York, some of whom also came to Miami Beach. The edit-page staff, most of the time, is openly pro-Nixon. The bureau reporters are considerably less ideological, and some of them, privately, are even liberal. The strain between New York and Washington sometimes shows.

Doomed it was, said Joe Alsop and, by inference at least, the *Journal*. The *Times*'s Johnny Apple wasn't so sure. ". . . if McGovern and his managers can maintain the amalgam of zeal and discipline they have demonstrated in Miami Beach this week," he wrote in a clearly labeled "News Analysis," "they just might have a chance to do in the country at large what they did in the caucuses in Virginia and the primary in Wisconsin and the convention in Florida."

Reporters for the *Post* went *both* directions. On the thirteenth, under a headline, "Party Out of Harmony," William Chapman and Don Oberdorfer wrote that "the usual thing for opposing forces in the Democratic Party is to bury the hatchet. . . . But it hasn't happened this year—at least not yet." Striking examples of intraparty bitterness followed.

The very next day, though, Haynes Johnson, in another Page One story, wrote that "despite the gloom emanating from such as Joseph Alsop [and Chapman and Oberdorfer too?] who began the convention writing about 'a Democratic death wish' and ended it raising the analogy of the disintegration of the British Labor Party early in the century, the Democrats have survived their 36th national gathering. The Democratic Party may be different, but it has not been destroyed." The next day, the fifteenth, David Broder, bedazzled, wrote that the final night of the convention "may have been one of the most euphoric hours of convention history." "Democratic Party Harmony Marks '72 Convention Close," the headline said. Broder was especially impressed by Ted Kennedy's speech, which, he thought, touched all the right chords. He was not as impressed by McGovern, who urged well after three o'clock in the morning that "America come home" from the war and from domestic strife.

"And on that note," Broder concluded his story, "the Democrats who had themselves 'come home' from the battle for the nomination to at least a temporary show of unity, went home to begin the campaign against Richard Nixon, the man McGovern called 'our unwitting unifier.' "

So put Apple and Broder, the nation's two best-known political writers, down on the side of euphoria. Me, too.

I think now that the ticket was always doomed, and that the seeds of its destruction were planted long before the convention began. At

Miami Beach, though, it wasn't obvious. Nothing at a political convention is very obvious, especially this convention, at which no one ever seemed to get any sleep. If I leaned in the direction of euphoria, perhaps it was because I thought we ought to wait and see how things went. Give the ticket a chance. Maybe there was enough alienation and frustration, enough anti-Nixon feeling among traditional Democrats, enough skill and know-how in the "outparty."

Just as there is a fine line between analysis and opinion, there is a fine line between skepticism and cynicism. In thinking that the Democratic ticket ought to be given a chance, knowing that it was an underdog, I thought I was exercising sufficient skepticism. Maybe, though, I decided to give it a chance because I wanted to give it a chance. My own ideology runs from the old Rockefeller on the right to the new McGovern on the left. In the center, but skewed a degree or two to the left. Nixon's position does not overlap with mine.

Surely, then, these things shaped my thinking and my attitudes. Professionally, as a columnist—permitted, even encouraged, to hold opinions, I'm entitled. As a political analyst, though, I'm threatened. It comes down to a matter of self-discipline. You have to keep telling yourself: don't be fooled, don't be misled, don't be diverted. For a professional, I suppose, this is where bias creeps in; it is locked in the mind, even in the subconscious. It seeps out in a decision to give the good guy a chance that you might refuse to give to the bad guy. It's a matter of inches, of exquisite nuance. It happens because we're human beings and, try as hard as we may, there's not a damn thing we can do about it.

So, I began my convention story on a skeptical note. I wrote:

"Members of the Virgin Islands delegation to the Democratic National Convention wore buttons that read, 'Try a Virgin.' In choosing a ticket, the party took their advice, twice. McGovern and Eagleton. . . ."

But I didn't really mean it. I thought, and said, that the convention went off better than anyone really had expected—at least until Thursday night, when the exhausted delegates ran amok by nominating Archie Bunker, Martha Mitchell, Mayor Daley, Roger Mudd, and Joe Smith of Scotts Bluff for Vice-president. Down on the floor, as prime time on the tube faded away, Jean Westwood told me: "Oh, they've been so good up until now. They deserve this." She meant it.

Then I said that for McGovern the priorities were these.

One. Survive the convention. He did.

Two. Unify the party. I said a start had been made on that.

Three. Prove to ordinary Democrats that he is not some kind of radical barn burner.

Four. Build at the same time this coalition of "outpeople."

Five. Run an exciting and different kind of campaign.

Six. Demonstrate that he is more than a pretty shrewd operator who managed to sneak victories in scattered primaries and win in caucuses with a small army of elitist volunteers. On that point, I was most skeptical of all.

Obviously enough, that was a tall order—too tall for McGovern, as it turned out. Maybe, though, he could have come close to meeting it—if, as his press secretary, Richard Dougherty, would write after the election was over, Tom Eagleton hadn't come skipping up to his cabin door "with an amusing little story of how he had gone off his rocker two or three times over the last ten years. Yes, a little shock treatment, George, but not too much. Such a trivial thing he just hadn't thought to mention it at the convention."

If, with the help of the press the seeds of destruction had been planted long ago, the seeds of terrible catastrophe, once again with the help of the press, were finally planted with one of the most bizarre episodes in the history of American politics. The Eagleton Affair.

14

Eagleton

"On three occasions in my life I have voluntarily gone into hospitals as a result of nervous exhaustion and fatigue."

—THOMAS F. EAGLETON, at a press conference, Custer, S.D., July 25.

With my usual facility for time and place, I was in Chicago that day, trying to determine how the McGovern-Eagleton ticket would fare in Richard Daley's hometown. I was talking to Norton Kay, press secretary to the man who is now governor of Illinois, Dan Walker, when the phone rang. Kay talked a few minutes. "My God!" he said, as soon as he had hung up, "Eagleton's just announced he's been in the nut house."

Not precisely, of course; not really the "nut house." But Eagleton did say that he had been hospitalized three times, and on two of those occasions his treatment included electric shock therapy. The final hospitalization was in 1966 and lasted three weeks. Since then, he said, "I've experienced good, sound health. . . . So I believe and I have every confidence that at the age of forty-two I've learned how to measure my own energies and know the limits of my own endurance."

"Well," said Senator McGovern, "I think Tom Eagleton is fully qualified in mind, body, and spirit to be the Vice-president of the United States and, if necessary, to take on the Presidency at a moment's notice. . . . I wouldn't have hesitated one moment [in selecting him] if I had known everything Senator Eagleton said today."

Of all the stories that came out of the 1972 campaign, including Watergate, none is more complex, more tragic, more mysterious than the Eagleton Affair. Months after the election, we still don't know all of the details—what, for example, do the hospital records show? Some things we may never know.

But I think we do know what the result of Eagleton's admission was: the Democratic campaign, already in trouble, was wrecked. The issue now became—not Richard Nixon and his policies—but George McGovern and his qualifications to be President.

The role of the press was crucial.

Because newspapers were on the scent of the story, the facts had to be disclosed. Because newspapers—especially the *Post* and the *Times,* in their editorials—said Eagleton had to go, he went. Muddying the waters, quite literally, was Jack Anderson, who, at the most delicate moment in the proceedings, broadcast a scurrilous allegation. Then, newspapers, which had insisted that Eagleton be dropped, reported that millions of Americans were angry and disillusioned because their advice had been taken.*

No one who participated emerged unscathed. The Eagleton Affair is a story of missed opportunities, misunderstanding, and misadventure. The story has been best told by Haynes Johnson, in a four-part series in the *Washington Post,* and by columnist Milton Viorst, in a lengthy article in *Esquire* magazine. Their post-election reporting will be included along with contemporaneous reporting in the day-to-day diary that now begins.

THURSDAY, JULY 13

At about 9 A.M., 20 or more of McGovern's advisors, friends, and assorted hangers-on met in a conference room at the Doral Hotel "to begin," in Viorst's words, "the process of selecting a Vice-presidential candidate." It was hardly a moment too soon—the deadline for submitting the candidate's name was four o'clock that afternoon. Earlier,

---

* Pat Caddell, McGovern's polltaker, discovered during the campaign that the most popular man in America was . . . Tom Eagleton.

perhaps the day before, McGovern had asked six of his advisors to "give him their four leading choices, seal them in an envelope, and not talk to anybody about them," Haynes Johnson wrote. Gary Hart picked, in order, Ted Kennedy, Senator Walter F. Mondale of Minnesota, Mayor Kevin White of Boston, and Representative Wilbur Mills of Arkansas.

Ted Kennedy, for obvious reasons, was almost everybody's first choice. McGovern wanted him and had talked earnestly with him two weeks earlier, but Kennedy ruled it out, flatly and finally. Still, McGovern didn't give up. On Wednesday night, McGovern talked (by phone) to Kennedy again and got the same answer.

With Kennedy unavailable, the talk at the morning meeting turned to others. Mankiewicz presided; it was, he recalled, a free-association sort of thing. Brainstorming. The brainstorms included Ralph Nader and Walter Cronkite. When the session got serious, Eagleton was still in the running. At that point, two people—Rick Stearns of McGovern's staff and "a prominent Democrat" not otherwise identified by Haynes Johnson—might have put a stop to it.

Stearns, when it came time to discuss Eagleton at the meeting, said a newspaper reporter had told him the day before that rumors were circulating about alcohol or psychiatric problems. The reporter was the Knight newspapers' Loye Miller but Stearns, exhausted, had trouble remembering his name.

Lieutenant Governor William Dougherty of South Dakota said he had heard the same rumors and, by accident, had talked to a physician from Missouri in the lobby of the Doral. The physician said there was no drinking problem, but, once, there had been a problem with "nervous exhaustion." Dougherty tended to dismiss the rumors as unfounded.

By noon, the list had been narrowed to seven names, including Eagleton's. One effort was made to check out the rumors, which, it was thought, principally involved alcohol. Stearns finally remembered that the reporter he had talked to the day before was Tom Ottenad of the *St. Louis Post-Dispatch*. He was mistaken, but never mind: Gordon Weil was detailed to call Ottenad, and he did. Ottenad, Weil reported back, knew nothing about a serious drinking problem. The first signal was missed.

The "prominent Democrat" awoke Thursday morning to read in the papers that Eagleton was under serious consideration. "The Democrat was alarmed," Johnson wrote. "He had first-hand knowledge that Eagleton had been hospitalized several times for psychiatric treatment." He picked up the phone and tried to get through to someone at the Doral, with no luck. He kept trying until he finally got a McGovern staffer, and he told him what he knew. The McGovern staffer —Johnson doesn't identify him either—said afterward that he relayed the message to still another staffer, who was supposed to get the message to McGovern. The second McGovern aide said later that he never got any such message. In any event, another signal was missed. Late that afternoon the "prominent Democrat" was stunned to learn that Eagleton was the choice. He called the staffer he had talked to originally. "For God's sake," he said, "didn't you understand what I told you?" Informed that the message had been passed along, he said: "What in the name of God are you people smoking up there?"

While all of this was happening, most of us were still asleep. None of us really knew anything—and few of us could find out anything. All conventions are chaotic, and this one was more chaotic than most. So many people have axes to grind, knives to sharpen. The night before, ax-grinders had floated the names of Larry O'Brien and Tom Eagleton at me. Someone tried to convince me that Mayor Moon Landreau of New Orleans should be taken seriously. Some reporters still believed Kennedy would accept. Nobody knew a damn thing.

When the meeting at the Doral finally ended, Boston's Mayor White was the front-runner. Mankiewicz took the consensus to McGovern, who, according to some reports, was still trying to get Kennedy to relent. Eagleton, in the early afternoon, was not taken very seriously, which may be a reason why the rumors about him were not taken very seriously.

In midafternoon, as the final choice edged closer and closer to Kevin White, McGovern made another call to Kennedy, who was still at Hyannis Port, where he had been sailing in his yacht, the *Patrician*.

Rumors persist that Kennedy vetoed Kevin White in the course of that telephone call. McGovern, in an interview with editors of the *Boston Globe* on January 12, 1973, refused to go into the details of the conversation. He did insist, though, that Kennedy "did not block

Kevin White's selection as Vice-presidential candidate." Yet, Mc-Govern conceded, "certain questions were raised." McGovern said he offered Kennedy the nomination again, and this time Kennedy said he needed some time to think about it. Kennedy called McGovern back: "I just can't take it," McGovern quoted him as saying. "If you decide on Mayor White I'm flying down in a private plane and I'll give him a ride down."

According to Haynes Johnson, some McGovern advisors who overheard the conversation between McGovern and Kennedy recall Kennedy "hitting the ceiling," saying White was not acceptable and that if it was going to be White, he, Kennedy, would have to reconsider and take it himself.

It's another mystery; we just don't know. It is agreed that John Kenneth Galbraith, the Harvard professor and member of the Massachusetts delegation, telephoned McGovern headquarters to report that White was not acceptable to that delegation. Of all the delegations, Massachusetts' was the most anti-Establishment, even antiparty. It was led by the fire-and-brimstone Jesuit Congressman Robert Drinan.

It is hard to believe that White was dropped—and dropped instantly—on the basis of that one telephone call from Galbraith. But dropped he was: McGovern called White and expressed his regrets. By then, the petitions required for nominating White had been completed. They were on Rick Stearns's desk and they had to be put aside. It was 3 P.M. now, only an hour to go until the deadline for coming up with a name—*somebody's* name.

Viorst reports that "from the original list of prospects [excluding White now, of course] McGovern dropped one name because of a wife's drinking problem, a second because of an impending divorce fight, a third because of objections from early supporters. Sargent Shriver was disqualified because he was out of the country and could not return in time for the convention." Viorst says McGovern strayed from the list to ask his good friend and Senate colleague Gaylord Nelson of Wisconsin to accept the nomination. Nelson turned it down, recommending instead *his* good friend and Senate colleague Tom Eagleton.

It was 3:25 when the conversation ended—35 minutes until the deadline. Reporters were gathered in the press room, awaiting the decision. Cameras were in place. The whole country was waiting. And still George McGovern didn't have a candidate.

Like Kevin White, Eagleton was young, Catholic, and reasonably liberal. He came from a large city (Saint Louis) in a reasonably sizable border state (Missouri). He was attractive and energetic, and he had a pretty wife and pretty kids. At the final minute, McGovern glanced at Gordon Weil's report. Viorst, alone, tells that story:

"Weil said that on several occasions in the sixties Eagleton had been hospitalized for what he publicly announced were stomach ailments. But Weil said that no knowledgeable observer of Missouri politics believed him, and that the consensus among reliable sources was that Eagleton had a problem with alcohol ingestion, though it was agreed he was not an alcoholic. Weil said he found no evidence whatever of psychiatric treatment. . . . In retrospect, Weil now says he believes that the story about Eagleton's incapacity to ingest alcohol was actually planted over the years by the Eagleton camp to throw investigators, like himself, off the track. He says he was sucked in by the 'cover story for the cover story.'. . . ."

At 3:40 P.M., McGovern called Tom Eagleton, waiting patiently and by now almost convinced that the call would never come. One of the persons in Eagleton's suite at the Ivanhoe Hotel, Viorst reports, was Bob Hardy, news director of KMOX in Saint Louis, who switched on his tape recorder almost as soon as the conversation began.

Only Eagleton's voice can be heard on the tape. "I'm flabbergasted, George. . . . Are you kidding me? . . . Why, ah, before you change your mind, I hastily accept. . . . Oh my God, George, well, I'm as pleased as I could be. I'm honored, I'm flattered and, uh, will do whatever I can. I hope I don't let you down. . . . Put Frank on. Thank you, George."

That part of the conversation lasted 32 seconds. It was followed by a conversation between Frank Mankiewicz and Eagleton, the conversation in which Mankiewicz insists he asked the crucial questions. Such as: Is there anything in your past we ought to know? Booze? Escapades? Embarrassments? To each of these questions, Mankiewicz told Viorst, Eagleton replied "No" or "Nothing at all." Eagleton says that Mankiewicz asked him only one question: "Are there any old skeletons rattling around in your closet?" The tape indicates that Mankiewicz and Eagleton talked for 29 seconds and there is nothing on it to suggest that the series of questions Mankiewicz says he asked were in fact asked—unless that happened later, when the tape was not running.

A little after 4 P.M., Mankiewicz appeared in the press room. Tom Eagleton, he announced, was George McGovern's choice. Rick Stearns crossed out Kevin White's name on the petitions and scratched in Eagleton's—illegal, but nobody cared.

FRIDAY, JULY 14

Eagleton, and just about everyone else the suddenly undisciplined delegates could think of, was nominated Thursday night, and the session caromed into the early hours of Friday. Eagleton gave his acceptance speech, and so did McGovern—for the benefit, it was said, of the folks in Guam.

McGovern, Eagleton, their wives, their advisors, their supporters returned to the Doral to celebrate the culmination of one of the longest political campaigns in American history. McGovern-Eagleton: the button makers were hard at work. At the party, Gordon Weil encountered Eagleton's principal aide, Douglas Bennet, who, on loan, had been the chief traveling advisor to Edmund Muskie in the twilight hours of his campaign. "Doug," Weil said, "we've been hearing these rumors . . ." There was no drinking problem, Bennet said, but Eagleton had been hospitalized for exhaustion. Johnson, in his account, says Bennet added, "and depression." Both accounts agree that Mankiewicz, when informed about Bennet's explanation, said that it could be cleared up when Eagleton appeared on CBS's "Face the Nation" on Sunday. "If they ask him about it, he'll just say that he's such a hell of a scrapper that, in 1960, he campaigned himself right into the hospital."

I don't suppose there was a reporter in Miami Beach who didn't hear some Eagleton gossip. I heard it and we tried to check it out. A member of our staff, Michael Putney, had worked in Missouri and he had known Tom Eagleton and, in fact, had covered some of his campaigns. Putney told us that Eagleton did not have a drinking problem but that, like almost everyone else in Jefferson City, Missouri's dull, remote little capital, he had been known to take an extra one for the road. Once, Putney recalled, a hotel manager had to ask Eagleton to keep his voice down. But that was it.

In our profile of Eagleton, we reported that Eagleton was a tough and almost inexhaustible campaigner. He was all of that. Our profile, like so many others, reflected the thought that Eagleton was a pretty good choice.

McGovern and Eagleton both flew out of Miami Friday, McGovern for home in Washington, Eagleton to keep a speaking engagement in Kansas City. They were not to see each other for another week.

Hart and Mankiewicz stayed on in Miami Beach, to iron out some details and then to head, with their wives, for the Virgin Islands and a few days of rest. McGovern, it was expected, would vacation at the Sylvan Lake Lodge in western South Dakota, deep in the Black Hills, near Mount Rushmore and not far from Little Big Horn, scene of Custer's last stand. Dick Dougherty, McGovern's press secretary, said it would be pretty much a real vacation and that little news could be expected from it. Only the regulars assigned to cover McGovern for the duration signed up to go to South Dakota with the candidate.

At about 3 P.M. Friday, Bennet put in a phone call to Mankiewicz. Viorst says the conversation went this way: "Frank, that technique we talked about last night, it won't work." "Why not, Doug?" "Well, it turns out Eagleton was hospitalized not once but twice." He wasn't just exhausted either; he was "kind of depressed." Mankiewicz told Viorst it was at that point that he first felt a tremor of anxiety. All that came of it, though, was an agreement that Eagleton and Mankiewicz should talk by telephone Saturday night. On that note, Hart and Mankiewicz headed for the islands.

SATURDAY, JULY 15

Eagleton returned from Kansas City to his home in the luxurious Spring Hill development, just off Massachusetts Avenue in suburban Montgomery County, Saturday night. He and his staff, plus—according to Haynes Johnson—two members of McGovern's staff, began a meeting that included discussion of how he would handle the health issue the next day on "Face the Nation."

Then, almost at midnight, Eagleton placed a call to Mankiewicz in the Virgin Islands. Mankiewicz and Hart were staying at the home of Henry Kimelman, a key fund raiser for McGovern. Viorst says Eagleton wanted to talk in generalities because he feared the line might be tapped. Johnson says the idea of talking in a kind of code was Mankiewicz's. In either event, both agree that the key question was asked by Mankiewicz and it went this way:

"Let us assume, Senator, that the FBI and the White House have all your medical records from Barnes and Mayo. Let's say the President and Chuck Colson [Charles W. Colson, a White House political advisor] are poring over them. What are they looking at? What words do they see?" According to Johnson, Eagleton answered, "Exhaustion, probably depression, maybe melancholy." According to Viorst, "Depression, exhaustion, melancholy."

Despite mounting apprehension, Hart and Mankiewicz sat tight. They were simply too depleted, too exhausted to leave the islands. Mankiewicz told Johnson: "Gary and I were worried and I think if we'd been in better shape we'd have come straight back to Washington. But it was so great being down there and we'd only been there such a short time."

SUNDAY, JULY 16

"Face the Nation" was no problem; Eagleton wasn't asked about personal problems. According to Johnson (but missing from Viorst's account), Hart and Mankiewicz talked to Eagleton Sunday afternoon. More probing questions were asked this time, and Mankiewicz told Johnson he learned then, for the first time, that Eagleton had been hospitalized twice. (Viorst, of course, says Mankiewicz learned of the second hospitalization from Bennet on Friday.) It may have been that same day that the two men called McGovern, now settled in at his vacation cottage in South Dakota. "We told him that what we found out was he got tired and had to go in the hospital for a rest and apparently—at least on the surface—there is not much to it," Hart recalled to Johnson.

MONDAY, JULY 17

That morning, Hart called his office in Washington to talk to his secretary, Marcia Johnston. Just routine: collect the messages for him, see what was happening. "Oh," Hart's secretary said, almost as an afterthought, "we got a crazy call at the switchboard that was taken down by a volunteer before I came in this morning." The volunteer—never identified—had written a note. The note said that the caller already had told the Knight newspapers about Eagleton's medical record, including the fact that he had received electric shock therapy.

The Knight papers did receive such a call on Monday. The call came into the *Detroit Free Press* and the anonymous man making the call asked for John Knight, who is owner of the chain. Instead, he was put through to John S. Knight III, a grandson and an editorial writer. Knight took some notes and told the "very nervous" caller to come up with details that could be checked out by reporters. Two days later, he did just that.

He also called back to McGovern headquarters in Washington and gave the same details to an assistant to Mankiewicz. Armed with the additional information, Mankiewicz and Hart set up a meeting with Eagleton Thursday morning. Then, they thought, they would finally get at the truth.

Now the Knight newspapers were on to the story. *Time* magazine also had some suspicions and even our old friends at Bill Loeb's *Manchester Union Leader* supposedly were alerted.

Out in South Dakota, though, reporters knew nothing. It was almost idyllic. One night, after dinner in the old lodge, McGovern's staff and the press joined in song.

"The candidate stood easily among them," William Greider reported later in the *Post,* "not demanding to be the center of attention like so many politicians. McGovern sang softly himself while his research man, John Holum, played guitar. . . . The Rev. Walter Fauntroy, the black preacher-politician from the District of Columbia, sang in his high tenor of that serene biblical promise: 'There Is a Balm in Gilead.' "

During that first week, McGovern "went horseback riding, wearing a silk ascot and looking only slightly more at ease than some of

the mounted reporters and staff aides who followed him up the trail.
. . . The next day, he airily signed a photograph which showed his
profile alongside the four presidential faces carved on Mount Rushmore—'From George McGovern, the fifth man.' "

"Everyone was loose," Greider wrote. "The hoard of reporters
and TV crews were camped about eight miles away at the Hi Ho
Motel in Custer, probably to give the nominee some privacy. But each
evening, they would gather at the Sylvan Lake Lodge to mingle freely
with the man and his staff, to share the grand view of Harney's Peak
and the 'hail storms,' a pioneer drink served in mason jars."

THURSDAY, JULY 20

Eagleton and Bennet and Mankiewicz and Hart met for breakfast
in the Senate dining room, at which time, Eagleton later insisted, he
told the full story. McGovern's two principal advisers learned, finally,
that Eagleton had been hospitalized *three* times; that treatment included shock therapy on two of those occasions, and that he still took
medication at home (according to Johnson) or that he still spoke to a
psychiatrist (according to Viorst).

"He was very vague on the question of restraints and the degree
to which his family was involved in his commitment," Hart told Johnson. Mankiewicz and Hart both pressed Eagleton about those medical
records. Mankiewicz believed Eagleton agreed then to make them
available. Bennet says no such agreement was made. Viorst wrote that
Eagleton, at the conclusion of the meeting, volunteered, "rather con-
tritely," to get off the ticket "if that was what McGovern wanted."
Mankiewicz and Hart did not respond to that, but they did agree that
Eagleton and McGovern should meet and talk it out as soon as possible.

They could have done it that very day—because McGovern had
flown in from South Dakota to vote for a minimum-wage bill. In fact,
the two men saw each other on the Senate floor and talked briefly—
but not, incredibly, about the problem that would soon destroy them
both.

FRIDAY, JULY 21

On the flight back to South Dakota, Mankiewicz and Hart finally told McGovern everything they knew. The private meeting on the plane was also attended by Mrs. McGovern, one of her husband's principal advisors. Viorst says that McGovern "seemed undisturbed, outwardly at least, by the news. He certainly gave no sign of grasping the report's implication for the campaign," even though Hart outlined to him the procedures for choosing a new running mate. Haynes Johnson, in his account, implied McGovern immediately grasped the significance of the report. "Everybody agreed that at the least it was a matter that deserved extremely serious thought and consideration and judgment—and that the implications were still not too clear."

According to Johnson, Mankiewicz argued strongly that Eagleton should be dropped. Hart, reverting to his legal training, told McGovern he had "a judiciary duty"—to assure himself "that Tom Eagleton was sound enough to be President of the United States." Hart also argued that McGovern would have to talk to Eagleton's doctors and see his medical records to properly carry out his "judiciary duty."

By then, four people knew "that a potentially fatal problem had dealt them a stunning blow"—George and Eleanor McGovern and Mankiewicz and Hart.

SATURDAY, JULY 22

But reporters from the Knight newspapers had been digging, trying to pin down the information they'd been given by their anonymous tipster, who had, it will be remembered, called their paper in Detroit on July 17. Clark Hoyt, from the Washington bureau, had done most of the reporting, and by now he was convinced there was almost enough in it to go with. On Saturday night, he and his bureau chief, Robert S. Boyd, arrived in Custer to lay what they had learned before McGovern's principal advisors. It was close to midnight when Boyd knocked on the door of Mankiewicz's cabin—but Mankiewicz wasn't alone; inside with him were Fred Dutton, a political specialist, and Jean Westwood, the new chairperson of the party. Boyd said the matter was urgent, and he wanted to talk to Mankiewicz alone. A meeting was set up for ten o'clock the following morning.

SUNDAY, JULY 23

Mankiewicz listened carefully to what the two Knight reporters had to say, never revealing that he knew more than they. Boyd and Hoyt "had come up with a very incoherent and largely unpublishable memo full of rumors and unsubstantiated material—but a memo that was clearly on the right track," Mankiewicz told Haynes Johnson. The "real crusher" in the memo "was a passage . . . that had quotation marks around it, as if it had been taken from a hospital record. It said that Tom Eagleton had been treated with electro-shock therapy at Barnes Hospital in St. Louis for, and this was the part that was quoted, 'severe manic depressive psychosis with suicidal tendencies.' And that," Mankiewicz said, "scared me."

Mankiewicz is one of the great dramatic actors of our time, and he turned it all on now. He appealed to the Knight reporters' patriotism. He promised them news breaks. He stalled and he fudged. One way or another, Boyd and Hoyt agreed to delay the publication of their findings. They lost the story, right there in Frank Mankiewicz's cabin.

That night, according to Johnson, Mankiewicz met George and Eleanor McGovern privately. "I remember that night I called him 'George,' which I had vowed I would not do during the campaign." The thrust of his advice: "Let's get rid of this guy."

Earlier in the day, Mankiewicz had been in touch with some of Eagleton's aides, trying again to get them to bring the medical records to South Dakota. It was Mankiewicz's impression that the records would be delivered by Eagleton personally, when he arrived in South Dakota Monday night. Eagleton's aides always have insisted no such binding agreement was ever reached.

TUESDAY, JULY 25

Tom and Barbara Eagleton, who had arrived at the lodge at midnight on Monday, met George and Eleanor McGovern early Tuesday morning for breakfast. No one else was there, not a single advisor on either side. Nor were the medical records there; no one would ever see those records. Yet, the decision was made at breakfast that Eagleton would remain on the ticket. Moreover, McGovern and Eagleton agreed that Eagleton's medical history would be revealed at a press conference—that very same morning. "We literally reached out our arms in compassion to him," Eleanor McGovern has said.

Johnson is harshly critical of McGovern's conduct. "Certainly," he wrote, "this was not the kind of session that Churchill recalled so vividly"—when 20 or more decision-makers were gathered and when Harry Hopkins would rap out "a deadly question." McGovern, at the moment of his greatest crisis, turned to no one. Viorst is more sympathetic. "McGovern assuredly made [his decision] not just out of a sense of expediency. He made it also out of consideration for Eagleton's future, a philosophical aversion to political concealment, and a sincere conviction that, whatever his history, Tom Eagleton would be a no greater or lesser risk to the country than any other man in possession of the awesome powers of the Presidency."

That's all very nice, but I'll stick with Johnson. McGovern needed all the tough advice he could get, and he refused to invite it. He made his decision without the facts to support it—he still didn't know what was in those medical records. "Suicidal tendencies?" He didn't know.

The advisors were called in after the decision was made—and handed a fait accompli. Mankiewicz, according to Viorst, "suspected strongly that his man had been had."

Mankiewicz and others argued that the press conference could at least be put off for a few days. No use. McGovern, and Eagleton, wanted to get it over with. The press conference began, even as Mankiewicz was on the telephone to Gary Hart back in Washington. Hart was incredulous. "Stop it! Stop it!" he shouted to Mankiewicz, according to Viorst. "It's too late," Mankiewicz replied.

And so, at last, the entire country—the whole world—knew that, in Norton Kay's words, Tom Eagleton had been in the nut house. Within hours, Eagleton, his wife, and his staff were on their way to the Rapid City airport. Mankiewicz insisted that Boyd and Hoyt ride in the Eagletons' car—their consolation prize for losing the biggest story of the Democratic campaign.

"For one fleeting period" (Johnson) . . . "at that moment" (Viorst), McGovern and Eagleton believed the worst was behind them. "We were agreed," an Eagleton aide told Johnson, "that electroshock treatment six years ago wasn't all that crucial, but we didn't see the press going wild. We just didn't calculate on the overkill of the press."

It was Eagleton's intention to ignore his own revelations—and to start talking about the issues in the campaign. But reporters wouldn't let him off that easily. Everywhere he went, the same questions kept popping up. In Los Angeles, NBC's Bob Abernathy began an interview by asking Eagleton if he "should" be President. "Is there anything about your physical or emotional condition that would even slightly affect your ability to do the job?" Eagleton tried to change the subject, but Abernathy was relentless. It was that way everywhere.

McGovern remained in South Dakota, "isolated" at the lodge, according to Viorst, "having for his principal advisors Fred Dutton and Dick Dougherty, both of whom were relative newcomers to the campaign." Mankiewicz had gone back to Washington.

There was no more group singing in the lodge at night. "Now," William Greider wrote in the *Post*, "McGovern dines privately in cabin 22 with his family, no more mingling with the reporters and tourists. . . . The press has his cabin staked out and the Secret Service agents keep them at a distance. What began as a vacation, mixed with political activity, is ending as an ordeal."

WEDNESDAY, JULY 26

One reporter, Carl Leubsdorf of the AP, managed to catch McGovern off guard and privately. McGovern had just finished playing tennis and he gave Leubsdorf a ride back to the lodge. From his conversation with McGovern, Leubsdorf wrote a story that said the candidate was "waiting and watching" to see what would happen.

When McGovern saw Leubsdorf's story, he got mad. He drafted a short statement. "I am 1,000 per cent for Tom Eagleton and have no intention of dropping him from the ticket," he said. The quotation, soon to take on a life almost of its own, appeared in the fifth paragraph of Douglas E. Kneeland's lead story in *The New York Times;* it appeared in the 24th paragraph, on page 17, of George Lardner Jr.'s story that had started on Page One in the *Washington Post.*

But the pressure to drop Eagleton was building—and reporters in South Dakota knew it, because the telegrams to McGovern were being received on a Western Union ticker in the press room. Eagleton, campaigning on the West Coast and in Hawaii, admitted he made a "mistake" in failing to tell McGovern about his medical record. Again and again, though, he refused to release the records. He said he was going to "educate" the country about the kind of personal depression he had been treated for.

McGovern himself was constantly on the telephone, and all the news he was getting was bad. To top it off, Mankiewicz learned late Wednesday that columnist Jack Anderson was preparing to write that Eagleton had been cited half a dozen times for drunken and reckless driving. Mankiewicz tried desperately to dissuade him, but Anderson would have none of it.

THURSDAY, JULY 27

Instead of writing the story in his column, Anderson decided to broadcast it on his daily radio show. "Eagleton has steadfastly denied any alcoholism, but we have now located photostats of half a dozen arrests for drunken and reckless driving," he reported Thursday morning. He had no photostats or any other kind of proof, it turned out. What he did have was a tip from True Davis, who ran a bank in Washington owned by Tony Boyle's Mine Workers and who had been defeated by Eagleton in the Democratic primary in Missouri in 1968. Davis, it turned out, also had tried to tip Maxine Cheshire, gossip columnist for the *Washington Post,* to the story. Later, in a column on the *Post*'s editorial page, Mrs. Cheshire said she worked for 10 hours Thursday trying to nail that story down. The more checking she did, the more obvious it became that it was Anderson who was reckless. "The Anderson charges, in short," she wrote, "are a classic example of precisely the sort of reporting practices that have brought the news business under increasing attack." Amen, Mrs. Cheshire.

Eagleton, campaigning in Hawaii, called a press conference to denounce Anderson's report as a "damnable lie."

Anderson is the nation's most celebrated investigative reporter, his credentials certified with a Pulitzer Prize. But he and all investigative reporters constantly face a deadly peril—the temptation to rush a story into print (or on the air) before all the facts are checked out. Investigative reporting is a little like fox hunting; in the thrill and competition of the chase, the hunters abandon caution and good common sense. They will jump any fence, leap any stream to catch the damn fox.

Some veteran investigative reporters become both cynical and self-righteous, at the same time. They can do no wrong; their victims can do no right. I've seen it happen, and it can be terrifying. Investigative reporting, sometimes, is the dark corner of American journalism.

It did not really matter that Anderson's charges were false. The damage was done. McGovern's people became even less enamored of Eagleton, and Eagleton became even more convinced that he should fight to stay on the ticket. It was now, he seemed to think, a matter of honor. A feeling of bitterness was growing, helped not at all by the fact that the candidates were thousands of miles apart.

If Anderson and his investigative colleagues represent the muscle of American journalism, the editorial writers—in principle, at least—represent the brains. Having been mugged by Jack Anderson, McGovern was now lectured by journalism's professors.

The *New York Post* weighed in first; Wednesday afternoon, it called upon McGovern to dump Eagleton. The *Washington Post* rendered its verdict Thursday morning. It was the same: get rid of Eagleton. "For it is our judgment," the *Post* said, "that the burden imposed by the presence of Senator Eagleton on the ticket can only be removed by his withdrawal as a candidate." *The New York Times,* the next morning, said "it would be a helpful contribution not only to the McGovern candidacy but to the health of the American political process for Senator Eagleton to retire from the field and permit the Presidential contest to be decided wholly on the issues."

Editorial writers tend to be very big on "issues." Yet, when Mc-

Govern took their advice, he became the "issue," and that, presumably, is not what the editorial writers had in mind.

FRIDAY, JULY 28

George McGovern went table-hopping Friday night in the dining room of the Sylvan Lake Lodge, in Custer, South Dakota. Reporters who were there are not likely ever to forget it, for George McGovern, the man of candor and decency, was trying to tell them that Tom Eagleton's fate was now in Tom Eagleton's own hands. It was a signal that McGovern was reassessing his own position— and that his support for Eagleton was no longer in the range of 1,000 percent. Under attack by party leaders and the nation's editorial writers, McGovern was retreating.

Earlier in the day, McGovern had called Eagleton in San Francisco, to say that he was "under pressure" and that he might have to reconsider his position. He read Eagleton a section from a speech he planned to deliver Saturday night in Aberdeen, South Dakota. The key words: "I do not know how it will come out, but I do know that it gets darkest just before the stars come out. So I ask for your prayers and your patience for Senator Eagleton and me while we deliberate on the proper course ahead."

It was on Friday too that McGovern had summoned Jules Witcover of the *Los Angeles Times* to cabin 22 for a little chat. Witcover, when he arrived, thought it would all be for background; McGovern made it clear that what he said he wanted to see in print, but not directly attributed to him.

What he wanted to see in print—in California, where Eagleton was campaigning—was a straight message that McGovern was convinced now that his running mate must withdraw.

"At the same time," Witcover wrote in his story that appeared on Page One of the *Times* the following day, "McGovern is determined to leave the initiative to Eagleton, convinced that when his running mate, just back from campaigning in Hawaii, takes his own soundings he will reach the same conclusion."

McGovern, Witcover said, "has been deep in thought and actively assessing the political impact of the Eagleton disclosure." Witcover talked to McGovern for almost two hours, gaining extraordinary insights that he could discuss in his story only in the most guarded terms.

"What that assessment has brought to him has been strong sentiment from political leaders and public supporters alike that Eagleton's continued presence on the ticket can only damage McGovern's own chances of defeating President Nixon in November.

"The reaction has been negative on two primary counts.

"—On Eagleton's failure to advise McGovern of his medical record when offered the Vice-presidential nomination.

"—Uncertainty in the public mind about Eagleton's ability to function in the Presidency, if necessary.

"McGovern is said not to have any question about the second point, but is fearful that the first touches on a basic aspect of the McGovern candidacy—credibility."

Speaking of credibility . . .

Back in Washington the same day, Frank Mankiewicz, McGovern's national political director, was telling *The New York Times*'s Johnny Apple, in a private interview, that "the decision to keep Tom Eagleton was made on Tuesday and will not change." Mankiewicz heatedly denied that either he or Hart was pressuring McGovern to drop Eagleton. All along, of course, Mankiewicz had been demanding Eagleton's replacement.

In his lead, in what was the major *New York Times* story on Saturday, Apple said that McGovern "was authoritatively reported today [Friday] to be resisting pressures from his staff to drop" Eagleton.

Just the opposite of what Witcover was reporting in the major newspaper at the other end of the country. Witcover had a slight advantage—he *knew,* because McGovern, personally, had told him so. Did Mankiewicz know about McGovern's interview with Witcover? Maybe not—the lines of communication all through this business were medieval—but Mankiewicz knew he was lying to *The New York Times.* He knew that.

What we had was McGovern signaling Eagleton he ought to step down, through the vehicle of Witcover and the *Los Angeles*

Times (and the table-hopping), while Mankiewicz, through Apple and *The New York Times,* was signaling that Eagleton was going to stay. It was baroque.

As we pieced together these and other events, we began to have growing doubts about the vaunted efficiency of the McGovern staff. More important, we became increasingly cynical about George Mc-Govern himself. The campaign was wrecked in Custer, South Dakota, and so was the relationship between us and him.

SATURDAY, JULY 29

Somehow, Tom Eagleton seemed to be missing all the signals. Saturday morning, in San Francisco, he told reporters he had just talked by telephone with McGovern. "All he said was, 'I'm for you 1,000 percent,'" not just once, but three times, Eagleton noted.

McGovern, at the same time, was telling reporters about that "pressure" he was under and saying he and Eagleton hoped to resolve the problem at a face-to-face meeting in Washington Monday night.

All day Saturday, Gary Hart kept trying to do something about Eagleton's medical records. He still wanted to see them, and he was still getting nowhere. Additionally, Hart was trying to cancel Eagleton's scheduled appearance on "Face the Nation" at noon on Sunday. According to Milton Viorst, Hart talked to Eagleton aide Doug Bennet three times Friday night and Saturday. Bennet told Viorst "that Hart led him to believe that McGovern was satisfied with the way events were moving, when in retrospect he [Bennet] is convinced McGovern had already made up his mind to get rid of Eagleton. Hart deceived him, Bennet says, into believing the question was still open. Hart answers that, on the contrary, he was not seeking to reassure Bennet at all. . . ."

SUNDAY, JULY 30

Sunday is a big day for interview shows—"Meet the Press," the father of them all, and "Face the Nation" and "Issues and Answers."

We watch them, even if the voters don't. This Sunday, two of the shows—"Face the Nation" and "Meet the Press"—made some history.

Eagleton appeared on "Face the Nation" (CBS) and the panel, incredibly, included Jack Anderson. For a moment, it appeared that Anderson was prepared to apologize for his unfounded charge that Eagleton had been cited for drunken driving. "I do owe you an apology," he said. "I've always told my reporters, Senator, that a fact doesn't become a fact for our column until we can prove it." Graciously, Eagleton accepted the apology—prematurely, it turned out. Anderson said he just couldn't "retract the story completely. I cannot do that," he said, "my conscience won't allow me to. . . ." Anderson, it seems, still felt the story might be true. It wasn't; it isn't; it never was, and Anderson's performance, as the *Washington Post* commented in an editorial, "has been a reckless and wholly regrettable excursion into the worst kind of 'journalism.' "

CBS's George Herman hardly distinguished himself either. Descending to a new low in bad taste, he commented that Eagleton was trembling and perspiring, proving, I suppose, that Eagleton was truly a serious case. "The lights in the studio are less than cool," Eagleton responded. ". . . But I feel very comfortable and relaxed. In fact, I'd like to go on for another half hour."

In between Anderson's posturing and Herman's probing, Eagleton managed to say it was his firm intention to stay on the ticket. But, if McGovern asked him to withdraw,"Well, I'd have to weigh it ."

If there was any doubt that McGovern wanted him to do just that, it was resolved on the rival "Meet the Press," which had, as guests, Jean Westwood, the party's chairman, and Basil A. Paterson, the vice-chairman. "I am convinced," Mrs. Westwood said, "that it would be the noble thing for Tom Eagleton to do to step down." Paterson, thereafter, joined Mrs. Westwood in "urging" Eagleton to quit.

After the show, Paterson told reporters that neither he nor Mrs. Westwood had talked to McGovern. In fact, Mrs. Westwood talked to him fifteen minutes before the program went on the air. Mankiewicz told the *Post*'s Haynes Johnson, "Jean had called George and said what I think I ought to say is such and such, and he said, 'Fine, why don't you say that.' "

Doug Bennet told Viorst that the Eagleton people, watching the show, were stunned. Bennet called the performance of Mrs. Westwood —"and, by implication, of McGovern—a terrible betrayal that came without any warning."

Having given, finally, a signal that no one could miss, Mrs. Westwood joined McGovern and his principal advisors at McGovern's home for a climactic meeting on how to dump Eagleton and how to find someone to replace him.

Hart, once again, stressed the fact that McGovern hadn't seen the medical records. Without them, he said, McGovern had no choice but to drop Eagleton. Mankiewicz, the foxiest of McGovern's advisors, speculated that the Republicans had the records, or might soon get them—and that they would use them. Everyone, in fact, agreed (including Eleanor McGovern, who was tougher than most): Eagleton was through. Mrs. Westwood outlined the steps that would have to be taken to convene the National Committee at a "mini-convention" and choose a successor.

According to Haynes Johnson, participants at the meeting also agreed that the successor to Eagleton should be someone with experience, party standing, and a proven record. People like Muskie and Humphrey, never considered before, could now enter the running. But who, now, would want it? Nobody asked that question.

MONDAY, JULY 31

Eagleton had been nominated in the early hours of Friday, July 14. Now, almost three weeks later, finally, *finally* it would end. First, though, George McGovern had to fly from Washington to Baton Rouge to attend the funeral of Senator Allen Ellender. When he returned to Washington, he went to the capitol and met in the Marble Room, off the Senate floor, with Eagleton and Senator Gaylord Nelson of Wisconsin, who had been so instrumental in getting Eagleton on the ticket.

Eagleton had not gone to the funeral. He kept himself busy during the day talking to Nelson and to other friends. He also talked to two of his doctors, who agreed that they would talk to McGovern later in the day.

"By all reports," Viorst says, "the meeting was extremely civilized. Eagleton presented the evidence he had assembled—crowd response, polls, favorable mail—to justify his contention that he remained an asset to the ticket." McGovern was adamant: "I think your being on the ticket will divert attention from the real issues," he said (according to Johnson). "In light of that," Eagleton replied, "why don't I step aside?"

Eagleton also placed the calls to the two doctors, and McGovern, out of everyone's hearing, spoke to both of them. McGovern has never revealed what he learned, but it is ironic that he finally learned something *after* the final decision to surgically remove Eagleton had been made.

The meeting lasted about two hours, after which the two principals went to their offices to shave and clean up. It was 9 P.M. when they returned to the Capitol to play out the final drama in front of the cameras and the reporters. As Johnson notes, "It was exactly three weeks since the gavel had pounded on the podium in Miami Beach opening the Democratic National Convention."

"I have consistently supported Senator Eagleton," McGovern began. But—but—"the public debate over Senator Eagleton's past medical history continues to divert attention from the great national issues that need to be discussed. . . . Therefore, we have jointly agreed that the best course is for Senator Eagleton to step aside. . . ."

"He and I are jointly in agreement," Eagleton said. "But I will not divide the Democratic Party, which already has too many divisions. . . . My conscience is clear . . . my spirits are high. . . . This is definitely not my last press conference, and Tom Eagleton is going to be around for a long, long time."

The final note to Haynes Johnson's series is telling.

"As the people were leaving that emotional press conference, Frank Mankiewicz encountered a young girl he had known during Robert Kennedy's 1968 campaign. 'Well, you lost me forever,' she said bitterly."

McGovern lost columnist Garry Wills forever too. In what may be the most devastating lead paragraph of the year, he wrote:

"Senator McGovern is giving sanctity a bad name. While he blessed the crowds with his right hand, his left one was holding Eagleton's head under water till the thrashing stopped. We'll all know we're in trouble if he should be elected and take his oath of office by saying he supports the Constitution 1,000 per cent."*

The "mini-convention" chose Sargent Shriver as Eagleton's replacement, but it didn't make much difference. For us and for them, it was finished.

Down Pennsylvania Avenue, in the White House, Richard Nixon may have rationed himself a smile.

---

* After reading that column, McGovern summoned Wills to his office, wanting to explain. Wills was not impressed. ". . . behind the politician," he asked later, "could there be—nothing?"

15

Nixon

In the first eight months of 1972, while the Democrats were tearing themselves apart, what was Richard Nixon doing?

Well, on January 2, he told Dan Rather during a nationally televised interview that he would not engage in "partisan political activities" until after the Republican convention in August—and then he went to Peking on February 21, looked at the Great Wall on February 24 ("It *is* a great wall," he said), visited the Forbidden City on February 25, journeyed to Hangchow on the twenty-sixth, flew to Shanghai on the twenty-seventh, and came home on the twenty-eighth, called on Congress March 17 to impose a moratorium on forced school busing, stopped the peace talks on March 24, launched air and naval attacks on North Vietnam April 6, sent the B-52s over Hanoi and Haiphong on April 10, ordered the port of Haiphong mined on May 8, arrived in Moscow on May 22, signed an arms treaty with Russia on the twenty-sixth, addressed the Russian people on their national television May 28, visited Iran on May 30 and Poland the next day, returned home on June 1 and addressed the Congress and the nation

30 minutes after his plane landed, denied on June 22 that the White House was involved in the Watergate break-in, revealed on July 8 that the United States would sell $750,000,000 worth of grain to Russia, said on July 22 that Spiro Agnew would be his running mate, played golf with George Meany on July 28, sent Kissinger to Paris on August 15 and to Saigon on August 17, vetoed a $30.5 billion appropriation for Health, Education, and Welfare on August 16, and accepted his party's nomination for President on August 22.

That's what he was doing.

It is difficult to separate the President as President from the President as Candidate. It is impossible to make the distinction when the reelection strategy is to run the President as President. Re-Elect the President, the bumper stickers said, in keeping with a strategy that was agreed upon as far back as early 1971 or even late 1970. The lessons learned from the off-year elections in 1970 had something to do with it. Nixon, in John Mitchell's words, ran for sheriff in one of the most awesomely demagogic campaigns of our time. The more Nixon and Agnew campaigned, it seemed, the better the Democrats running for Senate, House, and for governor looked. It was a disaster for Nixon and the Republicans.

This time, it was decided (and "the triad"—Nixon, Mitchell, and H. R. Haldeman—did the deciding), there would be no mistakes. No more amateurism: this would be a professional campaign and it would employ all the techniques that some Republicans had been borrowing from business and industry for the better part of a decade. Highly sophisticated polling, and lots of it; computers, for all kinds of purposes; direct mail; telephone banks; radio and television advertising, *good* advertising this time, not the stuff Joe McGinniss wrote about back in 1968. The Democratic contenders would be watched, analyzed, and every word they'd ever uttered would be filed away, to be retrieved electronically when the time came. And money, this campaign would have more money than any other campaign in American history, gobs of it, more than anyone could even spend. And, finally, security; the likes of Joe McGinniss wouldn't infiltrate *this* campaign. On that point, it seems clear, the triad was almost paranoid.

In retrospect, it is curious that we paid so little attention to these purely political efforts. Jeb Stuart Magruder, who ran Nixon's political committee in the early days, says he expected close scrutiny of all his activities, but he was amazed to find hardly anyone came around to see him. "Bob Semple [of *The New York Times*] was supposed to cover what we were doing and he kept saying he'd be around to see us, but we never saw much of him," Magruder recalls. "I guess, in the rush of covering the President, he didn't have much time for us."

Magruder would have us believe that the doors were always open and that he and his colleagues were eager to see us and tell us everything. He is somewhat disingenuous. The Committee for the Re-Election of the President (CREEP, it was christened by jealous rivals at the Republican National Committee) did open for business at 1701 Pennsylvania Avenue, just 150 yards from the White House, on May 1, 1971.* From the outset, though, it was a quiet, orderly place staffed by technicians—and a few saboteurs—who were not all that eager to talk to the press. We had to make appointments and we were required to spell out in some detail the nature of our business to the committee's press officer. If that was satisfactory, a day and an hour would be set for the appointment. We were then escorted from the reception room through a door that had to be unlocked to the office of the person with whom the appointment had been made. It was very formal and highly structured and nobody was going to give away any secrets. The presence of the ubiquitous shredding machines was evidence enough of that.

The first story I read about CREEP's activities, written by Broder and Oberdorfer, appeared in the *Washington Post* on June 13, 1971. "A '72 Head Start for Nixon," the headline on Page One said.

"Despite the President's repeated statements that he is not wearing his politician's hat this year," Broder and Oberdorfer wrote, "a squad of his men have slipped into their campaign togs and are scouting the battlefield for the army of Nixon workers that will be mobilized in the coming year.

"Some are lining up the financing for the 1972 race. Others are systematically canvassing public pollsters, television producers and advertising executives, computer experts and direct-mail specialists for the latest 'new politics' techniques that may be of use.

"Still others are touring the country, checking the degree of pre-

* In the beginning, CREEP stood for Citizens for the Re-Election of the President, in democratic deference to Republicans who might think someone else could be nominated.

paredness or unpreparedness of state and local Republican organizations and lining up prospects to head the 'Nixon committees' that will burgeon early next year to supplement the work of the regular GOP units."

Broder and Oberdorfer said this much early activity was "extraordinary," and so it was—but the single most important rule of the new politics is: start early. Broder and Oberdorfer also said the situation for Nixon was extraordinary. They wrote:

"Seventeen months before the election, the public opinion polls show Mr. Nixon vulnerable to defeat by any of the three most likely Democratic challengers. An insurgency is threatening in the Republican Party. Eleven million new voters in the 18-to-21 age group, not Mr. Nixon's area of political strength, have been enfranchised. And a third party and perhaps even a fourth party are in prospect. In short, 1972 shapes up as a wild and woolly presidential election year."

Broder and Oberdorfer found that the planning for the campaign had been divided three ways—the national committee, CREEP, and a small group of White House aides—resulting in a lack of overall coordination that was criticized by some people the two reporters interviewed. There was no "game plan," the critics said. The President's agents "don't seem to have any idea but sitting back and waiting for the Democrats to make the mistakes that will let Nixon win again."

The President's "agents" saw things from a different perspective. "We want to build our campaign slowly," one of them said, "and keep the President's public role limited. Last time, we peaked on September 5 in Chicago [at the first big rally] and we went downhill from there. Next time, we want to peak on November 7."

In fact, there was a "game plan" and it had been charted by the triad late in 1970 or early in 1971, but it was so closely guarded by Nixon, Mitchell, and Haldeman that not many people knew about it. Witcover of the *Los Angeles Times* says the essential element of the game plan came from a book Haldeman had been reading—*Working with Roosevelt,* by Sam Rosenman, a speechwriter for FDR. "His book," Witcover wrote, "discussed how Roosevelt delayed campaigning until the final three weeks in his fourth term campaign of 1944."* Roosevelt had a war to win and he ran as the President. Nixon had a war to end and he was going to run as the President.

There was never any doubt about "overall coordination" of the campaign. "From the outset," Witcover says, "it was determined that a separate campaign organization would be established to re-elect President Nixon, with Mitchell leaving the Justice Department at the appropriate time to head it.

"The separate re-election organization was necessary, Mitchell says now, 'basically so that you could control the campaign for the Presidency, and the fact that based on our own experiences in '68, many of the Republican organizations around the country are just paper organizations.' "

All along, too, members of the triad had anticipated a tough, even a nasty campaign and, in such a struggle, they did not plan to finish second. Late in 1970, Senator Robert Dole of Kansas, a partisan's partisan, was chosen as national chairman and instructed to carry the fight to the enemy. He took the assignment seriously. The attack strategy, which ultimately led to the arrest of the Watergate Seven, was a part of the game plan, always.

Polling responsibility was given to Robert Teeter of Market-Opinion Research Co., in Detroit. Teeter's firm broke new ground in political polling back in 1962, when it first went to work for George Romney, specializing in such things as "semantic differentials" and identification of ticket-splitters; its expertise is probably unmatched.

Peter Dailey, a West Coast advertising executive, was hired to run The November Group, an in-house agency assembled just for the campaign. Dailey began putting the agency together in December of 1971 —60 employes in New York, 10 in Washington. The buffoons Joe McGinniss wrote about in *The Selling of the President* in 1968 did not join the team in 1972.

Sixteen task forces were established to look into various aspects of the campaign, all reporting back to Magruder, who passed their recommendations on to the triad. Speechwriters Patrick Buchanan and

---

* A better example, closer at hand, was Eisenhower's 1956 campaign, when he visited only 15 states and delivered only a handful of speeches. His surrogate that year was . . . Richard Nixon.

William Safire were assigned, Witcover reported, "to write 'scenarios' analyzing the prospective fortunes of the leading Democratic hopefuls —how each could get the nomination, including Kennedy."

On March 6, 1972, the *Wall Street Journal,* in an article by James P. Gannon, outlined more of CREEP's activities.

Ken Rietz and 12 aides were working on a get-out-the-youth vote for Nixon with a Young Voters for the President Committee. "The accent will be on non-college youth, presumably more favorably inclined toward the President than are students."

Webster B. Todd, Jr., and his staff were organizing the elderly for Nixon.

Clayton B. Yuetter was organizing Farm Families for the President.

Alex Armendariz was "working up maps showing the biggest pockets of Spanish-speaking voters." Paul R. Jones, a Peace Corps veteran, was looking for ways to get as much as 18 percent of the black vote. Nixon, he said, got 12 percent in 1968.

And almost everyone at CREEP and in the White House was taking a covetous look at working-class, urban Roman Catholics. The President himself did his part, which included a visit to Poland that was not entirely statecraft. He also flew to Philadelphia to tell a crowd of priests and nuns that he was "irrevocably committed" to preserving parochial schools. He wrote a highly publicized letter to New York's Terence Cardinal Cooke in support of a church-led drive to repeal New York's liberal abortion law. He rejected his own population commission's recommendation in favor of liberalized abortion.

Such Presidential positions are "completely parallel to the Catholic point of view," the Reverend Martin J. McManus, Catholic-strategy consultant to the Republican National Committee, told the *Wall Street Journal.* "On issues of this kind," he said, "it's only a matter of making sure that ethnic people are aware of them."

On January 27, Secretary of Commerce Maurice H. Stans resigned to become, in Nixon's words, "chancellor of the exchequer of one of the two major parties."

On February 15, Attorney General John Mitchell resigned to manage the reelection campaign. It was pro forma; as attorney general, he had been managing the campaign.

So, everything was moving pretty much on schedule. One problem was Nixon's insistence that San Diego be the site of the truncated three-day Republican convention. San Diego isn't big enough—yet—for a national convention; worse, the town fathers didn't really want the Republicans. The decision was made, almost at the last moment, to switch the convention to Miami Beach. Magruder insists the reason for the decision was security. Miami Beach was safer. Whatever the reasons, the decision to switch made sense.

Another was the choice of a running mate. Some of us speculated that Agnew would be dumped, a theory that gained considerable currency after Agnew, in Williamsburg, Virginia, told reporters in what was supposed to be an off-the-record session that he didn't think much of the President's decision to travel to China. On July 22, though, Nixon announced that Agnew would be retained. That removed any chance for drama at the convention.

An unexpected problem was Martha Mitchell, the campaign manager's troubled and outspoken wife. On June 22 and again on June 25, she telephoned the UPI's Helen Thomas in a state of nervous collapse. During the second call, she said she was going to leave her husband until such time as "he decides to leave the President's reelection campaign." She talked darkly about security guards pulling her telephone off the wall and jabbing her in the "behind" with a needle.

Given the choice—Nixon or Martha—Mitchell chose his wife. He resigned July 1 and was replaced as campaign manager by Clark MacGregor, a personable former congressman who ran against Hubert Humphrey for the Senate in 1970, and lost.

The timing is interesting. Five days before Mrs. Mitchell's first telephone call, at about 1:50 A.M. Saturday, July 17, five men were arrested inside the offices of the Democratic National Committee in the Watergate complex. One of them was James W. McCord, Jr., former CIA agent, president of his own security firm, and "security coordinator" for CREEP and a consultant for the Republican National Committee. Later, police arrested two more men—E. Howard Hunt, a consultant on the White House staff, at least through the end of March, and G. Gordon Liddy, counsel for CREEP's finance committee.

"We want to emphasize," Mitchell said, "that this man [McCord] and the other people involved were not operating in our behalf or with our consent." Nixon's press secretary, Ronald L. Ziegler, dismissed the incident as "a third-rate burglary attempt" and warned that "certain elements may try to stretch this beyond what it is."

In the beginning, the White House denied that Hunt was involved in the break-in, despite the fact that the police had seized address books from the men arrested in the Watergate that contained his name. Police also seized an unmailed envelope that contained a check made out to the Lakewood Country Club in suburban Rockville that was signed by Hunt.

The White House conceded, though, that Hunt had worked in 1971 and 1972 for Charles W. Colson, special counsel to the President. That raised eyebrows all over town, for Colson is a very special counselor, known, in Witcover's words, as the Administration's "dirty tricks man." He began presiding as early as May over a committee that became known as "the attack group" and met each morning at 9:15 in his office in the White House.

On June 22, the President was asked about Watergate and he said the raid "has no place whatever in our electoral process." He also said "the White House has had no involvement whatever in this particular incident."

Well, Hunt had worked at the White House. He reported to Colson and Colson presumably reported to H. R. Haldeman, and no one was closer to the President than Haldeman. Later, the *Washington Post*'s Bob Woodward and Carl Bernstein would report that Watergate was just part of a much broader pattern of sabotage and espionage that reached deeply into the White House.

But their reporting—one of the great journalistic feats of our time—was not taken very seriously, until weeks after the election was over when the breathtaking dimensions of the scandal finally penetrated the nation's conscience.

Watergate did become a secondary issue in the general election, and we will return to it then. For now, though, it is reasonable to say that most voters were neither shocked nor angry about it. It was called the Watergate "caper" and that said something about the way it was perceived.

If most of us greeted White House denials of complicity in Watergate with something akin to cynicism, it is because we have learned not to trust everything the President, Mitchell, Haldeman, Ziegler, and all the rest tell us.

It is interesting to go back to the questionnaire I mailed to political writers in early 1972. In it, I asked each of them to sketch, in a few words, how he (or she) felt about Nixon and the leading Democrats. The responses on Nixon are especially illuminating. Out of 44 completed questionnaires, only three, maybe four, describe Nixon in words that could be interpreted as flattering. For example:

—"a square, works hard, rounded political skills."
—"superb but cold political professional."
—"astute, able, experienced."
—"a very competent political technician."

That's the positive stuff. Now, more typically, some of the rest:

—"plastic man, shrewd, ruthless."
—"mean, dark impulses."
—"aimless, improvisational, uninspirational."
—"shrewd, calculating, lacks moral conviction."
—"superb manipulator, hollow man."
—"slippery."
—"cunning, professional, but cracks under pressure."
—"modest ability, banal, contemptuous of people's intelligence."
—"basically a bad man."
—"deceptive, lies, plays games, dull."
—"cold, lacks moral leadership."
—"tricky."
—"tricky."
—"tricky."

Finally, from a veteran:

—"weathervane, hard to love, but beneficial to have man in White House with no fixed beliefs."

Nobody in the Washington press corps, it seems, loves Richard Nixon; even his stoutest defenders (of whom a representative sample responded to the questionnaire) recognize his personality defects. We do believe he is cold and ruthless.

The American people may not love Richard Nixon either—but

one supposes their thoughts about him have been somewhat more positive than ours. In our defense, though, we know him better than most people.

For Richard Nixon, we are a problem. He knows what we think about him and, quite naturally, he is resentful. Members of the White House staff—total loyalists—take a further step: it is hardly an exaggeration to say that some of them, some of the time, hate us. It is no wonder that the conflict between the press and this President is so furious.

It is curious, then, to discover that not very much of this animosity shows up in what we write. Leafing through 50 columns by more than a dozen of the best-known commentators in Washington, I can find only three that might be *personally* offensive to Nixon, Haldeman, and the rest. Two were written by Tom Wicker, one by Garry Wills.

In August we went back to Miami Beach to watch Richard Nixon accept his party's nomination for a second term at a convention most of us thought was cold and ruthless itself.

"What do you think?" a wealthy woman attending the convention asked Diane Shah of the *National Observer.* "They don't look too bad, do they? Certainly better than the Democrats. Did you see them on TV? It was disgusting." Then, sizing up her own party's delegates, she asked: "Do you suppose *they* look any better on TV?"

To most Americans, and to many of us, surely they did. The *Washington Post,* taking another survey, found the Republican delegates were wealthier, older, and more conservative than the Democrats. They ate lettuce and they responded warmly to Pat, Tricia, Julie, Mamie, Pat Boone, Charlton Heston, John Wayne, Art Linkletter, Jimmy Stewart, Frank Sinatra, and Sammy Davis, Jr.

According to Ms. Shah, everybody (except the demonstrators out in the streets) had a nice time. A member of the Cabinet, she reported, joined an evening cruise aboard a chartered yacht and had an especially nice time with one of the hostesses chartered for the evening.

The best story of the convention was dropped in the in-basket of the British Broadcasting Corp. It was the script for Tuesday evening's session, marking the exact time when Nixon would be nominated and the exact time when the impromptu demonstration in his honor would begin (and end). And just what John Wayne would say while introducing a film, *Richard Nixon—Portrait of a President.*

"8:54–8:55   INTRODUCTION OF DOCUMENTARY FILM
(2 Minutes)   ON PRESIDENT.

Mr. Wayne: . . . Don't get settled down for a speech, cause speech-making isn't my business. . . .

I came here because I believe with all my heart that Richard Nixon is the right man in the right office at the right time. And the same goes for Spiro Agnew. I've made enough pictures in my life to know the good guys from the bad guys, and I've sure seen enough in these last couple of years to know that Richard Nixon is a *good* guy. A *great* President and a *good* guy. . . .

Later, the script read:

10:33–10:45   DEMONSTRATION—"NIXON NOW"
(12 Minutes)
                 (Balloon Drop)

When the press office realized its mistake, representatives attempted to get the script back from BBC. Mrs. Kit Wisdom tried to grab it from the hands of Christopher Drake of the BBC. "Naughty, naughty," said Drake. Within minutes Dan Rather had a copy and was gleefully reading it down on the floor, as the cameras rolled (or whatever it is TV cameras do).

The only serious questions facing the convention involved seating a delegate from New Mexico pledged to Paul N. McCloskey, Jr., and acting upon a proposal that would have given the big, populous states a larger share of the delegates at the 1976 convention. The delegates voted against McCloskey and against the big, populous states.

The ragamuffin demonstrators out in the streets tried to interrupt the proceedings—one thousand two hundred of them were arrested the final two nights—but got nowhere. Delegates were a trifle discomfited the final night when a wisp or two of tear gas seeped into the hall itself. It was probably the last stand of the counterculture army and it ended with the crash of a few garbage cans tossed and rolled along Collins Avenue, followed by the footsteps of the troops, running like hell for the safety of Flamingo Park. Abbie Hoffman watched most of it on television in the working quarters we shared with the *Wall Street Journal*. So much for the revolution.

In his acceptance speech, which, in the official text, runs to 109 paragraphs, Nixon devoted 70 paragraphs to blistering attacks on McGovern (who is not named) and his policies. He condemned quotas as a means for ending discrimination, he condemned those (unnamed) who don't believe in the American system, attacked "our opponents" for their belief in the "politics of paternalism," declared that giving $1,000 to every American "insults the intelligence of the American people," estimated "they" have proposed legislation which would add 82,000,000 people to the welfare rolls, implied that his opponents are not dedicated to reducing the nation's crime rate, suggested that unnamed persons were ready to "betray our allies and destroy respect for the United States all over the world," declared that the "real heroes" were the 2,500,000 Americans "who chose to serve their country rather than desert it," predicted that "our opponents," if elected, would reduce the United States to "the second strongest nation in the world," and ridiculed "those who believe that we can entrust the security of America to the goodwill of our adversaries."

Summing up, the President said:

"Let us reject, therefore, the policies of those who whine and whimper about our frustrations and call us to turn inward. Let us not turn away from greatness."

Here was Richard Nixon, leader of the free world, the man who had gone to China and Russia, the President trying to end the most divisive war in our history—and he gave (we thought) a second-rate, partisan speech like that.

As much as anything else, I think, Nixon's acceptance speech demonstrates what it is about that man in the White House that troubles us.

It isn't a question of ideology; it could hardly be that, because we don't believe Nixon is any more ideological than we are. Basically, it's personal.

part five

US and ★ THEM

16

The Campaign

Would you vote for a Presidential candidate who:

Is a shy, introspective man to whom social chitchat appears to be as much fun as having his teeth drilled? . . . whose taste runs to movies like *Sound of Music* or *Patton?*

Who wants to end the Vietnam war, reluctantly accepts the necessity of wage and price controls, favors some sort of guaranteed income. . . ?

Who grew up in a family of modest means that struggled through the Depression, went to a small, obscure college, and became imbued with the Protestant work ethic? Who combined luck, ambition, and the iron-butt capacity for hard, grinding work with an apparently exclusive interest in politics to become his party's candidate for President? And who wants that office so badly that he has publicly embraced his former political enemies in a bid for their help and has trimmed his position on crucial and well-publicized issues?

The answer is: Yes. . . . You don't have any other choice. . . . Because Richard Nixon and George McGovern share all the attributes and attitudes listed above.

—James R. Dickenson,
The National Observer.

Not a dime's worth of difference, eh?

A dime's worth, surely. Yet, Dickenson has a point—Nixon and McGovern do share a great many attitudes and attributes, and maybe that was one of McGovern's real problems, created in no small part by us, because, in the beginning, we thought he was a little special.

Did this man want the office so badly he would publicly embrace his former political enemies? Damn right he did. On August 22, the second day of the Republican National Convention, McGovern and Shriver ate steak at the LBJ ranch in Texas. Afterward, McGovern said: "I asked for the President's advice . . . and he generously gave it and we were deeply impressed, both by his concern and by his wisdom. I'm proud to have the endorsement of President Johnson and I shall continue to treasure his friendship and counsel in the course of the campaign."

McGovern's kids once chanted, "Hey, hey, LBJ, how many kids did you kill today?"

What about that, George McGovern?

"My youthful supporters and others who are backing me understand that we cannot have 100 percent agreement with everyone who is backing my candidacy. I may not agree 100 percent with my campus supporters, but I think they're mature enough, intelligent enough to recognize there's a sharp difference between the things I stand for and what Richard Nixon stands for."

Earlier in the month, he sat down with Hubert Humphrey and offered him the nomination for Vice-president—Humphrey, Johnson's Vice-president; Humphrey, the candidate in California who had said McGovern was wrong on the war, wrong on Israel, wrong on unemployment compensation, wrong on labor law, wrong on welfare reform, and downright dangerous on national security.

He offered the nomination to Kennedy, Ribicoff, Nelson, Askew, and Muskie, too, and they all turned it down. Shriver was seventh on the list. He accepted.

On August 17, McGovern flatly denied a UPI report that Pierre Salinger had gone to Paris as his personal emissary to talk to the North Vietnamese. "I know nothing of any such report," he told reporters clutching UPI wire copy in their hands in Springfield, Illinois. "There's no truth in it at all."

A few hours later, after talking to Salinger in New York on the phone, he issued a statement that said:

"At my request he [Salinger] met with members of the North

Vietnamese delegation in Paris. The only purpose of the discussion was to determine if any change had occurred which would permit the return of the prisoners prior to the end of hostility. Mr. Salinger found no change in the publicly stated position of Hanoi. . . ."

On August 29, McGovern went to New York's Wall Street, where he laid to rest forever his controversial $1,000-a-person income redistribution plan. In its place he substituted what *The New York Times*'s James Naughton called "a more traditional liberal approach of guaranteed jobs and assured annual incomes for those who cannot work and have no money." It would be paid for by phasing out $22 billion in tax preferences for wealthy corporations and individuals.

Hobart Rowen, the *Washington Post*'s business editor, said McGovern's program was "comparable in some respects to President Nixon's Family Assistance program."

"What is good for business is essential for the country," McGovern told members of the New York Society of Security Analysts.

To soothe them further, he pledged to nominate Representative Wilbur D. Mills of Arkansas, chairman of the House Ways and Means Committee, as his secretary of treasury. Aides said McGovern had talked to Mills about the nomination. Mills said it was news to him. Then, thinking back a little harder, he said he did recall a telephone conversation in which McGovern mentioned it in passing. "I guess I didn't take it too seriously," he told the *Washington Post.*

Richard Dougherty, McGovern's press secretary, argued in a column in *Newsweek* after the election was over that the practice of journalism as an art is "primitively simple" and that one of its requirements "when a new figure appears on stage, is a label, preferably accurate but not necessarily. Following the Eagleton affair, he wrote, we came up with one for McGovern—'the sneaky bumbler.'

"What a label and what a running story. You could dictate it to monkeys."

So, "with the candidate bearing the stamp of the Sneaky Bumbler, every McGovern *faux pas,* every revision of policy—and there were actually few of either—helped to confirm the sneaky bit. Every squabble within the campaign organization—all small potatoes compared with getting your people arrested for burglary and wire tapping —reinforced the bumbler's image.

". . . the man who conducted the most open campaign in history, who answered questions put to him on everything from vivisection to philately, who took his message to the people daily over the long weeks, got for his troubles a reputation for dubious credibility. The man who captured the Democratic nomination with a superb self-made organization, who subsequently raised $20-odd million and wound up his campaign in the black, who made peace with Richard Daley and Lyndon Baines Johnson and anybody else who would listen to him, this man came across to the voters as a fellow of questionable competence."

Dougherty thinks it's very ironic.

It's all our fault, he says. And it shouldn't have happened, "when you consider that members of the press—far from conspiring to do him in—grieved every day as, responding to the dictates of their art, they pressed the knife a little deeper."

What we offered to the voters, Dougherty says, was a "caricature of the real man, and most reporters knew it. I would guess that 90 percent of the news people who covered McGovern voted for him."

Dougherty is wrong, I think, on a couple of points. One, we didn't think McGovern was a sneaky bumbler. We thought he was a forth-right bumbler. Second, most of us didn't "grieve" for him. Those days, by the time the campaign began, were far behind us. We believed he was, in fact, a bumbler, and we were appalled by the ineptitude of his campaign. By the time it was over, members of his staff were openly appalled too.

We want our candidates to be professionals. That's first. Then it helps if they're nice guys, by our own definition. Most of us liked McGovern—we thought he was a decent enough fellow, most of the time, and especially in his personal relationships—but we concluded he was not a professional.

Think of the bumbles.

His welfare-income distribution program was a bumble. He scuttled it himself.

His alternate defense budget was a bumble. In February of 1973, meeting with reporters for breakfast, he conceded that the most that could be cut from the defense budget was $7 to $9 billion, not the $32 billion he had proposed back in January of 1972. He had discovered after the election that manpower costs were fixed and climbing and nothing could be done about them. Even some of us knew that.

The selection of a running mate at the very last moment was a bumble. His staff—*somebody*—should have been thinking about a Vice-president. Saying he was behind Eagleton 1,000 percent was a bumble. Never seeing the medical records or talking to the doctors (until it was too late) was a bumble. Publicly offering the nomination to six different men, only to be rejected by all of them, was not only a bumble, it was humiliating.

The Salinger business was a bumble. Larry O'Brien was constantly in the middle of one bumble or another.

That McGovern saw fit to open his campaign on notes of explanation, amplification, and clarification was, if not a bumble, at least curious. The campaign opened officially on Labor Day in Ohio (not Cadillac Square in Detroit, the traditional site), and McGovern spent a good part of his time explaining—again—his positions on abortion, marijuana, and amnesty. The day before, he had flown to Hilton Head, South Carolina, to talk to 13 Democratic governors from southern and border states. That excursion hardly represented a lead from strength.

At the same time, Nixon was making what seemed to us to be a more effective appeal to labor. On September 3, *The New York Times* reported that the Nixon Administration had decided to scrap the Philadelphia Plan, "a highly publicized effort to place minorities in skilled jobs at federally assisted construction projects in Philadelphia through a system of quotas." The building-trades union—personified by Peter J. Brennan, later to become Nixon's secretary of Labor—strongly opposed the plan.

That afternoon, Nixon issued a Labor Day statement in San Clemente—highly demagogic, but effective. "We believe," he said, "it is wrong for someone on welfare to receive more than someone who works." Just who believed it is right wasn't made clear.

"We believe," he went on, "that a person's ability and ambition should determine his income, and that his income should not be redistributed by Government or *restricted by some quota system* [italics mine]."

Once again, he never mentioned McGovern by name—but it was

McGovern he had in mind when he said that the nation's "traditional values" were under challenge. "We are faced this year," he said, "with the choice between the 'work ethic' that built this nation's character— and the new 'welfare ethic' that could cause that American character to weaken. . . .

"The work ethic builds strong people.

"The welfare ethic breeds weak people.

"This year, you are not only going to choose the kind of leadership you want, you are going to decide what people Americans will be."

He went on from there to condemn "involuntary busing of school children" and he concluded by implying that a vote for McGovern was a vote for a nation that was "militarily weak and morally soft."

It was on Labor Day too that George Meany, AFL-CIO president, appeared on CBS's "Face the Nation" and declared that McGovern was an "apologist for the communist world."

This was what Nixon (and his allies) were doing and saying on Labor Day. McGovern was defending his positions on amnesty, abortion, and marijuana. A few days earlier, the Gallup Poll reported McGovern was trailing by 34 points. Nothing, in those early days, indicated to us that the gap would soon be narrowed.

It wasn't just how we felt; McGovern seemed to feel the same way. The *Post*'s William Greider wrote this lead:

"BARBERTON, Ohio, Sept. 4—The underdog presidential campaign of George McGovern was resumed today—and the candidate compared it frankly to the crippled B-24 bomber which he piloted home safely in World War II.

"We were scared, we were ready to bail out," McGovern said. "But I gave this order: 'Resume your stations, we're going to bring this plane home.'

". . . the South Dakota senator acknowledged that his own candidacy has taken a lot of damaging flak in recent weeks.

" 'We have had a difficult and trying time, during the weeks since the Democratic nomination,' McGovern said. 'But I say to you and to workers across America, to Democrats who may be a little fainthearted and to those who are anxious to fight on: Resume your stations— we're going to bring America home!' "

On September 7, the White House, continuing to orchestrate its appeal to working Americans, declared that Nixon, if reelected, "will not" propose any tax increases during his second term, barring major unforeseen developments.

Hobart Rowen, the *Post*'s financial editor whose son is married to one of McGovern's daughters, wrote that the White House pledge struck him as incredible. That prompted John D. Ehrlichman, Nixon's domestic counselor, to write the *Post* suggesting that each of Rowen's stories and columns be labeled "with a short, italicized paragraph showing he is an advisor to the senator and he has a family relationship to him."

The *Post*'s response, in an editorial, was predictably apoplectic.

"Perhaps," it said, "this is just a temporary condition brought on by Mr. Ehrlichman's reading too many installments of the Watergate mystery series; but it does him little credit to suggest that Mr. Hobart Rowen . . . is controlled in his judgments of the administration's economic policy by the fact that five years ago his son, then 22 years old, married Senator McGovern's 21-year-old daughter. And it does him even less credit to identify Mr. Rowen as an 'adviser' to Mr. Mc-Govern, a charge so patently untrue to be hardly worth denying. . . . Mr. Rowen has been fully as critical of some of Mr. McGovern's economic policies. . . ."

That, I think, gives some indication of the relationship between us and the people at the White House. We were being watched and we would be attacked as the occasion required, despite the much-publicized cease-fire declared by Nixon just before the Republican convention.

McGovern pushed on, preaching party regularity (in tandem with Ted Kennedy, who became his occasional traveling companion) and assaying a little demagoguery himself. He developed the "martini and bologna" theme. It went this way:

"A businessman can deduct the price of his $20 martini lunch and you help pay for it, but a working man can't even deduct the price of his bologna sandwich."

His aides, when queried on it, admitted there was nothing in McGovern's tax proposals that would eliminate the expense-account lunch. They explained that business would have to watch all its expenses more carefully once McGovern closed the tax loopholes and that would result in "internal discipline" that "would take out the bloat itself."

Bemused reporters arranged one day to serve McGovern a martini and a bologna sandwich. "You guys are spoiling my indignation," he laughed, and then he discovered the martini was only water. "Cheapskates!" he shouted.

Which serves to underline a more serious point: we were traveling with McGovern, night and day, week in and week out. Just as Dick Dougherty wrote, we had the opportunity to ask him about everything from vivisection to philately. Beyond that, his advisors were more available and more candid than any Presidential traveling staff I have ever known. Toward the end of the campaign, the advisors sometimes seemed to be lining up to talk to reporters like Naughton of the *Times,* Greider of the *Post,* Clymer of the *Sun,* Stout of *Newsweek,* and Fischer of *Time.* By then, though, they were trying to knife some other advisor in the back. Early on, they were just being helpful.

McGovern sensed the problem from the beginning. In New York on September 15, he charged Nixon was "hiding" because he was "afraid of the people." Later, he would say again and again that Nixon was "sitting in the White House on top of his Gallup Poll." He said it so many times that Gallup Poll became one word, "Gallupoll."

McGovern made the charge on the fifteenth because Herbert G. Klein, Nixon's director of communications, had been in town earlier in the day and had said at a news conference that McGovern was using Senator Kennedy as a "crutch."

"What did Mr. Klein think he was?" McGovern asked. "Is he campaigning for the Presidency? Instead of sending Mr. Klein up here, the President ought to come himself." Kennedy added that Nixon ought to accept McGovern's challenge for a debate, reminding reporters that brother John had debated him in 1960.

It was no coincidence Klein showed up in New York that morning. He was one of some 35 "surrogates" chosen to campaign in the President's place. "The surrogates," Lou Cannon wrote in the *Post* on September 1, "are an essential part of the re-election strategy, which is based on the belief that the President must perform as President rather than climbing down on the hustings for overt political combat with Sen. McGovern."

The list included two women, one black, one Spanish-speaking American, 11 Cabinet members, four agency heads, two members of the White House staff (Klein and Harry Dent), 10 senators, five governors, three members of the House, and one mayor. Helping out too were members of the President's family, and, of course, Spiro Agnew. Richard Kleindienst, the Attorney General charged with investigating Watergate, was one of the surrogates. By a curious logic, though, Defense Secretary Laird and Secretary of State Rogers were not surrogates; they aren't supposed to be partisans, it was explained.

"The whole operation," Witcover wrote in the *Los Angeles Times,* "was carefully coordinated. The attack group would select a theme; the surrogates would carry it around the country. . . . Though the surrogates got short shrift from the national press corps, they tapped a rich lode of publicity in the local press all over the country. Not only that, but they were routed into cities on the heels of the beleaguered McGovern or in advance of him. And later on, both.

"What evolved came to be called 'the sandwich theory.' Says one attack group member: 'At first we would send a surrogate in after McGovern. But after a while that was unsatisfactory. In effect, we were giving him a second ride. The surrogate would answer what he [McGovern] had said, but in so doing he would have to repeat McGovern's points. So we switched. We would send a surrogate into Philadelphia on Tuesday so that local papers would be full of his attacks on McGovern when McGovern came in on Wednesday. We placed him on the defensive locally.' Then, another surrogate would come in Wednesday night or Thursday morning to clean up."

Ben H. Bagdikian, the press critic, points up an even more ominous result of the surrogate effort. In an article in the *Columbia Journalism Review,* he said:

"Two major changes in day-to-day campaign reporting reflected wounds inflicted by the Administration's war on the press. One was the tendency of both print and broadcast media, when under fire for real or imagined unfairness, to retreat to mathematical editing: to give each major side the same play and same space each day, regardless of the inherent news value of each story. 'Twinning'—equal side-by-side Democratic and Republican daily campaign stories—was the rule in 1972. An uncoerced editor might decide that when George McGovern made a major statement on defense policy which was denounced rhetorically by a Republican campaign official that they were not of equal interest. But twinning made them so in the public eye, demeaning the President's opponent by seeming to accord him the same status as Administration underlings [meaning the surrogates]."

The second major change, according to Bagdikian, was the media's failure to take Nixon to task editorially and reportorially for his refusal "to make himself available for questioning." When this happened in earlier years, Bagdikian says, the press "pounded away."

The "news system" failed because "it was biased in favor of the President [93 percent of the nation's dailies endorsed Nixon, according to compilations by *Editor & Publisher*] or lazy or fearful of the operatives at 1600 Pennsylvania Ave., the Attorney General's Anti-Trust Division, the FBI, the Internal Revenue Service, the Securities and Exchange Commission, or the effect of government denunciation on a newspaper's standing in the stock market."

Bagdikian also deplored "a visible return to the sweeping orders for entire newspaper chains to back the President." He gave a stunning example of how it was done. The Scripps-Howard chain sent a teletyped editorial to all of its newspapers. It began:

"Fours years ago when the editors of (Name Your Paper) . . . met in editorial conference, they decided. . . ."

Surely some papers, the TV networks, and most TV and radio stations were worried about the Administration's campaign against the media, and maybe they retreated in the face of that threat. As often as not, though, I suspect the major reasons were laziness and puzzlement.

Irvin Horowitz, assistant national news editor of *The New York Times* and coordinator of the paper's election coverage, acknowledged to Witcover "that he never resolved the problem of balance in the one-candidate campaign. 'I worried about it for three months. . . . In the interests of fairness and balance you wanted to do something. But when you have one campaign completely open and the other side tighter than a clam, what do you do?' "

The *Chicago Sun-Times*'s Tom Littlewood made a valid point. "They kept telling us that Nixon might be out campaigning momentarily," he told Witcover. "First they used Congress as a reason for not going out, then there were the vetoes. There was always the possibility of tomorrow, and it kept us immobilized." Littlewood, of course, was being put on: Nixon never intended to go out—or, at least, not go out very often.

Even if he had, would it have made much difference? Highly questionable, says Witcover. "Even in 1968, when he was not the President, Nixon as a campaigner was carefully insulated from press interrogation. On the few occasions when he did campaign [in 1972] it was much more a presidential extravaganza than a candidate's tour. When he visited Westchester County, New York, one day in October, there were seven press buses in the motorcade. Most reporters, out of view, had to rely on a play-by-play account piped into the buses from a pool reporter riding behind Nixon's car."

I can second that notion. I traveled with Nixon to Atlanta in the middle of October, and it was the same thing. I wrote:

"Seven wire-service reporters, 37 newspaper reporters, six magazine reporters, 25 radio and television commentators and producers, and 28 engineers and electricians traveled with the Presidential party to Atlanta, and followed behind the President in a motorcade, which ended in a blinding storm of confetti at the Regency-Hyatt House Hotel. All of us were rushed to the press room, where we were joined by 25 or 30 more reporters and commentators and engineers from the local newspapers and radio and television stations.

"Ron Ziegler [Nixon's press secretary] was ready for us.

"He told us he knew some reporters had deadlines to meet. So, just to be helpful, he or some of his friends had picked up estimates of the crowd.

"One of the estimates came from Police Captain M. A. Hornsby, who said 700,000 to 1,000,000 people had seen the President. Later, upon further reflection, Ziegler gave the capain's estimate at 'more than 700,000.'

"J. D. Cooper, a battalion chief in the Fire Department, estimated the crowd at 'more than 500,000,' Ziegler told us. It was 'clearly' a record for Atlanta, the chief said, according to Ziegler.

"That evening, on the prime news shows, the nation was told that 500,000 or more people had welcomed Nixon to Atlanta. The next morning, most newspapers repeated that crowd estimate.

"And it's absolute nonsense.

"The crowd couldn't have been more than 100,000, and I think I can prove it.

"The mass of people greeting the President assembled along 15 blocks (probably closer to 12, I think, but let's give Ziegler the benefit of the doubt). I called the city's Public Works Department and a Mr. McDonald told me each block is about 400 feet long.

"So let's say that 400 people lined the curb of each 400-foot-long block, shoulder to shoulder and hip to hip. I doubt people can squeeze in that closely, but let's say they can. And they were lined up about five rows deep, on each side of the street. That means—400 times 5 times 2—that there were 4,000 people in each block. Multiply that by the 15 blocks involved, and you get 60,000 people.

"The side streets were closed off and people filled them in too. So add another 10,000. And there were some people who watched the motorcade before it got downtown. Add another 10,000.

"You can do some subtracting if you want to—because a minority of the people who came to see Nixon were for McGovern. They booed and hissed and chanted and jeered. . . .

"So, in an act of charity, I'm willing to say that 75,000 people turned out to welcome Richard Nixon to Atlanta. That's a little bit larger than the crowd that turned out to welcome George McGovern to Boston the week before.

"Ziegler set us up, and then Nixon finished us off. In a speech to some 250 supporters—piped into the press room to most of us—Nixon talked about the wonderful crowd he'd just seen.

" 'We have seen many very big crowds,' he said, modestly. 'We have seen some that are bigger. . . . However, I have never seen a bigger crowd in Atlanta. I understand it is the biggest crowd in Atlanta's history.'

"That's probably nonsense too. Old-timers recall that Nixon's crowd in Atlanta in 1960—12 years ago—was bigger. Nixon continued:

"'While there are some cities that are larger than Atlanta, and that would obviously account for a larger crowd in some places, I have never seen a crowd that has what I call a higher E.Q. We all hear about I.Q. That is very important. But E.Q. sometimes is even more important. That means Enthusiasm Quotient, and there was enthusiasm in that crowd.'

"Well, there was some enthusiasm. But all those high school bands—there must have been more than a dozen of them—were imported for the occasion. And all the confetti was coming from industrial vacuum cleaners operated by Nixon volunteers along the line of march.

"In his speech, Nixon did talk about other things—about busing (he's against it), about law and order (he's for it), about the Bible (he likes it), and about patriotism (it's an old-fashioned virtue).

"But this whole business of coming to Atlanta, it seems to me, was to demonstrate he can draw big crowds in the South—to prove to anyone who still doubts it that he will sweep the South next month.

"I don't doubt him. He'll do it. . . . The South is Nixon's, all of it.

"There are issues in this campaign, but Nixon isn't talking about them. It would be nice to know what he wants to do in his second term, but he's not telling. It would be nice to get some kind of valid explanation about this Watergate business, but no one's talking."

I concluded the column—bear with me—by suggesting the final trick up Nixon's sleeve might be a peace settlement; with it, I thought, he might carry everything but the District of Columbia.

"And what would Richard Nixon's final thoughts be then? Take that, *New York Times*. Take that, all of you who have ever said Nixon was dull and tricky and unprincipled and unscrupulous."

Even without a peace settlement, Nixon was heading for a great victory, I wrote. "He has pushed all the right buttons—to pull labor to his side, to woo the ethnics, to coddle the Catholics, to soothe the South. It has been a virtuoso performance.

"And here we sit on the sidelines—quibbling and nattering. But I think we should, because this is not a very good way to elect a President. The Presidency is not supposed to be a royal office. . . . There should be some kind of debate, even if it centers on Quemoy and Matsu.

"It's my impression we've allowed the Presidency to get away from us. The man and the office have become remote: I don't really sense Richard Nixon's *presence.* . . . In this campaign, there is no contest. It's 1 on 0, and 0 is winning. . . ."

That column, I'll stand on.

Bagdikian, at least, might have approved; he thought we should have "pounded away" at Nixon's refusal to make himself available. What else could we have done?

Investigate Watergate, I suppose.

"There was abundant evidence," Bagdikian says, "that the 'Watergate Affair' was an extraordinary and ominous story of major proportions. Serious men, including conservatives such as William F. Buckley, Jr., and U.S. Sen. Strom Thurmond, saw it as a dangerous corrosion of the American political system. There was little excuse for its not attracting massive press investigative and display attention." Besides, Bagdikian argues, "the story was in the classic tradition of cloak-and-dagger and cops-and-robbers. It exuded the odor of official corruption that sets conventional investigative and page 1 juices flowing. . . . But curiously, the allocation of fulltime journalistic investigation . . . was hardly lavish."

Bagdikian took a survey.

Out of 433 reporters employed by the 16 largest bureaus in Washington, fewer than 15 were assigned full time to Watergate. Newhouse, with 21 correspondents, assigned none. Gannett, with 12, assigned none. Copley, with seven, and the *Baltimore Sun,* with 13, had none. ABC and CBS didn't assign anyone, and NBC, the largest network bureau with 25 reporters, reported it assigned one to Watergate after the Republican convention.

The *Washington Post,* chief source for the original stories, assigned two reporters full time, backed up at various times by six others. The *Washington Star-News* assigned four full time. The *New York Times* buried the original burglary on page 50, got into the story late, and finally brought in Walter Rugaber from New York, with an assistant, full time. The *Los Angeles Times* assigned three reporters to the story; the *St. Louis Post-Dispatch* assigned two reporters full time and two part time, half of its eight-man bureau.

Time, with 19 reporters in Washington, had one working full time after the Republican convention. *Newsweek,* with 26 reporters, had one full time on the case. AP, the biggest bureau in town—65 reporters—assigned no one full time. Neither did UPI, with 51 reporters.

"It is possible," Bagdikian concludes, "that more man-hours of investigative journalism were put into the 1962 rumor (never confirmed) that John F. Kennedy had been secretly married in 1947 than were assigned to investigate the Watergate Affair."

Bagdikian made another survey.

He checked 30 newspapers representing 23 percent of American daily circulation to see how four major stories about Watergate were handled. The first story was the exclusive interview obtained by *Los Angeles Times* reporters Ronald Ostrow and Jack Nelson with Alfred C. Baldwin, one of the participants in the Watergate raid. The story was published in the *Times* on October 5, side by side with a verbatim taped account of Baldwin's recollections. The second story, written by Bob Woodward and Carl Bernstein of the *Washington Post,* alleged that Watergate was just part of a much larger campaign of espionage and sabotage. It appeared in the *Post* October 10. The third story was also written by Woodward and Bernstein; it connected H. R. Haldeman with the sabotage project. The fourth story studied was the White House denial of the Haldeman connection and its bitter denunciation of the *Washington Post* for alleging such a connection.

All of the stories were picked up by the AP and UPI and carried as well on the wires of the *Washington Post–Los Angeles Times* and *New York Times* services.

The results:

"There were 90 possibilities for publication of the three news breaks studied—30 papers times three stories. Of these opportunities, there were 31 failures to carry stories at all. Fourteen papers in the sample were listed by *Editor & Publisher* as having endorsed the President; 15 were listed as making no endorsement; one endorsed McGovern.

"Nixon-endorsing papers had 42 opportunities to print the stories but 52 percent of the time did not. The non-Nixon-endorsing papers . . . had 48 opportunities and only 23 percent failed to print the stories."

Papers endorsing Nixon put the stories on Page One only nine times. The non-Nixon papers put the stories on the front page 22 times.

The fourth story—the denial of the Haldeman connection from the White House—was carried by 11 of the 14 papers endorsing Nixon; two of them carried it on Page One. Thirteen of the 16 papers that did not endorse Nixon carried the denial story; six of them ran it on Page One.

"The most consistent and emphatic display of all the stories . . . was by the *Houston Chronicle,* an endorser of Nixon and a paper not always praised for professionalism." It ran every one of the stories, including the denial, on Page One.

Bagdikian's conclusion:

"The papers as a group, whether or not they endorsed Nixon, had a poor record of use and display of these stories—major events in the most ominous episode of high-level dirty politics in our history, occurring at a crucial time of national decision-making."

Bagdikian gives the *Washington Post* credit for turning up the most "significant findings"; lesser credit goes to *The New York Times, Time* magazine, and the *Los Angeles Times.*

Of all the networks, CBS alone gave serious coverage to Watergate. On two separate evenings, "CBS Evening News" with Walter Cronkite examined the case with the kind of detail and the allocation of time that is almost unprecedented in television news reporting. The first night—October 27—Cronkite began:

"At first it was called the Watergate caper—five men apparently caught in the act of burglarizing and bugging Democratic headquarters in Washington. But the episode grew steadily more sinister—no longer a caper, but the Watergate affair escalating finally into charges of a high level campaign of political sabotage and espionage apparently unparalleled in American history. . . ."

The reporter on the story was Daniel Schorr. He began by interviewing Alfred Baldwin, who, on October 10—17 days earlier—had told his story through the *Los Angeles Times.* ". . . I believed that we were working with the former Attorney General [John Mitchell] who was, or is, at the time he was in office, the top lawman in the United States," Baldwin told Schorr.

The report continued for almost 10 minutes, interspersed with comments like these, from Schorr, "So, though the indictments stopped at the seven, it was clear that there were links reaching into the White House and into the Nixon campaign organization," and, from Cronkite, "So far it has been White House policy to issue general denials, and to attack the *Washington Post,* which has made most of the serious allegations. The Administration has not, however, been willing to discuss in public and in detail any of the specific accusations by the nation's press reviewed here tonight."

Cronkite and the CBS reporters made their second report, concentrating on "the money behind the Watergate affair," four nights later, on October 31. Dan Rather hit hardest. "The President's men keep insisting that in our system everyone is innocent until proven guilty. They keep issuing general denials. They are depending upon that and silence to make the allegations go away."

For television it was strong stuff, even though the material was drawn from stories that already had appeared in newspapers and magazines. Predictably, it incensed the loyalists at the White House, who marked it down as still another example of the left-wing bias of television news.

The question Bagdikian asks is: Why wasn't there more investigation of Watergate by the networks and by the press? In part, I think I know the answer: because, it seemed to many of us, the *Washington Post* had a lock on the story. *The New York Times,* in its efforts to catch up, was desperate. At one point, the *Times* offered the White House almost unlimited space to tell its side of the Watergate story. "We just don't know if the *Post* has got anything or not," a *Times* reporter told a Nixon strategist. "We just can't prove anything. We believe there must be a reasonable explanation and we're willing to listen." The strategist said he'd think about it, and that's as far as it went. It wasn't until after the election, when investigative reporter

Seymour M. Hersh, who had exposed the My Lai massacre, was assigned to Watergate that the *Times* began to score.

It was a police story—the sources had to be cops, FBI men, criminal lawyers—and Washington news bureaus didn't have reporters that knew many people like that. The *Post,* as the town's premier local paper, did, and that's what made the difference.

We were all placed in an uncomfortable position: we had to accept the *Post's* judgment that there was a broad pattern of sabotage and espionage. The *Post* is one of the most readable and energetic newspapers in the world, but many of us have long felt that it is sometimes poorly edited and disorganized. That meant that some Washington reporters remained skeptical about some of the *Post's* reporting. That skepticism, as it turned out, was badly misplaced: the *Post's* investigation will become a classic in journalism. On May 1, 1973, press secretary Ronald Ziegler said, "I would apologize to the *Post* and to Mr. Woodward and Mr. Bernstein," the two young reporters responsible for most of the disclosures. Nixon himself, in his Watergate speech the night of April 30, 1973, praised "a vigorous, free press" for its role in exposing the Watergate scandal. Earlier that same day, he announced the resignations of Haldeman, John Ehrlichman, and Attorney General Richard Kleindienst. He fired his counsel, John W. Dean, III.

Bagdikian is right; we didn't work as hard on the Watergate story as we might have. There is no excuse for it. We can only say that other factors—distrust, jealousy, uncertainty—may have been more crucial than the broader questions Bagdikian raises.

To complete the CBS story, that network stepped out once again on the Cronkite show during the campaign. It examined in even more detail another scandal—the Russian grain deal, in which, it was thought, American grain dealers received windfall profits because they were given inside information. Unlike Watergate, though, the grain story never took hold.

NBC managed to outrage the White House just once, and that might have been largely unplanned. It happened the night of September 28 when Cassie Mackin appeared in a filmed report seen on "NBC Nightly News" with John Chancellor. Edwin Diamond, the press critic, described what happened in an article in *Columbia Journalism Review:*

"It looked like a typical item from the 'wind-in-the-hair' school of TV journalism: Mackin doing a 'standup' outside the hotel where President Nixon had spoken the night before, too late to make the network news program. But the script that accompanied the routine clips of Richard (and Pat) Nixon shaking hands, climbing into helicopters, and appearing at the fund-raising dinner was sharp and unequivocal.

"Mackin said that the Nixon campaign consists of 'speeches before closed audiences—invited guests only. . . .' She reported that the press was getting only glimpses of Nixon as he campaigned. Then she added:

" 'There is a serious question of whether President Nixon is setting up straw men by leaving the very strong impression that McGovern is making certain proposals which in fact he is not. . . .'

"The film cut to Richard Nixon speaking of 'some who believe' in defense budget cuts that 'would make the United States the second-strongest nation . . . with the second-strongest Army . . . with the second-strongest Air Force. . . .' Then back to Mackin: 'The President obviously meant McGovern's proposed defense budget, but his criticism never specified how the McGovern plan would weaken the country. On welfare, the President accuses McGovern of wanting to give those on welfare more than those who work—which is not true. On tax reform, the President says McGovern has called for "confiscation of wealth'—which is not true."

"It was," says Diamond, "a critical moment in NBC's coverage of the 1972 presidential campaign. Rather than merely amplifying a campaign attack, Cassie Mackin was offering a strong corrective—for NBC's audience of 10 million. Her gloss was too much for the men in the White House who monitor the media. NBC officials received three phone calls from Nixon Administration men protesting the Mackin item—the first call almost before the program's theme had faded."

It was a unique moment in TV journalism. Here was lovely little Cassie Mackin, blonde hair blowing in the wind, calling the President of the United States . . . a liar. On this one, I think I can see why the White House might have objected. This was editorial, and it wasn't labeled that way. NBC could have done two things—introduced Mackin's report for what it was (perfectly legitimate commentary) or asked her to handle it differently. For example, she had time to get McGovern or one of his aides to call the President a liar. I'm sure they would have cooperated.

A larger problem was that people who got their news only from the tube might not have known what McGovern's positions were on defense, taxes, or almost anything else. Bagdikian makes the telling point that, in 1972, "the most significant change in network behavior was the almost complete disappearance of prime-time political specials on issues between Labor Day and Election Day."

In 1960, for example, CBS gave four hours to the Nixon-Kennedy debates, plus three one-hour-long specials. In 1964, the network carried nine specials, most of them half-hours; in 1968, five specials. But in 1972 there were only two—"The Election Year" and another hour-long program called "Two Days to Go."

ABC ran no political specials at all. Diamond does not give a breakdown for NBC, but it ran two specials.

Bagdikian's final conclusion is grim:

". . . in the fall of 1972 the performance of the news media, the only communications mechanism that can possibly act as a balance to . . . awesome presidential power, shows that the prolonged attack on the most independent and competent of the nation's news organizations has inhibited the untrammeled interpretation by professional journalists of what the President and his subordinates say and do.

"Months before the presidential campaign began, in May of 1972, the Freedom of Information Center Report, No. 281, looking at the present state of the media and government, declared: 'The analysis concludes that the seeds have been planted for an era of stricter government control of the mass media.' Coverage of the 1972 presidential campaign suggests that the seeds have begun to take root."

Things are grim enough, but I'm not sure they're as grim as all that.

Some things really haven't changed. To say, for example, that the networks were—or seemed to be—cowed in 1972 is to say almost nothing at all. The networks always have been timid. Network reporters and correspondents follow in the footsteps of someone else;

Edward R. Murrow's legendary attack on Senator Joseph R. McCarthy came after, not before, the tide of public opinion had turned. To say, for another example, that 93 percent of the nation's dailies endorsed the Republican candidate for President is, again, to say nothing at all. Adlai Stevenson, talking to newspapermen in Portland, Oregon, in 1952, said:

". . . the overwhelming majority of the press is just against Democrats. And it is against Democrats, so far as I can see, not after a sober and considered review of the alternatives, but automatically, as dogs are against cats. As soon as a newspaper—I speak of the great majority, not of the enlightened 10 percent—sees a Democratic candidate it is filled with an unconquerable yen to chase him up an alley. . . . I am in favor of a two-party system in politics. . . . But I am in favor of a two-party system in our press too. And I am, frankly, considerably concerned when I see the extent to which we are developing a one-party press in a two-party country."*

We are still a one-party press—Republicans own the newspapers and the TV stations. Yet, I think, the owners aren't quite so obvious about it now. Just consider that the *Chicago Tribune,* once the most towering conservative newspaper in America, runs Nicholas von Hoffman's column. No above-ground journalist is more anti-Nixon, more contemptuous of centrist wisdom than von Hoffman.

While it is true that most newspapers still endorse Republicans most of the time, it seems to me that most reporters for those newspapers, especially reporters based in Washington, feel less intimidated by the policies of the people who employ them.

We are better trained now; we're better educated, a little more sophisticated, probably less irresponsible. We are no longer the natural ally of the Republican Party.

Nixon, Agnew, Clay Whitehead, and the rest may resent our newly found independence (such as it is), and that may be the root of the problem. Independent, outspoken judgment, in their minds,

* My source for Stevenson's quotation is William Safire's classic, *The New Language of Politics.* Safire, a Nixon speech writer, is credited with giving Agnew the phrase, "nattering nabobs of negativism." Safire left the White House in 1973 to write a column for *The New York Times.*

may border on radicalism. Walter Cronkite, when he turns over almost half of his news show to an examination of the Watergate scandal, is perceived by them as an enemy. Tom Wicker and Anthony Lewis, when they relentlessly decry America's role in Southeast Asia, may be seen as somehow un-American.

Patrick Buchanan, the White House aide who prepares for the President a daily summary of what the media has reported, really believes Nixon should "have the right of untrammeled [uninterpreted by media, that is] communication with the American people." Quite obviously, we don't agree; we can find no precedent for that in law or in custom.

We believe the First Amendment to the Constitution gives us the right to criticize, to natter, to quibble, even if we are foolish, mistaken, and misguided.

Some of us probably have been intimidated by the Administration's antipress campaign, especially those of us working for television and most especially those of us working in the networks' executive suites. But I know that I never felt intimidated during the campaign and I don't know any other reporter who covers national politics who felt intimidated. In fact, it's possible that some of us went out of our way to demonstrate we were *not* intimidated.

How, though, can this be reconciled with Bagdikian's findings? After all, we didn't do many things we should have done.

First, we were puzzled. We never figured out just what to do with a Republican noncampaign, so we didn't do much of anything.

Second, and possibly more important, we didn't think the Democrats had a chance. That's important: if McGovern's campaign was hopeless, what was the point? The drama, the excitement dribbled away, until we felt we were performing in a charade. Nobody wants to see a bad fight, go to a bad play, listen to a poor symphony: none of us wanted very much to cover this campaign. Alan Otten, a veteran of 26 years in the Washington bureau of the *Wall Street Journal,* says he was almost forced to dragoon reporters to write about it. I was responsible for the campaign coverage at the *Observer,* and only one or two people asked me if they could help. This is unheard of: every four years, most editors are besieged by staffers pleading for a chance to become involved. It didn't happen this time.

We were overwhelmed by what the polls were telling us. On September 25, a *New York Times*–Yankelovich survey of the nation's 16 largest states showed Nixon leading McGovern by a margin of 62 to 23. "Even in New York," Jack Rosenthal wrote, "the new survey found a Nixon lead of 57 to 26. . . ." If the election had been held at the time the survey was taken, "Mr. Nixon would have won by a landslide among virtually all ages, social classes, income levels, nationalities and regions." Nixon was even leading among Democrats—by three points.

Later that same month, the *Observer* surveyed all 477 Democrats running for the Senate, the House of Representatives, and for governor. Highlights were:

—Of 426 candidates running for the House, 212, or 49.8 percent, were supporting the McGovern-Shriver ticket unequivocally and on the record. Another 44 were supporting it with deep reservations. The rest were opposed or were not talking.

—Of 33 candidates for the Senate, 17 were behind McGovern.

—Of 18 candidates for governor, 9 fully supported the ticket.

The *Observer* used 56 of its correspondents and three members of its staff to make the survey, and it was a nightmare. Candidates simply didn't want to talk about the ticket; they wanted to evade the tough questions.

"Why are you doing this?" asked Representative Charles H. Wilson of California. "I would assume you are getting a very adverse reaction. Right now we all hate the son of a bitch."

Thomas R. Harkin, the congressional staff member who exposed the "tiger cages" in South Vietnam, said his views were not much different from McGovern's. "I get that across [he was running for Congress in Iowa], but people's perception of McGovern's stand is that it's something radical. He's got a big problem."

"He's wrong on amnesty, he's wrong on Vietnam, he's wrong on welfare, he's wrong on defense," said James Edward McNamara, a House candidate in Michigan. "Say," he added, "how long do you want to make this list?"

That's the sort of response we got, over and over again. It was devastating.

"Senator, do you think your standing in the polls is going to improve? Soon?" a reporter asked McGovern at a press conference in New York. "It can't get any worse," he replied.

McGovern plunged on, doggedly, stubbornly, and I suppose most of us admired him for his tenacity. It was never easy. At a Western Electric plant in Columbus, Ohio, some workers had been set up by the Republicans to ask him about amnesty, and the debate that ensued made good film and good copy—for us, if not for him.

Worker: "How come you want amnesty for traitors?"

McGovern: "I'm not for traitors."

Everywhere he went, the Republicans were just ahead of him and just behind him, and they were getting as much time on TV news as he was. In Tacoma, Washington, McGovern exploded. "It galls me," he said. Why should the President's "lackeys" get equal time? Because, he said, the networks were intimidated, that's why.

"I don't think they [the 'lackeys'] ought to get a thing. That's not what equal time means. I don't think the President ought to be allowed to sit there in the White House and have these lackeys of his running around the country getting equal time with me every day."

He was almost as angry about newspaper reporters and columnists who had been writing that he was trimming his views and trying to change his character. Maybe he had in mind Tom Wicker who, the day before, had written in the *Times* that "at some point compromise becomes flight, and if the Senator is wondering why he is making so little personal impact on the voters, it may well be because many people no longer can be sure who he is or where he stands."

McGovern responded:

"Those who say they'd like me to be the George McGovern of old—the George McGovern of the primaries—don't realize that I was only at 4 percent in the polls then. . . . Despite our critics in the press and elsewhere . . . I'm the same man I was then, except I'm more confident than ever that we're going to win this election."

It was, of course, an impossible dilemma for McGovern. He got the nomination because he was antiwar, anti-Establishment, and anti-things the way they are. But to win over the *other* Democratic Party—the Meany and Daley party—he had to prove he really didn't mean all those things. Damned if he did, damned if he didn't.

It was my thought then (and my thought now) that McGovern

and his advisors erred catastrophically in trying to run as the candidate of both Democratic parties. It was too sweeping a compromise; it was much too political. It was not believable. All it did was disillusion his early followers, disconcert people who might have become his followers, and degrade him in the eyes of those who would never become his friends.

Wicker, I suspect, was right. He concluded his column this way:

"It may be that political success in America still requires a candidate to avoid strong positions and play to the prejudices of the voters. But if so, Mr. McGovern has no hope of beating Mr. Nixon at that game; and anyway, there is growing evidence that millions of Americans are sick and tired of politics and politicians as usual, with their promises, their evasions, their pretensions, and their failures.

"So come home, George McGovern. . . . You were doing better when you seemed to be your own man."

The polls showed a staggering swing in how the voters perceived McGovern. In May, for example, Louis Harris reported that only about 33 percent of the voters agreed with the view that McGovern did not "inspire confidence as a President should." At that same time, 50 percent agreed that Nixon did not inspire such confidence. Late in September, 55 percent of the voters felt McGovern did not inspire confidence and only 33 percent felt that way about Nixon. It was almost a complete reversal.

For 20 years, George Gallup had been using a tool to test a candidate's personal popularity. McGovern scored lowest on that scale of any candidate in the 20-year span, excepting Goldwater.

At the *Post,* Haynes Johnson and other reporters continued what they had begun in the primary season—a depth analysis of voters' attitudes based on interviews with them. On October 2, Johnson reported that the latest wave of interviews (eight reporters were used, 443 persons were interviewed) showed that "George McGovern, the presidential candidate of candor and a different approach throughout the long primary season, is now regarded by many Americans as a man who lacks conviction, changes his mind, goes back on his word, says one thing in public and follows another course in private. He is, in this view, merely another politician after all—and you can't trust the breed."

Reporters felt much the same way.

"McGovern's unhappy because he's been unable to engage his opponent in direct debate on the issues," David Broder wrote in a column. "The press is unhappy because it doesn't have much of a campaign to cover, and worried that it's being manipulated into one-sided coverage. . . . It's my impression that few reporters are bleeding for the Democratic nominee. There's less personal partisanship in the press for either of the 1972 candidates than I've seen in any of the previous presidential campaigns I've covered."

Broder went on to describe how isolated Nixon was from the press trying to cover him. "There is no candidate to question and, really, no one authorized to speak for him. I know of no precedent for this. Between Labor Day and election day of 1956, President Eisenhower held five news conferences. In the same period of 1964, the last time an incumbent was involved in a presidential contest, Lyndon B. Johnson had five press conferences and innumerable informal sessions with reporters aboard his plane.

"By contrast, Mr. Nixon has held one press conference since his renomination, and his press secretary, Ronald Ziegler, says there is a '50-50 chance' he'll have another before election day. . . .

"The press was accused—and I think rightly—of being derelict in 1968 in not pressing Mr. Nixon to expound his strategy for ending the Vietnam war. How does the press justify itself this year, if the man who is likely to remain President is allowed to go through the whole campaign without answering questions on his plans for taxes, for wage-price controls, for future policy in Vietnam and a dozen other topics?"

An election, Broder said, is supposed to be the time a President "submits himself to the jury of the American voters. As a lawyer, Richard Nixon knows that if he were as highhanded with the jury as he's being in this campaign, he'd risk being cited for contempt of court."

The press, Broder concluded, "ought to be calling Mr. Nixon on this . . . for the sake of its own tattered reputation and for the public which it presumes to serve." Broder then laid out a proposal:

"The editors of the country and the television news chiefs ought to tell Mr. Nixon, in plain terms, that before they spend another nickel to send their reporters and camera crews around the country with him, they want a system set up in which journalists can be journalists again, and a President campaigns as a candidate, not a touring emperor."

It shouldn't be this way, but I'm not sure Broder's solution is workable. Between now and the next election, when Spiro Agnew may be the Republican candidate, we should try to think this through. Perhaps it's an assignment for our in-house associations of editors and publishers. It might be better if the working reporters and correspondents would get together and come up with some proposals. If we don't do something, the same problem will recur.

As attitudes exist today, probably we can't expect much sympathy from most Americans. It is, they may believe, *our* problem, and our credibility is not very high these days, either. It is, of course, *everybody's* problem, because when we can't report a Presidential campaign, nobody can vote with intelligence. When we have a noncampaign, the tendency not to vote at all may be overwhelming; in 1972, more than four out of every 10 Americans who could have voted chose not to. That is a national scandal.

When you think about it, what we tried to do in 1972 to make up for a noncampaign on the Republican side is faintly amusing. Wringing our hands, muttering to each other, chasing after poor George McGovern—and then rushing off with Agnew, as if that were a palliative for not being able to rush off with his boss.

And Agnew, when we arrived, was ready for us. We discovered a "new" Agnew—soft-spoken, programmed with obscure statistics, and, altogether, dull. After spending a few days with him, I wrote this lead:

"I have just seen the Republican Party's future—and he works, two or three hours a day.

"His name is Spiro Agnew and he is running (ambling, perhaps) for a second term as Vice-president of the United States. Beginning in 1976, it is thought, he may give his party 'eight more years' in the White House.

"On Monday, Tuesday, and Wednesday last week, Agnew traveled 4,789 miles in his chartered jet, the Michelle Ann III. He spent 9 hours and 27 minutes in the air. On the ground he gave four speeches, met privately once with about 35 of Sen. John Tower's richest and closest friends, and shook a few hands with some admirers at an airport."

At the Farm Progress Show near Galesburg, Illinois, Agnew told a field full of farmers that he took pride in the fact that "the sales of soybeans and soybean products abroad climbed to more than $2 billion" after a Nixon Administration decision in 1969 set the soybean support price at a "market-stimulating level." The market may have been stimulated; we weren't.

The only excitement in the Agnew campaign was supplied by his press secretary, Victor Gold, who has become a living legend. He has this thing about motorcades and buses. It started when he worked in the Goldwater campaign in 1964; it climaxed in 1972.

Bob Greene, the fresh young columnist for the *Chicago Sun-Times,* tells a typical Vic Gold story in his book, *Running.*

"It was late in the afternoon [of September 19] and the buses were parked at the curb in front of a hotel waiting for Agnew to come out of a meeting, and climb into his limousine, for the motorcade to start. Suddenly another bus drove by the press bus, and Gold saw it.

" 'GET THE HELL . . .' he screamed at the press bus driver. 'WHAT THE HELL DO YOU THINK YOU'RE DOING? HOW THE HELL DID THE GODDAM STAFF BUS GET AHEAD OF US IN THE MOTORCADE? WE ARE *ALWAYS* THE FIRST BUS! DAMMIT, GET IN FRONT OF HIM!'

"The driver was quivering. From the back of the bus a voice called, 'Sit down, Vic. Agnew's still in the hotel. That's a city transit bus taking people home from work.'

" 'Oh,' said Victor Gold."

On September 19, covering Spiro Agnew, that was the day's most exciting event.

No one paid much attention to Sargent Shriver, but he was out there campaigning too. At least, he was exciting. Reporters remember the day he misquoted both the Declaration of Independence and "The

Star Spangled Banner." I remember the day Shriver justified sending one of his kids to Exeter. Shriver, whose assignment was to carry the ticket's message to ethnics and the workingman, said he picked Exeter, a WASP institution, because he wanted his son, a Catholic like himself, to get a solid religious education. "These days," said Shriver, "you've got to receive an education in this kind of milieu. It's that kind of world." It is?

By October, hopes for a reasonable debate about the "issues" had vanished, as both sides engaged in an orgy of name-calling and obfuscation.

McGovern abandoned his efforts to spell out his positions on Vietnam, the cities, taxes, foreign policy, and the rest—and began charging that "this Administration is the trickiest, most deceitful Administration in our entire national history." He said too that it was "the most corrupt in history."

The most corrupt—more corrupt than Harding or Grant? "It's a historical fact," he told news executives in Buffalo. "I'm a former professor of history and I've been speaking in that capacity as well as a candidate for the Presidency. I say the Nixon-Agnew Administration is the most morally corrupt in the history of the United States."

Robert Abernathy, the NBC reporter in Los Angeles, wanted to know more about that. In a classic example of tough, persistent reporting, he and McGovern had this exchange:

Abernathy: "Are you saying that you and the Democrats are more politically moral than President Nixon and the Republicans?"

McGovern: "Exactly. I think a McGovern Administration would raise the whole moral and political tone of this country."

Abernathy: "But are you morally superior to Nixon?"

McGovern: "I'm just saying that I think I have the sense of responsibility. . . ."

Abernathy: "But are you convinced your moral standards are higher?"

McGovern: "Well, I think I could set a higher moral tone. . . ."

Abernathy: "In short, you feel a McGovern Administration would be morally superior."

McGovern: "Well, I don't like to put it that way. It sounds kind of unctuous to say I'm morally superior to Nixon."

The moral question was best summed up by C. Barsotti, in a cartoon in the *New Yorker.* Two men are arguing at a bar. One says to the other: "Look, Nixon's no dope. If the people really wanted moral leadership, he'd give them moral leadership."

The *Washington Post* reprinted the cartoon at the same time it reprinted an article from the *San Diego Union* by James S. Copley, chairman of the corporation that publishes the Copley newspapers. Copley had just visited the President in the Oval Room at the White House and, while he couldn't report anything of substance he and the President had talked about, he could say that, "I was humbled by the thought that the President would find a half hour to discuss the issues with me—when the whole world clamored for his attention."

This too:

"Observing his straightforward manner and listening to his resonant voice, as we sat in the White House, I reflected that perhaps the most important quality that Mr. Nixon brought to his high office was his Quaker heritage—his belief that there can be no compromise with right and truth and his firm conviction that whatever he feels is worth doing also merits his total dedication."

At almost the same time, Nixon was attacking "the leaders of the media" and university presidents and some businessmen for their failure "to understand the importance of great decisions and the necessity to stand by the President when he makes a terribly difficult, potentially unpopular decision. . . ." That's unfair: James Copley is one of "the leaders of the media" and he understands.

Agnew, in the closing days of the campaign, seemed to be reverting to the Agnew we've always known so well. He said, among other things, that "about all that the factional and truncated plans that he [McGovern] offers seem to do is make him popular in some sections of North Vietnamese society."

And Nixon's surrogates, no doubt alerted by the "attack group" that Watergate was finally beginning to take hold, opened a co-ordinated attack on the messengers, chiefly the *Washington Post,* that had brought us the unpleasant news. The campaign strategists chose Clark MacGregor, until now the campaign's nice guy, to open it. "The *Washington Post*'s credibility has today sunk lower than that of George McGovern," he told reporters.

Then, on October 26, Henry Kissinger appeared at a White House briefing and told reporters that "peace is at hand" in Vietnam. Was that part of the political plan too?

"I don't think so," a member of the attack group told Jules Witcover. "I'm sure Henry [Kissinger] and Haldeman and others perceived the political impact."

But, according to Witcover, "another member [of the attack group], asked in another context for an example of things that were said or done to avert attention from the Democrats' escalating charges on the Watergate affair, replied: 'Try peace is at hand. We can thank Watergate for that.'

"MacGregor acknowledges that he saw Mr. Nixon at a White House breakfast that morning and raised the possibility. 'I told him I felt it would be very helpful—if Henry felt he could—to speak in some detail on the Hanoi report.' He made the recommendation, MacGregor says, 'because Henry does it superbly, and there were questions to be answered. My first judgment was that it would be helpful, but only minimally. I felt the McGovern voters wouldn't be won over by it, but what Henry did would solidify those who were going to vote for the President. Henry solidified opinion of the high degree of competence in this Administration.' "

Political considerations, one can therefore assume, were at least a part of the decision to announce how handy peace had become.

I saw McGovern for the last time during the campaign a few nights later. He was exhausted and he looked haggard, and he thought peace was *not* at hand. "I think we've been had," he told me. Either he—we—had been had or Nixon and Kissinger were far too eagerly premature. The talks did break down, and the B-52s attacked Hanoi and Haiphong, but that would come later.

Finally, almost two years after it began, the McGovern campaign came limping home, in tatters. "Oh, dear God," one of his aides said, "let it end soon."

It was just as bad as we anticipated—McGovern took the District of Columbia and Massachusetts—and David Broder, our most famous political writer, tried to analyze what had happened.

"What Goldwater and McGovern had in common—and what defeated both, so resoundingly—was that in the course of their campaigns, the voters came to the same conclusion that political and journalistic Washington had previously reached: that they were light-weights in the heavyweight division of presidential politics. They were men of good heart and good spirit, open and honorable, whose failing was their tendency to see public questions in one-dimensional, almost simplistic terms."

McGovern read the column and sat down to write Broder a letter in longhand.

"Bullshit," he said.

part six

US★—II

17

What We Did

When the election was over, *The New York Times*'s James Reston wrote a memo to his editors, analyzing the performance of the press.

". . . we overestimated the tangibles and underestimated the intangibles; we relied too much on techniques of reporting which are no longer fool-proof; just as he [the candidate] was too isolated with other reporters, so were we too isolated with other reporters, and we, too, were far too impressed by the tidy statistics of the polls."

Reston wrote that memo after the 1948 election, when Truman "upset" Dewey, to the consternation of the pollsters and the pundits.

It's just a way of saying that if we blew this election, it's nothing new: we've blown them before.

Did we blow it?

By now, I would hope, readers who have come this far know the answer. I have laid out the evidence as fully as I knew it, with as much candor and fairness as I could provide. The evidence is not complete—it never can be—and the fairness and the candor may be suspect, as they always are.

But, did . . . we . . . blow . . . it?

The temptation is to squirm and quibble. To be sure (my friends at the *Wall Street Journal* would say), there were occasions when we were brilliant. There were admirable innovations in the techniques we used. Most of us worked hard, and a few of us need apologize to no one, especially those among us who never gave up on Watergate.

Admit it, though. We did—on balance—blow it.

In a column that appeared in the *Washington Post* on Tuesday, April 11, 1972, David Broder wrote:

"The hardest thing for any newspaperman to learn, if my own case is any example, is how to wait for the story to end before leaping into print to tell its meaning."

It is good advice, and I have glued it to my typewriter. For Broder and for most of us, 1972 was leap year.

We leaped into print to award the nomination to Muskie, even before the first of 23 primaries took place. We read Dr. Gallup's famous poll and we leaped into print to write off George McGovern. We never imagined George Wallace would run in the Democratic primaries, and we leaped into print to award Florida to Jackson or Muskie or almost anyone else. We waited breathlessly for John Lindsay to make up his mind; when he did, we leaped into print to say he would put an end to the McGovern nonsense. We thought Hubert Humphrey was old and foolish, and we couldn't wait to leap into print to say so.

It didn't make any difference if we were liberal or conservative, Consciousness I or Consciousness III. The gift of prophecy is not ideological and it has no life-style. Most of the time we were just wrong, because there was no way on this earth we could be right.

This sort of thing is sheer folly. It is a kind of group self-immolation which allows us to read what we've written by the light of our own fire.

It does us no good and it does the candidates and the public real harm. Because we selected Muskie as the front-runner before a single vote was cast, we hand-delivered him very special problems that he couldn't handle (and probably shouldn't have had to handle, *then*). At the same time, we put all the other candidates in also-ran positions from which some of them could never recover.

We have developed a system of primaries, caucuses, and conventions for choosing the nominees of our two major parties. We are mischievous and misguided when we move into that system and begin setting our own rules and then keeping the score.

It would be naive to suggest that this kind of who's-ahead, instantly analytical reporting can ever be stopped entirely. Our editors and even our publishers want to know who's ahead and what's happening. We are under great pressure to respond.

What we need in the face of that pressure is a deep and abiding faith in the perishability of our own logic. We need, ultimately, to be more humble. We are such prigs when it comes to analyzing politics: pompous, ponderous, full of ourselves. When the political season begins, you can almost hear the collective clearing of our throats.

Most political reporters I know have a sense of humor; they could hardly survive without it. Somehow, though, most of us don't seem very amused when we sit down at the typewriter. We should be.

Amused—and skeptical, especially about such things as the Gallup poll. National surveys don't mean much when the nation isn't paying attention to the questions the pollsters are asking. It is absurd to ask a voter to name his choice for a Presidential nomination before he knows who's running.

The progression is all wrong.

First, we ought to be telling the voters who these people are and what they believe in and what they hope to do. By "we" I mean everybody—*Rolling Stone, The New York Times,* CBS, and the *Ashtabula Star-Beacon,* each in its own way, each of us in our own way. Everybody should have his say—liberals, conservatives, neutralists, old journalists, new journalists, straight reporters, columnists. We need more variety and more controversy—not less.

Having done this, *then* we and the pollsters can begin to measure how the candidates are doing with people who know who these candidates are and what they want to do.

In 1972, we decided who was going to win, and *then* we began to analyze who the candidates were and what they believed in.

I think Professor Nelson W. Polsby is on to something when he says the worst sins of the news media are *"incoherence,* stemming from a style of news coverage and reporting that is highly mechanical. . . ; *sparseness,* a characteristic that is mostly a consequence of the pressures on reporters to converge and concentrate on a narrow range of phenomena; and *inexpertise,* a quality that has its roots in journalistic craft norms that value amateurism . . . and egalitarianism."

We need to think seriously not only about what we cover and in what order, but *how* we do it.

Our techniques are, in fact, "highly mechanical." Newspapers assign reporters to travel with the candidates and write something every day. Other reporters may be assigned to look into special areas— television advertising, for example, or fund raising. Some newspapers have their own columnists, who appear regularly as clockwork. Then there are the nationally syndicated columnists who appear just as regularly and who always write exactly the same number of words, be the subject a Presidential assassination or a governors' conference.

It is so predictable—and so dull.

The columnists, especially, are dull—and pedantic, and lazy, and predictable. There are some lawyers whose life ambition is to become a judge, so, finally, after a career of hard work, they can relax. Journalism is a little like that; a reporter, after a long and successful career, becomes a columnist, so he can relax. If someone asked me to pick a stable of columnists for a brand-new newspaper, I would hardly know what to say. On the left, Nicholas von Hoffman, I think; he's rarely dull and always contentious. I'd surely pick Garry Wills because he's the toughest and probably the brightest we have. On the right? Surely not William F. Buckley, Jr. He's a dilettante, mesmerized by his own fustian rhetoric. James Jackson Kilpatrick is a better writer, and he makes more sense. Evans and Novak? I think maybe so, because they are at least hardworking, most of the time, even if they are intransigent. I'd take Jack Anderson too, because he makes news—right or wrong. Down the middle, and for respectability, Joseph Kraft might add a little something. Finally, to make sense of it all—Art Buchwald.

But it's not much of a list. When you think of how many journalists we have in this country, it's a disgrace. It should be a feast of talent, with people representing all kinds of views and writing in all kinds of styles.

It is not accidental that the list of really good people is so short. It's intentional, because so many of our publishers and editors are scared of real controversy. They want their columns to be short, safe, and sound. Which is nonsense. If an editor is scared of Nick von Hoffman, he can go out and hire somebody just as good and just as outrageous on the right. There must be people who can take a conservative position with elan.* Balance—or, at least, the appearance of it—covers a multitude of sins.

It is my own impression that we should go even further: we should reconsider the idea of the column itself. I don't think even our best people can make much sense in 700 words a day, three days a week. Some columnists should be writing 3,000 words, once a week. Others should be writing 100 words, five times a week. I can think of some journalists who could be superb columnists—writing one "column" every month, 10,000 words long.

If we are to survive, I think we must break out of all these rigid molds. Does it make sense, for example, for a reporter to travel with a candidate and write one 1,200-word story every single day?

After a few weeks of this, even his own editors are bored to tears. They start processing the copy, like cheese.

The old *Philadelphia Record*—God rest its soul—once ran a sports story that said, in its entirety: "The Phillies lost their 102d game yesterday, and left town."

Just once, I would enjoy seeing a story like this:

MILWAUKEE, Oct. 12—Senator John Smith, Democratic candidate for President, campaigned in Wisconsin yesterday, and nothing happened.

We do have a problem with "incoherence" and part of that problem stems from our refusal to make simple, basic judgments, day to day, about what is important and what is trivial. "Sparseness" and "inexpertise" flow from that failure. Stories tend to be "sparse" because we try to shoehorn everything, important and trivial, into a paper that has just so much space. We are liable to a charge of "inexpertise" because our "highly mechanical" techniques don't allow us to show we know what's important and what's trivial. Sometimes, of course—

* My own paper, within limits, does this. My column, which the readers perceive as "liberal," I suppose, is balanced by a column written by Edwin A. Roberts, Jr., a provocative spokesman for "conservative" positions.

but just sometimes—we don't know. That cannot always be helped.

For example:

It takes no genius to understand that McGovern's decision to drop his tax-reform–welfare plan is a more important story than a routine speech by one of Nixon's surrogates. So the editor puts the McGovern story on Page One and puts the surrogate inside, if he wants to use that story at all.

The question of what to do about a Nixon noncampaign would have been easier to answer if editors had made such commonsense, everyday decisions.

Improving coverage of politics in newspapers really isn't so difficult. Our obvious sins—making careless predictions, for example—can be corrected. One tough editor could straighten out an entire staff: all he has to do is pick up a reporter's story—and "spike" it. That kind of message is rarely subject to misinterpretation.

A newspaper can decide at the outset of a campaign that its news reporting will be tough and disciplined. The reason that *The New York Times* continues to be our most reliable newspaper is that its news reporting is disciplined; the reason the *Washington Post* remains in the *Times*'s shadow as a reliable recorder of the news is because it is *not* disciplined.

I have heard all the arguments for the "new journalism" and for "advocacy" reporting and I remain unimpressed. There is a place for straight, hard, objective reporting of the major events of the day—in the news columns. If, for example, George McGovern releases an alternate defense budget, I want to know what it says and I want to hear what other people think about it. I would prefer to hear about it from a specialist—a Defense Department reporter, perhaps—who really knows what he's writing. It is a mistake, I think, to expect that political reporters can write all of the major stories that come out of a political campaign. Expertise is important and, when we have it, we should use it.

But, an advocate of the "new journalism" would argue, news doesn't exist in a vacuum. By reporting what somebody said, we don't reflect reality. That's true, but no one really recommends that kind of reporting. In most stories, some analysis is vital.

It is on this point that we enter a shadowy world of semantics.

Where does analysis end and opinion begin? Almost every major newspaper in the country is trying to resolve this problem. The *Los Angeles Times,* for example, felt that a reporter who said in a news story that McGovern supporters were a part of Nixon's crowds in Westchester County, New York, was stating an opinion. Nonsense. That's not even analysis; that's just basic reporting.

Of course there is no easy solution. Nobody ever wrote a completely "straight" news story and nobody ever will. No one can make an analysis of anything without permitting some "opinion" to seep into his thinking. So, we have to deal with the problem case by case, using common sense as the only proper guideline.

If we keep in mind that a newspaper's initial responsibility is to tell its readers what the story in its essentials is all about, we have a departure point. After we've done that, anything goes. Properly labeled and carefully positioned, the more commentary, opinion, and advocacy the better. It is important, though, that we let the reader know what we're doing; it is, in essence, a matter of truth in labeling and it goes straight to our credibility which, recently, has been in very serious question. We have been "incoherent," just as Professor Polsby says, because neither we nor our readers have understood exactly what it is we're trying to do.

The problem for television reporting is more serious. I agree with Sander Vanocur:

"We cannot continue to shoehorn all those [news] items into a half-hour evening news show without making it into a wire service budget with pictures. Nor do we get anywhere by adding another half hour, for we simply fill it up with the same staccato fare. Just because we have been doing it that way for the first 15 years is no reason why we have to continue it for the next 15. Events have become too complex to be explained away in a minute and 30 seconds; we must be aware by now that pictures we put up every night do not necessarily portray reality."

We are talking here about the regularly scheduled evening news shows—not about the great dramatic traumas of our time, in which television preempts its whole schedule and permits us to share these events in ways no print medium can possibly match.

In February of 1972, the A. C. Nielsen Co. found, 24,700,000

TV households watched the network evening news shows, down from 25,600,000 households in 1971. The audience is huge, but declining. And what are the viewers getting from it?

A study conducted by Andrew Stern of the University of California at Berkeley "indicated the disconcerting fact that even if television remained the nation's prime source of news, it did not mean anyone was necessarily paying attention.*

"Of 232 respondents who were asked, 'What do you recall from tonight's broadcast?' with an average of 19 items to point to, 51 percent could not recall a single story a few minutes after the newscast was off the air. Among the 49 percent who could summon up at least one item, the last thing they heard, the windup commentary by Eric Sevareid or Harry Reasoner, was least remembered."

That's devastating, especially when you consider that Agnew and others have been terribly disturbed because they believe a TV commentator can shift the focus of a story by the mere tilt of his eyebrow. Most people, it seems, can't remember the story, much less the commentator or his eyebrow.

TV news "reporting," pretty obviously, isn't working. For one thing, as I've noted earlier, there isn't much reporting on television. These little items are thematic; they have a point of view, and most of the time they presume the facts.

I am pessimistic that much can be done about it. The people who run the networks and the local stations live and die by the rating books. That means that TV reporting, by definition, is show business. To survive, a TV news show must have a celebrity—a Walter Cronkite or a Harry Reasoner. They aren't reporters; they can't be reporters. Reporters emulate them, and hope some day to be one of them. Sometimes, I think, every young television reporter in America sounds like David Brinkley.

Documentaries are valuable, except we didn't have many of them in 1972. And, even if we had, not many people would have watched them. Programs like "First Tuesday" and "60 Minutes" are sometimes extraordinarily good, but they suffer in the ratings too.

* From *The Politics of Broadcasting:* the Alfred I. duPont–Columbia University Survey of Broadcasting Journalism, 1971–1972, an invaluable source.

I suspect most Americans don't want to watch very much tough, controversial news just before or after dinner (or maybe any other time). ". . . the problem with television," John Chancellor has said, "is that to see any news you pretty much have to see it all. . . . You can't pick and choose. I think this has bothered people because they have been exposed not only to dull and serious news, but also to news that is embarrassing to them as Americans or embarrassing to them as Southerners, or embarrassing to them as liberals or conservatives. People around in the country don't like news the way they're getting it. The only problem we have is that we don't know any other way to give them that news on television."

I can think of other and better ways. Get rid of the show-biz anchor men, let reporters really report the stories. Bring in some outside people as analysts and advocates. Concentrate more on the important stories, get rid of some of the trivia. Break out of the format; do something one night, something else the other night. Put the news shows on the air at 10:30, instead of 7 or 7:30. Produce minidocumentaries; use animated cartoons. *Be different.*

But I can't imagine that any of these proposals would be taken seriously. The trend is to retreat from controversy.

In 1971–1972, the *Survey of Broadcast Journalism* reported, "The choice before the nation's electronic newsmen seemed to be: Do what you know you should and, for the moment, lose listeners and cash; or ignore your own best interest—make money—and risk, perhaps a long way off, a well-deserved oblivion."

We are under attack for all of the wrong reasons. We should be criticized for being mistaken so often, for being incoherent, for not telling the full story, for being so mechanical, for being rigid and old-fashioned.

Instead, we are attacked because, in Daniel Patrick Moynihan's words, we are a corps of Ivy League "elitists" or because, in Edith Efron's words, we are "strongly biased in favor of the Democratic-liberal-left axis of opinion."

More provocative, perhaps, is the criticism of columnist Robert Novak, who is one of us. In a paper delivered at a symposium at Kenyon College and later printed in the *Congressional Record,* Novak said:

". . . the journalist working for the television networks, the big news magazines and the important metropolitan press had now [in 1972] become part of the liberal establishment, both in his manner of living and in his ideological commitment. . . . These journalists were increasingly advocating causes of the moment rather than functioning as neutral observers. Taken together, the developments widened the gap between the mass media and the great mass of citizens, a gap that can only result in diminished credibility by the media. . . .

"The national media is a melting pot where the journalists, regardless of background, are welded into a homogenous ideological mold joined to the liberal establishment and alienated from the masses of the country."

To support his contention Novak framed seven "axioms" that he said were "shared by the Washington press of 1972"—which, in capsulated form, are: 1) the Vietnam war has been shameful and immoral; 2) the military-industrial complex is a sinister conspiracy; 3) severe measures must be taken against pollution, even if the result is increased unemployment; 4) white racism is a cancer that must be removed, by forced busing, if necessary; 5) the forces of repression, becoming a sinister reality under Nixon and Mitchell, threaten our liberties; 6) priorities must be reordered so that great amounts of federal cash can be pumped into our cities; and 7) it is time for a redistribution of the nation's wealth.

Ben Bagdikian, the press critic, responded to Novak's paper by making still another survey. With the help of Burns W. Roper, the polltaker, Bagdikian put together a questionnaire and mailed it to a random sample of 10 percent of the correspondents based in Washington. Of the 222 questionnaires, 97 were returned. The 44 percent return, it was said, was satisfactory. The results were published in the *Washington Post*.

Of the seven "axioms," three—No. 2 (the military-industrial complex), No. 4 (white racism), and No. 5 (repression)—were rejected outright. Two were accepted by healthy majorities—No. 6 (reordering of priorities) and No. 7 (redistribution of income). The final two —No. 1 (the shameful war) and No. 3 (pollution)—were accepted narrowly.

From this, perhaps a "neutral observer" (which Novak is not) could deduce that Washington correspondents may be slightly more "liberal" than the nation at large. Surely, though, we are not welded into a "homogenous mold joined to the liberal establishment."

"What are Washington correspondents like?" Bagdikian asked.

"There are more than 2,200 of them doing a variety of jobs, and they are hard to generalize about. There is a lot of fake romanticism about the Washington correspondent, not often discouraged by the correspondents. The romantic correspondent speaks only with Presidents and Secretaries of State, who listen to his advice respectfully. . . . (But) the average correspondent works in a small office doing part-time pieces for a string of unrelated papers whose editors would think he had taken leave of his senses if he wrote cosmic stories about high policy."

True enough, but in fairness to Novak he was not talking about the "average" correspondent. He was talking about the big-timers who do write cosmic stories about high policy.

Or do they?

What we have seen in this book is evidence that, big-timers or little-timers, we really don't care that much about "high policy." We are mechanistic, interested chiefly in personalities, power plays, squabbles, the degree of "professionalism" of the various candidates. Above all else, we are fascinated by one question: Who's ahead?

If we are interested in "high policy," we should have analyzed McGovern's tax reform proposals; after all, they did call for a redistribution of income, which, supposedly, we favor. Or, we should have analyzed McGovern's defense proposals, because they would make a reordering of priorities possible, and, supposedly, we want that.

But we paid no attention to either program—because we weren't interested in George McGovern, who was obviously the candidate of this very same "liberal establishment" we are supposed to be welded to.

Muskie, remember, was our Democratic candidate. First, because we thought he was ahead. Second, because we thought he and the "masses of the country" were not far out of tune. That meant, we thought, that he had the best chance to defeat Richard Nixon.

We were probably right too. The Muskie we thought we knew *was* ahead before the New Hampshire primary (when it didn't make much difference) and he *was* perceived by us, and by voters who knew something about him, as a centrist (which should have made a difference). We were probably right back then about McGovern too: he was almost a fringe candidate and he was not an exceptional politician.

But Muskie had weaknesses we didn't know about—couldn't know about—in the beginning. As we came to understand those weaknesses, we exposed them, even if he had been our choice. The original Muskie might have been the man to defeat Richard Nixon, but he couldn't win the nomination. McGovern, because of the chaotic conditions in the Democratic Party, was the man who could win the nomination, but could never hope to win the election.

Almost surely, we underestimated Richard Nixon, but, in fact he did seem vulnerable before he went to China and Russia and before he imposed Phase II wage and price controls. Watergate, even if the full truth of it came too late, did confirm our suspicions that he was the kind of man who could lose an election he should have won.

We failed in a large sense to understand what was happening to the Democratic Party. We failed in a much smaller sense to gauge the mood of the nation.

I said in the beginning we are ordinary people, and this is not an ordinary time in our history. We are professional craftsmen, not artists, and we tried in 1972 to make sense out of a political campaign that reflected all of the turmoil and chaos that is rooted in a swiftly changing society. That we failed so often should be no surprise. It was predictable.

We can never be perfect, but we can be better. We cannot continue to do things the way we've always done them. We desperately need new people, new techniques, and much more variety. We need to break out of a mold that serves neither us nor our readers (or viewers).

I detest flag-waving about the press; the pretty little speeches about the First Amendment, Peter Zenger, and the neighborhood carrier boy. We are not what some of us think we are, and we never were.

The best that can be said of us may have been said best by Marya Mannes, the essayist and critic.

"In the business of informing the American public (often against its prejudiced will or—worse—its indifference), I suspect that my friends the 'biased elitists' are as a whole much less perverted or tarnished by their power than the powerful who attack them."

I suspect that too.

18

Epilogue

Most of this book was written in December of 1972 and January of 1973, before the nation learned just how deeply "Watergate" reached into the White House. Even now, weeks later, we don't know how much more deeply it may go.

We do know enough to say that the Presidential election of 1972 always will be remembered by that one word: Watergate. Without question, it is the most monstrous political scandal this nation has known.

As the revelations tumble into the headlines day after day, we can see just how close we came to living in a totalitarian state. Attempts were made to corrupt the FBI and the CIA; witnesses were, in effect, bribed to remain silent; special favors were given to special people who gave Nixon's agents bundles of political cash. The $100 bill became, in fact, the symbol of Watergate.

If Nixon himself was not a part of it (and that still isn't certain), it was he who set the tone—and the style; it was he who picked these men. He says he wasn't aware *specifically* of these high crimes and misdemeanors. Maybe not—but he should have been. More than that, these men—his men—thought they were doing what he would want them to do.

The press should take no pleasure in Watergate, but, of course, dozens of reporters do. This is the Nixon we've been trying to tell you about. This is why we've always disliked the man. You can't trust him, we have said. He is tricky, we have agreed. We were—we are—right.

No wonder he and his disgraced followers—Mitchell, Haldeman, Ehrlichman, and the rest—feared and detested us. From the beginning, it was the press and, finally, it was a stubborn and uncompromising judge (John J. Sirica) who pushed and shoved and at last brought this Administration to its knees.

The *Washington Post* won a Pulitzer Prize for its Watergate coverage.* Next time around, it's a safe bet the *Post*'s two brilliant reporters Carl Bernstein and Bob Woodward will win Pulitzers too. The *Post, primus inter pares,* stuck to the story and saw it through. Almost alone in the beginning, it was joined by other papers, especially after the election was over.

McGovern advisor Gary Hart believes that if George Wallace had run as a third-party candidate and if we had known on Election Day what we know now about Watergate, McGovern might have won. Who knows? All we can say is that Watergate should have been an issue in the election, and it really wasn't.

If we had worked harder and dug deeper, could we have made Watergate the issue it should have been?

I rather doubt it. It isn't just Watergate—the break-in itself, the illegal cash, the Ellsberg burglary, all of it—that bothers so many Americans; it is, even more, the incredible efforts of Nixon and his henchmen to cover it up.

To millions of Americans, that's really bad. We were on to some of the cover-up, but there was much more that we didn't know and really couldn't know. In essence, the cover-up was a post-election story, and at this writing it is still being reported.

Watergate itself: that's different. Bagdikian's complaints that the

---

* Others we met in this book won Pulitzers too—the *Post*'s David Broder for his columns and the Knight papers' Robert Boyd and Clark Hoyt for their reporting of Eagleton's history of mental illness.

press had the story (from the *Post,* mostly) and downplayed it most of the time take on a new urgency in light of what we know now. But I don't think more thorough reporting and coverage would have made much difference: the voters, at that point, were not awed by the story and most of them had decided George McGovern was not a serious alternative.

Watergate raises other questions. Without Republican sabotage of the candidacies of Muskie, Jackson, and others, would McGovern have won the nomination? So far, the evidence of really damaging sabotage to these other Democrats is unconvincing. The most successful stroke was the phony "canuck" letter that led to Muskie's tears in New Hampshire. The reaction, though, was pure Muskie: who's to say it wouldn't have happened on some other occasion? McGovern, I think, won the nomination honestly.

Some good should come out of Watergate. From now on, for one example, candidates and their managers should be more reluctant to spy, bug, cheat, and lie. For another, Watergate should force Congress to reform the methods by which campaigns are financed. We must have federal financing of federal campaigns and now may be the time to see it through.

The press takes pride in the way it investigated Watergate, conveniently forgetting that in the beginning not very many of us did very much. Watergate, we think, has done a lot for our credibility gap.

I hope so—but I'm not sure. Even now, it seems to me, another wave of protest about how we do things is building up out there. If Nixon remains as clever as I think he is, he could ride the crest of that wave back to shore. We'll see.

We should not deceive ourselves. We are no better because of Watergate, and no worse.

Index

271